How to be an Even Better Manager

EIGHTH EDITION

How to be an Even Better Manager

Michael Armstrong

KoganPage

LONDON PHILADELPHIA NEW DELHI

First published in Great Britain in 1983, entitled *How to be a Better Manager*
Second edition, 1988, entitled *How to be an Even Better Manager*
Third edition 1990
Fourth edition 1994
Fifth edition 1999
Sixth edition 2004
Seventh edition 2008
Eighth edition 2011

120 Pentonville Road	1518 Walnut Street, Suite 1100	4737/23 Ansari Road
London N1 9JN	Philadelphia PA 19102	Daryaganj
United Kingdom	USA	New Delhi 110002
www.koganpage.com		India

© Michael Armstrong, 1983, 1988, 1990, 1994, 1999, 2004, 2008, 2011

ISBN   978 0 7494 6329 8
E-ISBN   978 0 7494 6330 4

British Library Cataloguing-in-Publication Data

A CIP record for this book is available from the British Library.

Library of Congress Cataloging-in-Publication Data

Armstrong, Michael, 1928–
    How to be an even better manager : a complete A-Z of proven techniques and essential skills / Michael Armstrong. – 8th ed.
        p. cm.
    Includes bibliographical references and index.
    ISBN 978-0-7494-6330-4 (alk. paper)
1. Management.   I. Title.
    HD31.A73 2011
    658.4–dc22

2011014282

Typeset by Graphicraft Limited, Hong Kong
Printed and bound in India by Replika Press Pvt Ltd

CONTENTS

FOREWORD TO THE EIGHTH EDITION

This eighth edition of *How to be an Even Better Manager* covers 50 key aspects of management and has been extensively revised since the seventh edition was published in 2008. Nine new chapters have been added, dealing with how to benchmark, how to budget, how to cut costs, how to empower, how to increase engagement, how to listen, how to manage culture, how to improve organizational capability and how to troubleshoot.

The book therefore covers a wide range of the skills and approaches used by effective managers – what they need to understand and be able to do to be fully competent in their roles.

It will be an invaluable handbook for existing and aspiring managers, and will be particularly useful for those seeking to obtain qualifications such as NVQs in management or those studying for the Leading, Managing and Developing and Developing Skills for Business Leadership modules of the Chartered Institute of Personnel and Development qualification scheme.

PREFACE

How to use this book

This book is for those who want to develop their managerial skills and competences. It covers all the key skills that managers use, and refers to the main aspects of managing people, activities and themselves with which they need to be familiar.

You can dip into this book at any point – each chapter is self-contained. But it would be useful to read Chapter 1 first. This defines the overall concept of management and the areas in which managers need to be competent, thus providing a framework for the succeeding chapters, which deal with the specific skills and techniques involved in managing people and processes.

How to be a better manager

Better managers recognize that the art of management is something they need to learn. No one becomes a fully competent manager overnight. There are, of course, many ways of learning how to be an effective manager. There is no doubt that experience is the best teacher – the time you have spent as a manager or team leader and your analysis of how good managers you come across operate. You can learn from your own boss and from other bosses. This means accepting what you recognize as effective behaviour and rejecting what is inappropriate – that is, behaviour that fails to provide the leadership and motivation required from good managers and that does not deliver results.

There is an old saying: 'People learn to manage by managing under the guidance of a good manager.' This is just as true today, but to make the best use of experience it is helpful to place it in a framework that defines your understanding of what management is about, and helps you to reflect on and analyse your own experience and the behaviour of others. There is also a wealth of knowledge about the skills that managers need to use and the aspects of managing people, activities and themselves that they need to understand. None of these skills provides a quick fix that is universally applicable. It is useful to know about them, but it is also necessary to develop an understanding of how they are best applied and modified to meet the particular demands of the situation in which you find yourself. This is not a prescriptive book – 'Do this and all will be well' – rather, its aim is to present approaches that have been proved to be generally effective.

But they have to be adapted to suit your own style of managing and the circumstances where their application is required.

To become a better manager it is necessary to develop each of the 50 areas of skills and knowledge covered by this handbook.

But you will be better prepared to do this if you have a general understanding of the process of management. This will provide a framework into which you can fit the various approaches and techniques described in each chapter. The aim of this introductory chapter is to provide such a framework under the following headings:

- what management is about;
- the aims of management;
- the purpose of management and leadership;
- the processes of management;
- managerial roles;
- the distinction between management and leadership;
- the fragmentary nature of managerial work;
- what managers actually do;
- what managers can do about it;
- managerial qualities;
- managerial effectiveness;
- developing managerial effectiveness.

What management is about

Essentially, management is about deciding what to do and then getting it done through people. This definition emphasizes that people are the most important resource available to managers. It is through this resource that all other resources – processes and systems knowledge, finance, materials, plant, equipment, etc – will be managed.

However, managers are there to achieve results. To do this they have to deal with events and eventualities. They may do this primarily through people, but an overemphasis on the people content of management diverts attention from the fact that in managing events managers have to be personally involved. They manage themselves as well as other people. They cannot delegate everything. They frequently have to rely on their own resources to get things done. These resources consist of experience, know-how, skill, competences and time, all of which have to be deployed not only in directing and motivating people, but also in understanding situations and issues, problem analysis and definition, decision-making and taking direct action themselves as well as through other people. They will get support, advice and assistance from their staff, but in the last analysis they are on their own. They have to make the decisions and they have to initiate and sometimes take the action. A chairman fighting a takeover bid will get lots of advice, but he or she will personally manage the crisis, talking directly to the financial institutions, merchant banks, financial analysts, City editors and the mass of shareholders.

The basic definition of management should therefore be extended to read 'deciding what to do and then getting it done through the effective use of resources'. The most important part of management will indeed be getting things done through people, but managers will be concerned directly or indirectly with all other resources, including their own.

The aims of management

Management is a process that exists to get results by making the best use of the human, financial and material resources available to the organization and to individual managers. It is very much concerned with adding value by the use of these resources, and this added value depends on the expertise and commitment of the people who are responsible for managing the business.

The purpose of management and leadership

The Management Standards Centre stated that the key purpose of management and leadership is to 'provide direction, facilitate change and achieve results through the efficient, creative and responsible use of resources'. These purposes were analysed as follows:

Providing direction

- Develop a vision for the future.
- Gain commitment and provide leadership.
- Provide governance – comply with values, ethical and legal frameworks and manage risks in line with shared goals.

Facilitating change

- Lead innovations.
- Manage change.

Achieving results

- Lead the business to achieve goals and objectives.
- Lead operations to achieve specific results.
- Lead projects to achieve specified results.

Meeting customer needs

- Promote products and/or services to customers.
- Obtain contracts to supply products and/or services.
- Deliver products and/or services to customers.
- Solve problems for customers.
- Assure the quality of products and/or services.

Working with people

- Build relationships.
- Develop networks and partnerships.
- Manage people.

Using resources

- Manage financial resources.
- Procure products and/or services.
- Manage physical resources and technology.
- Manage information and knowledge.

Managing self and personal skills

- Manage own contribution.
- Develop own knowledge, skills and competence.

The processes of management

The overall process of management is subdivided into a number of individual processes that are methods of operation specially designed to assist in the achievement of objectives. Their purpose is to bring as much system, order, predictability, logic and consistency to the task of management as possible in the ever-changing, varied and turbulent environment in which managers work. The main processes of management were defined by the classical theorists of management as:

- Planning – deciding on a course of action to achieve a desired result.
- Organizing – setting up and staffing the most appropriate organization to achieve the aim.
- Motivating – exercising leadership to motivate people to work together smoothly and to the best of their ability as part of a team.
- Controlling – measuring and monitoring the progress of work in relation to the plan and taking corrective action when required.

But this classical view has been challenged by the empiricists, such as Rosemary Stewart[1] and Henry Mintzberg,[2] who studied how managers actually spend their time. They observed that the work of managers is fragmented, varied and subject to continual adjustment. It is governed to a large degree by events over which managers have little control and by a dynamic network of interrelationships with other people.

Managers attempt to control their environment but sometimes it controls them. They may consciously or unconsciously seek to plan, organize, direct and control, but their days almost inevitably become a jumbled sequence of events.

To the empiricists, management is a process involving a mix of rational, logical, problem-solving, decision-making activities, and intuitive, judgemental activities. It is therefore both science and art.

Managers carry out their work on a day-to-day basis in conditions of variety, turbulence and unpredictability. A single word to describe all these features would be chaos. Tom Peters,[3] however, has suggested that it is possible for managers to thrive on chaos.

Managers also have to be specialists in ambiguity, with the ability to cope with conflicting and unclear requirements, as Rosabeth Moss Kanter[4] has demonstrated.

Managerial roles

During the course of a typical day a chief executive may well meet the marketing director to discuss the programme for launching a new product, the HR director to decide how best to reorganize the distribution department, the production director to ask why costs per unit of output are going up and what he or she is going to do about it, and the finance director to review the latest set of management accounts before the next board meeting.

He or she may have had to meet a journalist to be interviewed about how the company is going to deliver better results next year. Lunch may have been taken with a major customer, and the evening spent at a business dinner. Some of these activities could be categorized under the headings of planning, organizing, directing and controlling, but chief executives would not have attached these labels when deciding how to spend their time (in so far as there was any choice). The fact that these processes took place was imposed by the situation and the need to take on one or more of the roles inherent in the manager's job. These roles are fundamentally concerned with:

- Getting things done – planning ahead, maintaining momentum and making things happen.
- Finding out what is going on.
- Reacting to new situations and problems.
- Responding to demands and requests.

They involve a great deal of interpersonal relations, communicating, information processing and decision-making.

The distinction between management and leadership

Managers have to be leaders and leaders are often, but not always, managers. But a distinction can be made between the processes of management and leadership.

Management is concerned with achieving results by effectively obtaining, deploying, utilizing and controlling all the resources required, namely people, money, information, facilities, plant and equipment.

Leadership focuses on the most important resource, people. It is the process of developing and communicating a vision for the future, motivating people and gaining their commitment and engagement.

The distinction is important. Management is mainly about the provision, deployment, utilization and control of resources. But where people are involved – and they almost always are – it is impossible to deliver results without providing effective leadership. It is not enough to be a good manager of resources, you also have to be a good leader of people.

The fragmentary nature of managerial work

Because of the open-ended nature of their work, managers feel compelled to perform a great variety of tasks at an unrelenting pace. Research into how managers spend their time confirms that their activities are characterized by fragmentation, brevity and variety. This arises for the following six reasons:

- Managers are largely concerned with dealing with people – their staff and their internal and external customers. But people's behaviour is often unpredictable; their demands and responses are conditioned by the constantly changing circumstances in which they exist, the pressures to which they have to respond and their individual wants and needs. Conflicts arise and have to be dealt with on the spot.

- Managers are not always in a position to control the events that affect their work. Sudden demands are imposed upon them from other people within the organization or from outside. Crises can occur that they are unable to predict.

- Managers are expected to be decisive and deal with situations as they arise. Their best-laid plans are therefore often disrupted; their established priorities have to be abandoned.

- Managers are subject to the beck and call of their superiors, who also have to respond instantly to new demands and crises.

- Managers often work in conditions of turbulence and ambiguity. They are not clear about what is expected of them when new situations arise. They therefore tend to be reactive rather than proactive, dealing with immediate problems rather than trying to anticipate them.

- For all the reasons given above, managers are subject to constant interruptions. They have little chance to settle down and think about their plans and priorities or to spend enough time in studying control information to assist in maintaining a 'steady state' as far as their own activities go.

What managers actually do

What managers do will be dependent on their function, level, organization (type, structure, culture, size) and their working environment generally (the extent to which it is turbulent, predictable, settled, pressurized, steady). Individual managers will adapt to these circumstances in different ways and will operate more or less successfully in accordance with their own perceptions of the behaviour expected of them, their experience of what has or has not worked in the past, and their own personal characteristics.

There are, however, the following typical characteristics of managerial work:

Reaction and non-reflection

Much of what managers do is, of necessity, an unreflecting response to circumstances. Managers are usually not so much slow and methodical decision-makers as doers who have to react rapidly to problems as they arise and think on their feet. Much time is spent in day-to-day troubleshooting.

Choice

Managers can often exercise choice about their work. They informally negotiate widely different interpretations of the boundaries and dimensions of ostensibly identical jobs, with particular emphasis upon the development of 'personal domain' (ie establishing their own territory and the rules that apply within it).

Communication

Much managerial activity consists of asking or persuading others to do things, which involves managers in face-to-face verbal communication of limited duration. Communication is not simply what managers spend a great deal of time doing but the medium through which managerial work is constituted.

Identification of tasks

The typical work of a junior manager is the 'organizational work' of draw-ing upon an evolving stock of knowledge about 'normal' procedures and routines in order to identify and negotiate the accomplishment of problems and tasks.

Character of the work

The character of work varies by duration, time span, recurrence, unexpected-ness and source. Little time is spent on any one activity or, in particular, on the conscious, systematic formulation of plans. Planning and decision-making tend to take place in the course of other activities. Managerial activities are riven by contradictions, cross-pressures, and the need to cope with and reconcile conflict. A lot of time is spent by managers accounting for and explaining what they do, in informal relationships and in 'participating'.

What managers can do about it

To a degree, managers have simply to put up with the circumstances in which they work as described above – they have to manage in conditions of turbulence, uncertainty and ambiguity. That is why one of the character-istics of effective managers is their resilience – they have to be able to cope with these inevitable pressures. But there are competencies as described below and skills as discussed in the rest of this book that can help them to manage in these circumstances. To a considerable extent it is up to man-agers to be aware of these requirements, the behaviours expected of them and the skills they can use to help in carrying out their often demanding responsibilities. They must treat these as guidelines for personal develop-ment plans.

Managers can learn from the example of their bosses, by guidance from those bosses and from mentors, and through formal training courses, but self-managed learning is all-important. The starting point is an understand-ing of the key managerial qualities and the criteria for measuring managerial effectiveness, as described in the next two sections.

Managerial qualities

Michael Pedler and his colleagues[5] suggested on the basis of their exten-sive research that there are 11 qualities or attributes that are possessed by successful managers:

- command of basic facts;
- relevant professional knowledge;
- continuing sensitivity to events;
- analytical, problem-solving and decision/judgement-making skills;
- social skills and abilities;
- emotional resilience;
- proactivity;
- creativity;
- mental agility;
- balanced learning habits and skills;
- self-knowledge.

Studies carried out on the qualities displayed by successful top managers as quoted by Rosemary Stewart[1] show a number of common characteristics, such as:

- willingness to work hard;
- perseverance and determination;
- willingness to take risks;
- ability to inspire enthusiasm;
- toughness.

Managerial effectiveness

As a manager and a leader you will be judged not only on the results you have achieved but on the level of competence you have attained and applied in getting those results. Competence is about knowledge and skills – what people need to know and be able to do to carry out their work well.

You will also be judged on how you do your work – how you behave in using your knowledge and skills. These are often defined as 'behavioural competencies' and can be defined as those aspects of management behaviour that lead to effective performance. They refer to the personal characteristics that people bring to their work roles in such areas as leadership, teamworking, flexibility and communication.

Many organizations have developed competency frameworks that define what they believe to be the key competencies required for success. Such frameworks are used to inform decisions on selection, management development and promotion.

Importantly, they can provide the headings under which the performance of managers and other staff is assessed. Managers who want to get on need to know what the framework is, and the types of behaviour expected of them in each of the areas it covers.

The following is an example of a competency framework.

- *Achievement/results orientation.* The desire to get things done well and the ability to set and meet challenging goals, create own measures of excellence and constantly seek ways of improving performance.
- *Business awareness.* The capacity continually to identify and explore business opportunities, understand the business opportunities and priorities of the organization and constantly seek methods of ensuring that the organization becomes more businesslike.
- *Communication.* The ability to communicate clearly and persuasively, orally or in writing.
- *Customer focus.* The exercise of unceasing care in looking after the interests of external and internal customers to ensure that their wants, needs and expectations are met or exceeded.
- *Developing others.* The desire and capacity to foster the development of members of their team, providing feedback, support, encouragement and coaching.
- *Flexibility.* The ability to adapt to and work effectively in different situations and to carry out a variety of tasks.
- *Leadership.* The capacity to inspire individuals to give of their best to achieve a desired result and to maintain effective relationships with individuals and the team as a whole.
- *Planning.* The ability to decide on courses of action, ensuring that the resources required to implement the action will be available and scheduling the programme of work required to achieve a defined end result.
- *Problem*-solving. The capacity to analyse situations, diagnose problems, identify the key issues, establish and evaluate alternative courses of action, and produce a logical, practical and acceptable solution.
- *Teamwork.* The ability to work cooperatively and flexibly with other members of the team, with a full understanding of the role to be played as a team member.

Some organizations illustrate their competency frameworks with examples of positive or negative indicators of performance under each heading. These provide a useful checklist for managers willing to measure their own performance in order to develop their career. An example is given in the Appendix.

Developing managerial effectiveness

The development of managerial effectiveness should be focused on the qualities and competencies listed above. The fundamental question that is addressed by this book is: 'How can I learn to be a manager?'

A familiar answer to this question is to say that 'managers learn from experience'. But can experience alone be the best teacher? Several writers have expressed their doubts on this score. Tennyson called it a 'dirty nurse'. Oscar Wilde noted that 'experience is the name everyone gives to their mistakes.' And the historian Froude wrote that 'experience teaches slowly and at the cost of mistakes.'

Experience is an essential way of learning to improve but it is an imperfect instrument. We also need guidance from a good manager and from other sources such as this book that will help us to interpret our experience, learn from our mistakes and make better use of our experience in the future.

What you can do

Perhaps Francis Bacon provided the best answer to this question when he wrote: 'studies perfect nature and are perfected by experience.' The art of management, and it is an art, is important enough to be studied. The aim of such studies should be to help us to make better use of our natural attributes – our personality and intelligence – and to ensure that past experience is better interpreted and more fully used, and that future experience is more quickly and purposefully absorbed. The rest of this book provides practical guidance on what you need to know and be able to do in order to become a better manager.

Ten fundamental ways of becoming a better manager

1 Know where you are, where you are going, how you are going to get there and how you will know you have arrived.
2 Aim to master the present and pre-empt the future.
3 Communicate effectively – about what is happening, why it is happening, what is going to happen and why.
4 Make it clear to people what you expect them to do.
5 Realize each person is different.
6 Let people know how they are getting on.
7 Let people make mistakes.
8 Be prepared to say 'no'.
9 Don't worry about being liked.
10 Build trust.

Notes

1 Stewart, R (1967) *Managers and Their Jobs*, Macmillan, London

2 Mintzberg, H (1987) Crafting strategy, *Harvard Business Review*, July–August

3 Peters, T (1988) *Thriving on Chaos*, Macmillan, London

4 Kanter, R M (1989) *When Giants Learn to Dance*, Simon & Schuster, London

5 Pedler, M, Burgoyne, J and Boydell, T (1986) *A Manager's Guide to Self-Development*, McGraw-Hill, Maidenhead

How to be assertive

Assertion and aggression

Assertiveness is:

- standing up for your own rights in such a way that you do not violate another person's rights;
- expressing your needs, wants, opinions, feelings and beliefs in direct, honest and appropriate ways.

When you are being assertive you are not, therefore, being aggressive, which means violating or ignoring other people's rights in order to get your own way or dominate a situation.

Aggressive behaviour causes one of two counterproductive reactions: fight or flight. In other words, aggression either breeds aggression, which gets you nowhere, or it forces people to retreat in a demoralized or dissatisfied way. Indulging in this sort of behaviour will not help to achieve your aim of getting them to go along with you.

Assertive behaviour

Behaving assertively puts you into the position of being able to influence people properly and react to them positively. Assertive statements:

- are brief and to the point;
- indicate clearly that you are not hiding behind something or someone and are speaking for yourself by using words such as: 'I think that...', 'I believe that...', 'I feel that...';
- are not overweighted with advice;
- use questions to find out the views of others and to test their reactions to your behaviour;
- distinguish between fact and opinion;

- are expressed positively but not dogmatically;
- indicate that you are aware that the other people have different points of view;
- express, when necessary, negative feelings about the effects of other people's behaviour on you – pointing out in dispassionate and factual terms the feelings aroused in you by that behaviour, and suggesting the behaviour you would prefer;
- point out to people politely but firmly the consequences of their behaviour.

Handling aggression

If you are faced by aggression, take a breath, count up to 10 and then:

- Ask calmly for information about what is bugging the aggressors.
- State clearly, and again calmly, the position as you see it.
- Empathize with the aggressors by making it plain that you can see it from their point of view, but at the same time explaining in a matter-of-fact way how you see the discrepancy between what they believe and what you feel is actually happening.
- Indicate, if the aggressive behaviour persists, your different beliefs or feelings, but do not cut aggressors short – people often talk, or even shout, themselves out of being aggressive when they realize that you are not reacting aggressively and that their behaviour is not getting them anywhere.
- Suggest, if all else fails, that you leave it for the time being and talk about it again after a cooling-off period.

Influencing styles

Assertiveness is about fighting your own corner. You have to believe in yourself and what you are doing and express these beliefs confidently and without hesitation. It is about using influencing skills.

There are four influencing styles you can use:

- Asserting – making your views clear.
- Persuading – using facts, logic and reason to present your own case, emphasizing its strong points (benefits to the organization or the individual(s) you are dealing with), anticipating objections to any apparent weaknesses and appealing to reason.

- Bridging – drawing out other people's points of view, demonstrating that you understand what they are getting at, giving credit and praise in response to their good ideas and suggestions, joining your views with theirs.

- Attracting – conveying your enthusiasm for your ideas, making people feel that they are all part of an exciting project.

There is more about influencing people in Chapter 22.

How to benchmark

To establish how well – or badly – you are doing, to identify areas for improvement and, importantly, to get new ideas, it pays to compare your organization with its best-performing peers. You need to study what the 'best-in-class' companies are doing – how well they perform generally in comparison with your business, how well they carry out specific activities and processes, and what they are doing that is new and different and might work well in your company.

Asked what he thought of his wife, James Thurber replied: 'Compared with what?' Whatever we are comparing – products, practices, processes, output levels, performance achievements – we all seek yardsticks or measures to enable meaningful comparisons to be made. This is what benchmarking is about.

How does benchmarking work?

The purpose of benchmarking is to identify areas for improvement and stimulate change. It can be defined as:

> A continuous, systematic process of evaluating companies recognized as industry leaders, to determine business and work processes that represent 'best practice' and establish rational performance goals.

Benchmarking processes can be analysed under four headings:

- *Competitive analysis* – the systematic analysis of competitive activity so that performance can be improved.
- *Best practice* – looking for best practice in the ways in which companies operate.
- *Performance comparison* – assessing company performance against that achieved by comparators.
- *Standard setting* – providing guidance on setting appropriate and stretching performance standards.

The underlying logic of benchmarking is compelling: unless you know what the competition is doing, and how your customers rate your efforts on a comparable basis, how can you establish meaningful goals for improvement? Without benchmarks, the impact of improvement programmes can be a lottery; raising standards to an industry average, for example, is not the same as leap-frogging rivals. Benchmarking helps to sets target that enable companies to achieve sustainable competitive advantage.

What do you benchmark?

Anything that drives or measures performance can be benchmarked. Examples include productivity, product quality, standards of service delivery, cycle times, pay, fund management performance, product and service characteristics, employment ratios and employee engagement data.

Benchmarking sometimes concentrates on overall performance indices and ratios, but it often produces the best results when it compares operational or process performance levels so that specific standards and targets for improvement can be set. When valid and reliable comparative data are available on, say, delivery times, managers who will not accept that it is possible to improve their performance can be told: 'If they can do it, then so can you.'

With whom do you benchmark?

Ideally, you benchmark with direct competitors, especially those that are operating in similar circumstances to your own. But direct competitors may be unwilling to exchange information. In any case, useful comparisons on similar aspects of management or business operations can be made with out-of-sector companies.

How do you benchmark?

Some organizations seek outside help but it is possible to run your own benchmarking exercise. This could consist of the following stages:

1 *Plan* – make decisions about what is to be benchmarked. You cannot do everything at once, so you must focus on those areas that are likely to deliver the greatest returns – the drivers of performance.
2 *Collect data* – decide on sources of data (other organizations, published benchmarking data, information from employers' or trade associations, etc). Approach any organizations you select, making sure you contact

the right people, ask the right questions and evaluate the information you receive. You have to bear in mind that some organizations will put forward the most favourable picture of their performance. They may not deliberately distort it, but it is probably best to treat any information you are given by competitors with several large pinches of salt.

3 *Analyse results* – compare the figures and other information provided by different organizations and ensure that, as far as possible, you are comparing like with like. Make allowances for any operational differences that might affect the data. If you are getting information on policies, practices or processes, remember that what works well in one organization might not necessarily work well in yours. People talk about best practice as if it were universally applicable. But it is not. What you do must fit the circumstances of your own organization. Best fit is more important than best practice.

4 *Decide on action* – on the basis of the analysis take a realistic view of what the data tell you needs to be done. Following that assessment, decide on any changes or innovations that emerge as appropriate and that can be implemented without difficulty. A cost–benefit analysis can usefully be made at this stage to show whether any contemplated action is worthwhile.

5 *Implement* – plan the implementation programme carefully – good ideas can too easily go wrong if they are initiated without sufficient care. It is generally best to pilot test any new system. Any changes will have to be managed with equal care.

6 *Review progress* – take stock of how the innovation or changed arrangement is going and take swift corrective action if required. If problems have arisen, it may be necessary to obtain new information from different sources to provide further guidance.

What factors should be taken into account?

The following factors should be taken into account in analysing and using benchmark data:

● Benchmarking is likely to be most effective if the company has a clear vision of where it wants to go and well-articulated strategies for realizing that vision. It should know what its critical success factors or distinctive capabilities are – the drivers of organizational performance.

● Even if like-for-like comparisons can be made between the results achieved by different companies, if these are just in the form of numerical data they may well be insufficient – figures do not tell the whole story. It's what was done to achieve those figures that counts.

That is why benchmarking should cover processes and practices as well as outcomes.

- Because practices are not necessarily transferable, it is necessary to analyse what aspects of them might work if they were modified to fit the requirements of your organization.
- Even if you obtain good, reliable information from a number of sources, it still requires considerable skill and effort to translate this into meaningful and actionable terms for your organization.
- Make sure that organizations provide information on what they are actually achieving, not their intentions for the future.
- There is often as much to learn from the failures and bad practices of comparator organizations (if you can find them out) as there is from their successes.

04

How to budget

The need for budgets

Budgets don't win friends but they do influence people. They can be painful to create and can be agonizing to manage. But they do translate policy into financial terms and, whether we like it or not, that is the way in which plans must be expressed and, ultimately, performance controlled.

Budgets are needed for three reasons:

- to show the financial implications of plans;
- to define the resources required to achieve the plans;
- to provide a means of measuring, monitoring and controlling results against the plans.

The process of budgeting

The process of budgeting consists of the following steps:

1 Budget guidelines are prepared that are derived from the corporate plan and forecasts. They will include sales and outputs targets, the activity levels for which the budget has to cater, and assumptions on inflation, costs and prices. Policies will be set on the profit margins or financial contribution to be achieved. Targets for reducing the budget may be set.

2 Initial budgets setting out proposed expenditure under each heading are prepared by the budget holder. Changes to previous budgets that are not in line with changes in activity levels or inflation, costs and price assumptions have to be justified. Naturally, a budget that failed to achieve the targeted reduction would have to be explained.

3 Draft budgets are checked first by budget accountants and then by higher management to ensure that they meet the guidelines and any increases in expenditure are justified.

4 Subject to any amendment, which may arise from iterative discussion, approved budgets are issued to budget holders as a control document.

5 Control is exercised over expenditure by comparing actuals with the budgeted figure. If there is a difference – a 'variance' – this will have to be justified.

Limitations of budgets

The main problems of budgets are:

- The basic budgeting procedure is inadequate: imprecise guidelines, unsatisfactory background data, cumbersome systems, lack of technical advice and assistance to managers, arbitrary cuts by top management.
- There is an unskilled or cynical approach by managers to budgeting resulting from inadequate basic procedures, lack of guidance, training or encouragement, or a feeling that budgets are simply weapons to be deployed against them rather than tools for them to use.
- There is a lack of accurate forecasts of future activity levels.
- Unrealistic assumptions are made as a basis for budgeting.
- Targets for reducing costs are unrealistic and unachievable.
- It is difficult to amend the budget in response to changing circumstances.
- The fundamental weakness of basing budgets on past levels of expenditure that are simply 'plussed up' rather than subjecting the whole budget to a critical examination.
- There are weaknesses in reporting or controlling procedures that prevent the budget being used to monitor performance.

Preparing budgets

The problems concerning the preparation of budgets mentioned above can be eliminated or at least reduced if the following actions are taken:

- Prepare budget guidelines that set out policies on where you want to go and, broadly, how you intend to get there. These could be set as targets for activity levels such as sales or output, or as an outline of major operating plans. Base any assumptions to be used in budgeting, such as rates of inflation and predicted increases in costs or prices, on properly researched information.

- Set realistic targets for cost reductions. If a corporate cost reduction exercise is laying down the cuts required, at least explain why it is necessary. Help and guidance might be required on the priorities to be attached to different activities and therefore the scope for cutting costs.

- Ensure that those responsible for preparing budgets are given advice and encouragement by management or budget accountants. These experts should be there to help, not to prod or threaten, as they have been known to do.

- Train budget holders in the budgeting process, especially newly appointed managers. It will be a technique with which many people are unfamiliar and they will need all the help they can get.

- Get people to think hard about their budgets. They should be discouraged from simply updating last year's actual expenditures. Wherever there is any choice on how much is spent, they should be asked to go back to first principles and justify the expenditure. For major items they could be required to make out a proper business case that sets out the returns expected on the expenditure. Budget estimates should be based on reliable forecasts of future activity levels and costs, which should be included in supporting documentation. As far as possible each existing and proposed activity should be analysed to establish: its objectives, what is involved, why it is being carried out or is to be carried out, the present and projected costs of the activity, the benefits resulting from the activity and the key performance indicators that can be used to assess the success of the activity.

- Do not accept any large increase on last year's budget without an explanation and a justification.

- Be wary of even a large decrease. This could mean that a significant activity is being marginalized to be replaced by one that is not going to be so productive.

- Probe to ensure that budgets submitted to you are realistic and do not include a 'fudge' factor – sums of money that will be put on one side to cover overspends.

- Do not slash budgets arbitrarily. Give reasons. If you don't, you will get fudge factors or a 'couldn't care less' attitude.

- Update or 'flex' budgets regularly, especially when activity levels and costs are subject to large variations.

Flexible budgets

If it is possible, with a reasonable degree of accuracy, to relate changes in income and costs to levels of activity, the use of flexible budgets is worthwhile. Budgets are 'flexed' when the original budget is deliberately amended to take account of changed activity levels. A static budget is prepared for only one level of activity, such as the volume of sales. This means that both fixed and variable costs are assumed to remain constant at any level of activity. Fixed costs may do so, but variable costs by definition will not. Because the actual activity or output is almost certainly different from the budgeted activity, the original budget will be inaccurate and a false picture will be presented of variances from that budget. It is therefore necessary to flex the budget to reflect different levels of activity. This is done by assuming different levels of activity and preparing cost and overhead budgets for each level.

The control of a flexible budget is carried out on the same basis as any other control process; that is to say, actuals are compared with budget to show any variance. However, the budget with which the actuals are compared is the adjusted budget based on actual activity levels.

Budgetary control

Expenditures against budget have to be monitored by the budget holder so that variances can be dealt with in good time. Budget actuals will be scrutinized by budget or management accountants and variance reports prepared for budget holders and higher management. Budget holders are held to account for any variances and will be expected to take corrective action.

This sounds simple but isn't. A successful budgetary control procedure is not easy to achieve. You have to work at it. There is no problem in designing a system with computer-generated reports containing lots of information. But there is a danger of generating information overload with excessively complex data. The answer is to keep it simple so that variances stare budget holders and their managers in the face and provide a driving force for action.

05

How to communicate

People recognize the need to communicate but find it difficult. Like Schopenhauer's hedgehogs, they want to get together; it's only their prickles that keep them apart.

Words may sound or look precise, but they are not. All sorts of barriers exist between the communicator and the receiver. Unless these barriers are overcome the message will be distorted or will not get through.

Barriers to communication

Hearing what we want to hear

What we hear or understand when someone speaks to us is largely based on our own experience and background. Instead of hearing what people have told us, we hear what our minds tell us they have said. We have preconceptions about what people are going to say, and if what they say does not fit into our framework of reference we adjust it until it does. (Advice on how to listen is given in Chapter 23.)

Ignoring conflicting information

We tend to ignore or reject communication that conflicts with our own beliefs. If it is not rejected, some way is found of twisting and shaping its meaning to fit our preconceptions.

When a message is inconsistent with existing beliefs, the receiver rejects its validity, avoids further exposure to it, easily forgets it and, in his or her memory, distorts what has been heard.

Perceptions about the communicator

It is difficult to separate what we hear from our feelings about the person who says it. Non-existent motives may be ascribed to the communicator.

If we like people we are more likely to accept what they say – whether it is right or wrong – than if we dislike them.

Influence of the group

The group with which we identify influences our attitudes and feelings. What a group hears depends on its interests. Workers are more likely to listen to their colleagues, who share their experiences, than to outsiders such as managers or union officials.

Words mean different things to different people

Essentially, language is a method of using symbols to represent facts and feelings. Strictly speaking, we can't convey meaning – all we can do is to convey words. Do not assume that because something has a certain meaning to you, it will convey the same meaning to someone else.

Non-verbal communication

When we try to understand the meaning of what people say, we listen to the words but we also use other clues that convey meaning. We attend not only to what people say but to how they say it. We form impressions from what is called body language – eyes, the shape of the mouth, the muscles of the face, even posture.

We may feel that these tell us more about what someone is really saying than the words he or she uses. But there is enormous scope for misinterpretation.

Emotions

Our emotions colour our ability to convey or to receive the true message. When we are insecure or worried, what we hear seems more threatening than when we are secure and at peace with the world. When we are angry or depressed, we tend to reject what might otherwise seem like reasonable requests or good ideas.

In a heated argument, many things that are said may not be understood or may be badly distorted.

Noise

Any interference to communication is 'noise'. It can be literal noise that prevents the message being heard, or figurative in the shape of distracting or confused information that distorts or obscures the meaning.

Size

The larger and more complex the organization, the greater the problem of communication. The more levels of management and supervision a message has to pass through, the greater the opportunity for distortion or misunderstanding.

Overcoming barriers to communication

Adjust to the world of the receiver

Try to predict the impact of what you are going to write or say on the receiver's feelings and attitudes. Tailor the message to fit the receiver's vocabulary, interests and values. Be aware of how the information might be misinterpreted because of prejudices, the influence of others and the tendency of people to reject what they do not want to hear.

Use feedback

Ensure that you get a message back from the receiver that tells you how much has been understood.

Use face-to-face communication

Whenever possible talk to people rather than e-mail or write to them. That is how you get feedback. You can adjust or change your message according to reactions. You can also deliver it in a more human and understanding way – this can help to overcome prejudices.

Verbal criticism can often be given in a more constructive manner than a written reproof, which always seems to be harsher.

Use reinforcement

You may have to present your message in a number of different ways to get it across. Re-emphasize the important points and follow up.

Use direct, simple language

This seems obvious. But many people clutter up what they say with jargon, long words and elaborate sentences.

Suit the actions to the word

Communications have to be credible to be effective. There is nothing worse than promising the earth and then failing to deliver. When you say you are going to do something, do it. Next time you are more likely to be believed.

Use different channels

Some communications have to be in writing to put the message across promptly and without any variations in the way they are delivered. But, wherever possible, supplement written communications with the spoken word. Conversely, an oral briefing should be reinforced in writing.

Reduce problems of size

If you can, reduce the number of levels of management.

Encourage a reasonable degree of informality in communications. Ensure that activities are grouped together to ease communication on matters of mutual concern.

06

How to coordinate

Coordinating – 'achieving unity of effort' – is not a separate function of a manager. The concept of coordination does not describe a particular set of operations but all operations that lead to a certain result.

Coordination is required because individual actions need to be integrated. Some activities must follow one another in sequence. Others must go on at the same time and in the same direction in order to finish together.

Approaches to coordination

Obviously, you can achieve good coordination if you get people to work well together. This means integrating their activities, communicating well, exercising leadership and team building (all subjects covered in individual chapters). But you should also pay attention to the specific techniques discussed below.

Planning

Coordinating should take place before the event rather than after it. Planning is the first step. This means deciding what should be done and when. It is a process of dividing the total task into a number of sequenced or related sub-tasks. Then you work out priorities and timescales.

Organizing

You know what should be done. You then decide who does it.

When you divide work between people you should avoid breaking apart those tasks that are linked together and that you cannot separate cleanly from each other.

Your biggest problem will be deciding where the boundaries between distinct but related activities should be. If the boundary is either too rigid or insufficiently well defined, you may have coordination problems. Don't rely too much upon the formal organization as defined in job descriptions, charts and manuals. If you do, you will induce inflexibility and set up communication barriers, and these are fatal to coordination.

The informal organization that exists in all companies can help co-ordination. When people work together they develop a system of social relationships that cut across formal organizational boundaries. They create a network of informal groups that tend to discipline themselves. This frees management from detailed supervision and control and leaves it more time for planning, problem-solving and the overall monitoring of performance.

Delegating

The informal organization can help, but you still need to delegate work to individuals in a way that ensures they know what is expected of them and are aware of the need to liaise with others to achieve a coordinated result.

The art is to make everyone concerned understand the points on which they must link up with other people and the time in which such actions have to be completed. You should not have to tell people to coordinate; they should do so almost automatically. This they will do if you delegate not only specific tasks but also the job of working with others.

Communicating

You should not only communicate clearly what you want done, you should also encourage people to communicate with one another.

Avoid situations in which people can say: 'Why didn't someone tell me about this? If they had, I could have told them how to get out of the difficulty.' Nobody should be allowed to resort to the old excuse that 'no one tells me anything.' It is up to people to find out what they need to know and not wait to be told.

Controlling

If you use the processes described above, and they work, theoretically you will not have to worry any more about coordination.

But, of course, life is not like that. You must monitor actions and results, spot problems and take swift corrective action when necessary. Coordination doesn't just happen. It has to be worked at – but avoid getting too involved. Allow people as much freedom as possible to develop horizontal relationships. These can facilitate coordination far more effectively than rigid and authoritarian control from above.

A case study

There is no one right way of coordinating a number of activities.

It all depends on the nature of the activities and the circumstances in which they are carried out: for example, the present organization structure, the existence of coordinating committees and the facility with which communication can take place between those involved. Ultimately, good coordination depends upon the will of everyone concerned – to coordinate or be coordinated. Formal devices such as committees will not necessarily do the trick.

An example of good coordination took place in a company that was developing a new product in a new market. Neither the product nor the market fitted conveniently into the existing divisional structure and it was therefore decided to appoint one man as project manager to get the product launched. He would have a staff of two: a brand manager and a secretary. The work of development, production, marketing, selling and customer servicing would be carried out by the relevant departments in various divisions of the company.

The project manager had the status and authority to get things done by each department. The board was right behind the project and had allocated the priorities and resources required. But the different activities had to be coordinated and only the project manager could do it.

The easy way out would have been to set up a massive coordinating committee and leave it at that. This would have failed. Projects of this complexity cannot be coordinated just by creating a committee.

The project manager developed a different approach that proved to be highly successful. His first objective was to make everyone concerned enthusiastic about the project. He wanted them to believe in its importance so that they would be committed to working closely with the other departments involved.

His next step was to hold separate discussions with departmental heads so that they completely understood the programme of work required in each area. With the help of a project planner he then drew up a chart showing the key events and activities, and the relationships between them and the sequence in which they needed to take place in order to complete the project. This chart was distributed to all the departmental heads and supplemented by an explanatory brief on the work required at each stage of the programme. Only then did he call a meeting to iron out difficulties and to ensure that everyone knew what had to be done and when.

He set up a system of progress reports and held progress meetings with departmental heads. But these were only held as necessary and he did not rely upon them to achieve coordination. He depended much more on personal contacts with individual managers, reviewing problems, noting where adjustments to the programme were needed, and stimulating the managers to even greater efforts when required. It was time consuming, but it kept him closely in touch so that he could anticipate any likely delays, setbacks or failures in communication, and be in a position to take action. He used the chart as his main instrument for checking that the critical events took place as planned.

The successful coordination and completion of the project were not achieved by one method but by the judicious use of a combination of techniques relevant to the situation: motivating, team building, planning, integrating, monitoring and controlling.

07

How to achieve continuous improvement

If you want to be a better manager, you have to strive constantly to improve your own effectiveness and the effectiveness of the operation or service for which you are responsible. This involves playing a significant part in any organizational programmes for continuous improvement as well as subjecting your own activities to scrutiny so as to ensure that operational problems are identified and overcome.

What is continuous improvement?

The philosophy of continuous improvement at organizational level is that businesses must constantly seek ways of improving their operational systems, the quality of their products and services, and the customer appeal of those products and services.

Continuous improvement involves enlisting the ideas and efforts of everyone in the organization to ensure that a steady stream of suggestions are obtained and acted upon to provide for incremental improvements to operational and quality performance. 'Incremental' is the key word in continuous improvement. It is not about making sudden quantum leaps in response to crisis situations. It is about adopting a steady, step-by-step approach to improving the ways in which the organization goes about doing the things required to deliver value to its customers. This philosophy and the principle of incrementalism applies to everyone in the organization, especially its managers.

The significance of continuous improvement

In Japan the process of continuous improvement is called *kaizen*, which is a composite of the word *kai* meaning change, and *zen* meaning good or for the better. The *kaizen* management style relies on a foundation of gradual change, building up a culture of quality awareness and constant learning. It is almost the opposite of the Western culture of innovation, which is based on sudden change and great leaps forward in business.

The significance of continuous improvement is that it is a day-to-day process in which everyone is involved. Continuous improvement changes the way people think about their work, and it is the *process* of change that is important as well as the results achieved. Its significance also rests on the fact that continuous improvement uses the contributions of all employees. It encourages the production of a stream of suggestions for modest improvements that can be translated into immediate changes in working practices.

How to introduce continuous improvement

Continuous improvement can be introduced by means of communications, involvement, process development and training. Managers play a key role in these activities.

Communications

Top management takes the lead by communicating the values governing continuous improvement, emphasizing the need for everyone to be involved, and setting out strategic goals. Line managers develop the top management message in association with their teams, translating it into their own departmental context and agreeing team goals.

The communications should emphasize that everyone is expected to operate proactively in the search for improvement rather than let problems arise and then react to them.

Involvement

The achievement of continuous improvement should involve everyone in the organization. It is necessary to consider how involvement can take place, either in the form of group activities or by getting individuals and teams to act as assessors or verifiers. Setting up improvement groups means that an intensive training programme has to be planned and implemented.

Involvement can be organized formally by means of:

- *Improvement groups* – these act upon broad management-given directives and advice. They are often inter-departmental.
- *Problem-solving teams* – these are teams brought together to solve specific management-directed problems.
- *Quality circles* – teams made up from members of one department or work area, identifying their own projects to develop. They may be

composed of volunteers and management or supervision may not be directly involved in the teams' deliberations, though they will take part in evaluating proposals and ensuring that they are implemented.

Facilitators may be made available from within the organization to act as educators, trainers and coaches to teams, not only on specific problem-solving techniques but also on the general philosophy of continuous improvement.

Process development

The development of continuous improvement is partly about creating an infrastructure of involvement processes, including suggestion schemes and improvement groups, but it is also concerned with developing appropriate tools and assessment procedures.

Developing and training

The purpose of education is to increase awareness of the need for continuous improvement. Training courses may be held to impart problem-solving and decision-making skills. The use of the various analytical and statistical tools can be demonstrated and practised.

Holding the gains

Evaluation should lead to action 'holding the gains'. The gains can include better practices and processes, cost savings and improved service to customers. Continuous effort is required to ensure that incremental gains are consolidated and become part of normal working practices to the benefit of customers and, therefore, the organization.

Continuous improvement techniques

Improvement is based on building knowledge of what works and does not work and then applying it appropriately. The three basic questions are: 1) What are we trying to accomplish? 2) What changes can we make that will lead to an improvement? And 3) How will we know that a change is an improvement?

The plan–do–check–act cycle is used as the basis for developing and testing changes: plan the change strategy, including who will be involved, what data will be collected and when the data will be considered adequate for study; do the intervention; check the results; act on the knowledge gained from the data – maintain the plan, modify the plan, add to the plan. If the change is successful, embed it by expanding it to the rest of the system, establishing processes to support it and identifying ways in which further improvements can be made.

Continuous improvement involves the use of problem-solving techniques as discussed in Chapter 45. There are a number of analytical techniques also available as described below.

Critical evaluation

Critical evaluation techniques are used to assess the degree to which a proposal or a concept is appropriate or valid. There are five steps:

1 Analyse and describe the requirement.
2 Identify alternative approaches to meeting the requirement.
3 Assess the advantages and disadvantages of each approach.
4 Summarize factors influencing the choice of approach.
5 Define criteria for determining the success of the selected approach.

Cause-and-effect diagrams

Cause-and-effect diagrams are used to clarify the causes of a problem. They are sometimes called 'fishbone diagrams' (because of their shape) or 'Ishikawa diagrams' (after Kaoru Ishikawa, the Japanese quality expert who championed their use).

Suppose a customer complains at a restaurant. The fault may be caused by the raw materials, the cooking, the staff or the facilities. Problems with the raw materials may in turn be caused by suppliers, storage or costs. A cause-and-effect diagram draws these relationships as leading to spines like a fish bone, as shown in Figure 7.1.

Pareto charts

Pareto charts are used to focus on key problems. They are based on Pareto's Law. Pareto, an Italian economist, observed that 20 per cent of the population owned 80 per cent of the wealth. Dr Joseph Duran in the 1940s recognized a universal principle that he called 'the vital few and trivial many'. This principle – that 20 per cent of something produces 80 per cent of the results – became generally known as Pareto's Law. In his original work, Juran noted that 20 per cent of the defects caused 80 per cent of the problems. Many investigations have revealed that this law applies in a wide range of areas. For example, 80 per cent of stock comes from 20 per cent of suppliers, and 80 per cent of sales come from 20 per cent of sales staff. It is also sometimes argued that 20 per cent of an organization's staff will produce 80 per cent of the problems, but it works the other way round: that is, another 20 per cent of staff will produce 80 per cent of added value. The principle has also been applied to the process of management, suggesting

FIGURE 7.1   Cause-and-effect diagram

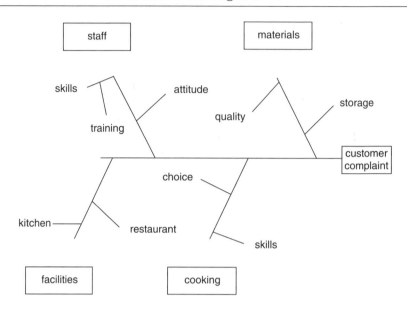

that people should identify the 20 per cent of important things they do during a day and concentrate more on these than on the remaining 80 per cent.

The problem is that of identifying the vital 20 per cent, and Pareto charts are used for this purpose. They illustrate the relative importance of problems by showing their frequency or size in a descending bar graph as illustrated in Figure 7.2. They are constructed by listing the problems and then assessing how significant they are in relation to one another.

FIGURE 7.2   A Pareto chart

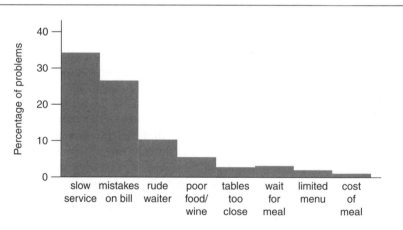

Brainstorming

Brainstorming gets a group to generate as many ideas as possible without pausing to evaluate them. The rationale for the process is that people are more likely to come up with ideas if they are not subjected to criticism or even ridicule. Any idea goes and no one is allowed to comment on what others say. The aim is to produce as many ideas as possible. The majority (possibly 80 per cent) are likely to be useless, but some practical ideas (20 per cent perhaps) will emerge. Evaluation of the ideas only takes place after the session has finished and no one gets the credit for any accepted ideas or the blame for any of those rejected.

Nominal group technique

The nominal group technique gets a group to achieve consensus on the ranking of problems, issues or solutions in order of importance.

Benchmarking

Benchmarking involves identifying good practices in other organizations, comparing them with practices within the benchmarker's organization and drawing conclusions on the lessons learnt from good practice elsewhere that can be applied within that organization. The comparisons concentrate on the areas for improvement that have been identified, and the aim is to learn as much as possible about how other organizations have tackled similar problems, bearing in mind that what works well in one organization does not necessarily succeed in another.

The conditions required to make continuous improvement work

The conditions under which continuous improvement will work well are:

- Top management provides the leadership and direction and ensures that the values underpinning continuous improvement are made clear to all concerned and are acted upon.
- Middle management supports the philosophy of continuous improvement and is prepared actively to support its introduction and to ensure that effort is sustained.
- There is a high-involvement, high-commitment culture in the organization.
- There is trust between management and employees and vice versa. Management must trust employees to act independently and employees

must trust management not to exploit their ideas to their detriment. This trust must be earned. Management must deliver their promises and employees, with guidance, encouragement and help, must show that they can be trusted to get on with it.

- Continuous support must be provided by management to the improvement process. This will include facilitating improvement groups and providing the education and training required.

- Action learning must take place – people should learn from the actions they take. This means that processes of evaluation and action planning are required.

- The organization must function as a learning organization: that is, one that facilitates the learning of all its members, thus continually improving by rapidly creating and refining the capabilities required for future success.

- Employees are rewarded for their contributions to continuous improvement, but these rewards should be non-financial and take the form of various kinds of recognition, to teams and individuals, publicly and privately.

How to control

08

Basically, you are seeking to control two areas – input and output – and the relationship between them, which is productivity or performance. All managers will know Murphy's two laws: if anything can go wrong, it will; and of the things that can't go wrong, some will.

The aim of good control is to protect your plans from the operation of these laws as far as possible, to detect trouble spots before they erupt, to prevent those accidents that are just waiting to happen. Prevention is better than cure.

Essentials of control

Control is relative. It does not deal with absolutes, only with the difference between good and not-so-good performance.

The basis of control is measurement. It depends on accurate information about what is being achieved. This is then compared with what should have been achieved and with what has been achieved in the past. But that is only a starting point. Good control also identifies responsibility and points the way to action.

Effective control

If you want to exercise good control you need to:

1 Plan what you aim to achieve.
2 Measure regularly what has been achieved.
3 Compare actual achievements with the plan.
4 Take action to exploit opportunities revealed by this information or to correct deviations from the plan.

Note that control is not only a matter of putting things right. It also has a positive side – getting more or better things done on the basis of information received.

Problems of control

A good control system is not easy to set up. There are two essentials:

- To set appropriate and fair targets, standards and budgets. (This may be difficult where the scope for quantification is limited or if circumstances make forecasts unreliable.) Note that targets are good, within reason, but too many can cause resentment, confusion and focusing on producing the right numbers rather than doing the right things.

- To decide what information is crucial for control purposes and design reports that clearly convey that information to the people who need it and can use it to point the way to action. This also produces problems. Too many control systems generate a surfeit of indigestible data that go to the wrong people and are not acted upon. You can have too little information, but there is also such a thing as information overkill. There is, moreover, a tendency for some people to report good results and cover up poor ones. In any case, the figures may not tell the whole story.

Overcoming the problem

There are five steps to take if you want to achieve good control:

1 Decide what you want to control.
2 Decide how you are going to measure and review performance.
3 Use ratio analysis to make comparisons and to identify variations and problems.
4 Set up a control system.
5 Manage by exception.

Controlling inputs and outputs

In controlling input and output, and hence productivity, an overview is essential. It is no good concentrating on inputs, mainly expressed as costs, unless you look at the benefits arising from these expenditures and the effectiveness with which the costs have been incurred. Cost–benefit and cost-effectiveness studies are an essential part of the control process.

Input control

When you control inputs you should aim to measure and assess the performance of:

- *Money* – its productivity, flow, liquidity and conservation.
  - You need to know what return you are getting on investments compared with the return you want.
  - You should ensure that you have the cash and working capital to run the business. Cash-flow analysis is vital. One of the golden rules of management, as stated by Robert Heller, is 'cash in must exceed cash out.'
  - You must conserve and provide the money needed to finance future trading and development projects and for capital investment.
  - Management has to know how effectively its financial resources are being used to produce goods, services and profits, and this requires continuous and close attention to the control of direct and indirect costs and overheads generally.
- *People* – the effectiveness of the people you employ in terms of their quality and performance.
- *Materials* – their availability, condition, convertibility and waste.
- *Equipment* – machine utilization and capability.

Output control

- *Quantitative control measures* – the units produced or sold, the amount of services provided, the sales turnover obtained and the profits achieved. Key performance measures will vary between organizations. You need to determine through analysis which are the crucial indicators of success or failure.
- *Qualitative control measures* – the level of service provided by an organization (eg a public corporation) or by a non-productive department within an organization (eg HR). It is more difficult to select valid performance measures in these areas, but the attempt should be made.

Control systems

What you need from a control system

Your basic requirement is reports that clearly identify areas of good and bad performance so that appropriate action can be taken.

At higher levels 'exception reporting' should be adopted so that significant deviations, on which action should be taken, can be highlighted. Overall summaries of performance against plan and of trends will also be necessary at this level, but these may disguise significant underlying deviations that would be pointed out in an exception report.

The reports themselves should:

- contain measurements that are accurate, valid and reliable, and that permit a direct and easy comparison between planned and actual performance;
- analyse trends, comparing one period's performance with that of the previous period or of the same period the previous year and, where appropriate, summarizing the year-to-date position;
- be given to the person who is responsible for the activity concerned;
- arrive promptly, in time to allow the necessary action to be taken;
- provide succinct explanations of any deviations from plan.

Measurements

Measurement is a good thing, but all figures need to be treated with caution. They may conceal more than they reveal. The weaknesses to look for are:

- *Non-representative reporting* – data selected that do not cover the key issues, disguise unfavourable results or overemphasize favourable performance.
- *Not comparing like with like* – the 'apples and pears syndrome'. For example, a trend or projection that does not take account of changing or new factors that have altered or will alter the situation since the base data were collected.
- *Not starting from a common base* – this is a variant on the 'like with like' problem. Trend comparisons should be related to a common base in terms both of the period and the elements covered by the information.
- *Misleading averages* – averages do not always tell you the whole story. They may conceal significant extremes in performance.
- *Unintentional errors* – simple mistakes in calculation, presentation or observation.
- *Measurements out of context* – almost any single measure is influenced by, or inseparable from, other measures. Figures in isolation may not mean very much. You have to know about relationships and underlying influences.

Management by exception

Management by exception is a system that rings alarm bells only when the manager's attention is needed. The principle was invented by the father of scientific management, Frederick Taylor. In 1911 he wrote in *Principles of Scientific Management*:[1]

Under the exception principle the manager should receive only condensed, summarized and invariably comparative reports covering, however, all of the elements entering into the management and even these summaries should all be carefully gone over by an assistant before they reach the manager, and have all the exceptions to the past averages or standards pointed out, both the especially good and the especially bad exceptions, thus giving him in a few minutes a full view of progress which is being made, or the reverse, and leaving him free to consider the broader lines of policy and to study the character and fitness of the important men under him.

Management by exception frees the boss to concentrate on the issues that matter. It gives the subordinate more scope to get on with his or her work while knowing that events out of the ordinary will be reported upwards.

Deciding what constitutes an exception is a useful exercise in itself. It means selecting the key events and measures that will show up good, bad or indifferent results and indicate whether or not performance is going according to plan.

The chosen indicators or ratios can be studied so that the significance of changes or trends is readily understood. More important, the possible causes of deviations can be analysed and kept in mind. Investigations can then be quickly launched in the right direction and swift remedial action can be taken.

Most of us have come across the boss or manager who seems to have the almost magic facility for studying a mass of figures and immediately spotting the one really important deviation or the item that does not ring true. It sometimes seems to be pure instinct, but of course it is not. Such managers are practising the art of management by exception, even if they never call it by that name. Their experience and analytical powers have told them what constitutes normal performance. But they can spot something out of the ordinary at a thousand paces. They know what the key indicators are and they look for them, hard. This is a skill that anyone can develop. And the effort of acquiring it is well worthwhile.

Note

1 Taylor, F (1911) *Principles of Scientific Management*, Harper & Row, New York

09

How to be creative and innovative

Walter Bagehot wrote: 'It is often said that men are ruled by their imagination; but it would be truer to say that they are governed by the weakness of their imagination.'

Unimaginative management is a sure way to failure. Creative thinking that leads to innovation aims to overcome the danger of being governed by this weakness.

Creativity

Creative and logical thinking

Creative thinking is imaginative thinking. It produces new ideas, new ways of looking at things. It relates things or ideas that were previously unrelated. It is discontinuous and divergent.

Edward de Bono[1] invented the phrase 'lateral thinking' for it and this term has stuck; it implies sideways leaps in the imagination rather than a continuous progression down a logical chain of reasoning.

Logical or analytical thinking is a step-by-step process. It is continuous, one step leading to the next until, ideally, you converge on the only possible solution. It is sometimes called 'convergent' thinking; de Bono refers to it as 'vertical thinking' because you go straight down the line from one state of information to another.

De Bono summed up the differences between vertical and lateral thinking as follows:

Vertical thinking	Lateral thinking
Chooses	Changes
Looks for what is right	Looks for what is different
One thing must follow directly	Makes deliberate jumps from another
Concentrates on relevance	Welcomes chance intrusions
Moves in the most likely direction	Explores the least likely directions

Creative thinking is not superior to logical thinking. It's just different. The best managers are both creative and logical. Eventually, however creative they have been, they have to make a decision. And logical thinking is necessary to ensure that it is the right decision.

The process of creativity

In *The Act of Creation*, Arthur Koestler[2] described the process of creativity as one of 'bisociation': putting together two unconnected facts or ideas to form a single idea. The establishment of the relationship or bisociation is usually accompanied by a release of tension. There is a flash of illumination leading to a shout of 'Eureka!' or at least 'Aha!' As Koestler remarks, it is like the release of tension after the unexpected punchline of a joke – the 'haha' reaction. Or even the less dramatic release of tension when confronting a work of art.

If we assume that it is desirable to increase our capacity for creative thinking, there are three steps to take:

1 Understand the barriers to creative thinking.
2 Develop individual capacity for creative thinking.
3 Use the collective capacities of groups of people to develop new ideas by brainstorming.

Barriers to creative thinking

The main barriers to creative thinking are:

● Allowing your mind to be conditioned into following a dominant pattern – the mind is a patterning system and this means you can be trapped into a fixed way of looking at things, what de Bono calls a 'concept prison' or a 'tethering factor'.

- Restricting the free growth of your ideas within rigidly drawn boundaries that are treated as limiting conditions.
- Failure to identify and examine the assumptions you are making to ensure that they are not restricting the development of new ideas.
- Polarizing alternatives – reducing every decision to an 'either/or' when there may be other ways of looking at things.
- Being conditioned to think sequentially rather than laterally and looking for the 'best' idea, not different ideas. As de Bono says: 'It is better to have enough ideas for some of them to be wrong than always to be right by having no ideas at all.'
- Lack of effort in challenging the obvious – it is tempting to slip into the easy solution.
- Evaluating too quickly – jumping to conclusions and not giving yourself enough time to allow your imagination to range freely over other possible ways of looking at things.
- A tendency to conform – to give the answer expected.
- Fear of looking foolish or being put down.

How to develop your ability to think creatively

If you want to think more creatively, the first thing to do is to analyse yourself. Go through the list of barriers to creativity and ask yourself the question 'Is this me?' If it is, think about ways in which you can overcome the difficulty, concentrating on:

- breaking away from any restrictions;
- opening up your mind to generate new ideas;
- delaying judgement until you have thoroughly explored the alternative ideas.

Breaking away

To break away from the constraints on your ability to generate new ideas you should:

- Identify the dominant ideas influencing your thinking.
- Define the boundaries (ie past experience, precedents, policies, procedures, rules) within which you are working and try to get outside them by asking questions such as:
  - Are the constraints reasonable?
  - Is past experience reliable?
  - What's new about the present situation?
  - Is there another way?

- Bring your assumptions out into the open and challenge any that restrict your freedom to develop new ideas.
- Reject 'either/or' propositions – ask 'Is there really a simple choice between alternatives?'
- Keep on asking 'Why?' (But bear in mind that if you do this too bluntly to other people you can antagonize them.)

Generating new ideas

To generate new ideas you have to open up your mind. If you have removed some of the constraints as suggested above you will be in a better position to:

- Look at the situation differently, exploring all possible angles.
- List as many alternative approaches as possible without seeking the 'one best way' (there is no such thing) and without indulging in premature evaluation (which can at best lead to partial satisfaction).
- In de Bono's words, 'arrange discontinuity', deliberately set out to break the mould. The techniques for triggering off new ideas include:
  - free thinking, allowing your mind to wander over alternative and in many cases apparently irrelevant ways of looking at the situation;
  - deliberately exposing yourself to new influences in the form of people, articles, books, indeed anything that might give you a different insight, even though it might not be immediately relevant;
  - switching yourself or other people from problem to problem;
  - arranging for the cross-fertilization of ideas with other people;
  - using analogies to spark off ideas; the analogy should be suggested by the problem but should then be allowed to exist in its own right to indicate a different way of looking at the problem;
  - 're-framing', placing the problem in a different context to generate new insights.

Delaying judgement

Your aim in creative thinking should be to separate the evaluation of ideas from their generation. The worst mistake you can make is to kill off new ideas too quickly. It is always easy to find 10 ways of saying 'no' to anything. For example:

- It won't work.
- We're already doing it.
- It's been tried before without success.
- It's not practical.
- It won't solve the problem.

- It's too risky.
- It's based on pure theory.
- It will cost too much.
- It will antagonize the customers/the boss/the union/the workers/the shareholders, etc.
- It will create more problems than it solves.

Some of these objections may be valid. But they should be held back until you have generated as many ideas as possible. Allow ideas to grow a little. Don't strangle them at birth.

It is too easy to say 'no', too easy to ridicule anything new or different. In creative thinking it is the end result that counts, and if you want it to be original you must not worry too much about the route you follow to get there. It doesn't matter if you stumble sometimes or take the wrong turning, as long as delays are not protracted and you arrive in the right place at the end.

As de Bono (1971) says:

> In vertical thinking one has to be right at every step. So, no matter how many steps are taken, the end point (idea, solution, conclusion) is automatically right if all the intervening steps have been right... In lateral thinking one does not have to be right at each step, but one must be right at the end.

Delaying judgement is difficult. It goes against the grain. You have to make a conscious effort to hold back until the right moment arrives, which is when you feel that you have collected as many new ideas as you can in the time available.

Our training, our inhibitions, our reluctance to look foolish or to go out on a limb all work against us. We should certainly try to do it ourselves and persuade other people to go along with us. But we can help the processes of opening up, introducing discontinuity and releasing new ideas by the technique of brainstorming.

Brainstorming

Brainstorming has been defined as a means of getting a large number of ideas from a group of people in a short time. It is essentially a group activity that uses a formal setting to generate as many ideas as possible without pausing to evaluate them.

The main features of a brainstorming session are as follows:

1 A group of between six and twelve people is assembled. Some will be directly involved with the problem, some should be drawn from other areas from which they can bring different ideas and experience to bear on the problem.

There is a chairman and a note-taker.

2 The chairman defines the rules, emphasizing that:
- The aim is to get as many ideas as possible.
- No attempt will be made to evaluate any ideas.
- No one should feel inhibited about coming up with suggestions.

3 If necessary there is a warm-up session to familiarize the group with the procedure. For example, they could be asked to suggest how many uses they can think of for a paper clip.

4 The chairman states the problem, avoiding the trap of defining it too narrowly.

5 The chairman opens the session by a phrase such as 'In how many ways can we...?'

6 The chairman encourages people to contribute and prevents any attempt to evaluate ideas. From time to time he or she may restate the problem.

7 The note-taker condenses the ideas suggested and lists them on flip charts, not attempting to act as an editor or worrying about duplications at this stage. The session should not be tape-recorded, as this may inhibit ideas.

8 The chairman keeps on encouraging the group to contribute, trying to get people to freewheel and produce as many ideas as possible – good, bad, indifferent, sensible or silly. He or she keeps the pace going and never comments or allows anyone else to comment on a contribution. Every idea is treated as relevant.

9 The chairman closes the meeting after 30 minutes or so – 45 minutes at most. The session must not be allowed to drag on.

10 Evaluation takes place later, possibly with a different group. At this session the aim is to:
- Select ideas for immediate use.
- Identify ideas for further exploration.
- Review any different approaches that have been revealed by the session.

Brainstorming is a useful technique for releasing ideas, overcoming inhibitions, cross-fertilizing ideas and getting away from patterned thinking. It needs to be planned and executed carefully and proper evaluation is essential.

Use it selectively, where there seems to be ample scope for different ideas. It will not solve all your problems but can help you to crash through the barriers erected by the traditional approaches to decision-making.

Remember that however creative you are, what you finally decide on has to work. Brainstorming and other techniques for increasing creativity will help you to break new ground, but eventually you will have to think clearly and analytically about the pros and cons of the preferred solution before making your final decision.

Innovation

Innovation is the lifeblood of an organization. There is nothing so stultifying to a company – or the people in it – as a belief that the old ways must be the best ways. An organization that tries to stand still will not survive.

Innovation requires a blend of creativity, clear thinking and the ability to get things done. It requires thinkers and doers to work closely together. Top management must create a climate in which managers have the scope to develop new ideas and the resources to implement them.

The success of innovative projects, therefore, can be seen to depend on two issues: the characteristics of the organization and those of the individual manager.

Organizational characteristics

The organizational characteristics that encourage innovation are:

- a free flow of information that allows executives to find ideas in unexpected places and pushes them to combine fragments of information;
- close and frequent contact between departments, and an emphasis on lateral as well as vertical relationships, providing resources, information and support;
- a tradition of working in teams and sharing credit;
- senior executives who believe in innovation and will make the necessary resources available;
- managers with the ability and desire to seize opportunities and to make time available for innovation.

Individual characteristics

To be an effective innovator you need:

- To have a clear initial view of the results you want to achieve – you should not worry too much to begin with about the ways of achieving them.
- To define clearly the aims and benefits of the project.
- To argue the case for the project persuasively, making a compelling business case (see Chapter 22).
- To elicit support not only from your boss but also from your colleagues and subordinates – you need to build a coalition in which everyone shares equally in the belief that the project is worthwhile.

- Courage – to take calculated risks and to weather the storm when the inevitable setbacks occur.
- To be good at getting people to act – mobilizing people to contribute fully to the project means using a participative management style.
- Power to mobilize support and resources and to achieve results.
- The ability to handle interference or opposition to the project – resistance can be open, but it often takes a passive or covert form: criticism of the plan's details, foot-dragging, late responses to requests, or arguments over the allocation of time and resources among projects. Covert resistance can be the most dangerous.
- The force of character to maintain momentum, especially after the initial enthusiasm for the project has waned and the team is involved in more tedious work.

Notes

1 de Bono, E (1971) *Lateral Thinking for Managers*, McGraw-Hill, London
2 Koestler, A (1984) *The Act of Creation*, Hutchinson, London

10

How to cut costs

Costs always need controlling. You should start with the assumption that costs are too high and can be reduced. This assumption is based on the knowledge that many companies have not only survived but also flourished after drastic cost-cutting exercises. When you remove the fat that always exists you are left with a leaner and more powerful organization.

What to cut

Your attack on costs should concentrate on these six areas:

- *Employee costs* – in labour-intensive companies employee costs may exceed 50 per cent of income. Over-employment, especially in service and staff departments, is a major contributory cause of excessive costs. Employment costs will include the direct costs of salaries, wages, pensions (a considerable item) and other benefits, and the indirect cost of the HR and training functions.

- *Manufacturing costs* – these are the actual costs incurred in making products; they reflect labour, material and operating costs, but also, importantly, the way the product has been designed.

- *Selling costs* – these may be largely accounted for by the cost of employees in the sales, customer service or distribution functions, although this will be covered under employee costs. The figures will also include advertising, promotions, public relations, packaging and display material.

- *Development costs* – these are the costs of developing new products, processes, materials and systems, especially IT, and of acquiring new businesses.

- *Material and inventory costs* – the cost of buying materials and bought-in parts and of maintaining optimum stock levels. The latter can be particularly high if inventory control systems are ineffective.

- *Operating costs* – all the other costs incurred in running the business. These include space, facilities, IT, the provision of plant and equipment and all the services required to keep the organization going.

Waste and costly activities

Any examination-of-costs exercise should first focus on wasteful practices and costly activities. The areas where they can occur should be identified before conducting a cost-cutting exercise so that attention can be directed to likely trouble spots. Concentrate on both practices or procedures that can lead to waste or pointless costs, and on areas where employees can waste time or incur unnecessary expenditure.

Waste can incur in any of the following areas:

- over-complex procedures with unnecessary forms and reports;
- too much unnecessary traffic on the intranet;
- focusing so much on achieving output or service standards that attention is diverted from the cost of doing so;
- too much checking and verifying of work;
- too many indecisive meetings;
- too many layers of management and supervision;
- delays in decision-making because authority is not delegated down the line;
- over-rigid adherence to rules and regulations;
- bottlenecks and inefficient work flows.

Time-wasting practices by staff can include lateness or leaving early, prolonged tea or meal breaks, unnecessary breaks for any other reason, spending time on the internet and dealing with personal matters in company time. Other wasteful practices include extravagant use of the company's facilities.

Cost-creating practices can include absenteeism and frequent absences through illness. A major cost for all retail companies and other businesses too is pilfering.

Planning to cut costs

First you build cost-effectiveness into your plans. Then you introduce or improve procedures such as budgeting that define and justify the costs that it is reasonable to incur. You later control expenditure against the budget, probing into over-expenditure, finding out why it is happening and initiating corrective action.

Plans should be based on cost–benefit studies that aim to find the best ratio between expenditure and results; in other words, to minimize costs and maximize benefits. The emphasis should be on realism. It is good to be forward looking and entrepreneurial. But if you are like that, you are always in danger of becoming euphoric about the future, overestimating the benefits and underestimating the costs. At the planning stage you must think hard about the costs you are likely to incur. You must be realistic. It will almost certainly cost more than you think (or than your suppliers tell you it will cost). Find out what you are really going to spend by analysis and obtaining estimates from a number of people. Add at least 10 per cent for contingencies. Insist on penalty clauses to recover costs in the event of an overspend. Query every request for a change in a specification or for something extra, and insist on a cost estimate. Allow for inflation and fluctuation in exchange rates. Always expect the worse.

You should be equally realistic about benefits. Business cases are littered with overestimates of benefits as well as underestimates of costs. Challenge every assumption. Carry out a 'sensitivity analysis' to determine the effects on income and costs of optimistic, realistic and pessimistic forecasts of performance.

The cost-reduction exercise

A cost-reduction exercise is a planned campaign aimed at cutting costs by a specified amount. It requires three initial steps, the careful allocation of responsibility for the exercise and the application of a searching, deliberate, carefully controlled and consistent approach to conducting it.

Initial steps

Set targets, either for immediate cuts in crisis conditions or for specific reductions in the short term (defined in weeks rather than months). Targets may call for an overall reduction of costs by, say, 10 per cent or for cutting overheads by a certain percentage. Or they may be set in specific areas, eg a 10 per cent reduction in staffing. They can be expressed in the form of ratio improvement, for example reducing the ratio of labour costs to sales from 11 to 10 per cent.

The significant impact of overheads on profits should be emphasized to everyone. It is interesting to note that in a company where profits are 10 per cent of sales, a reduction in the ratio of labour costs to sales from 11 to 10 per cent would increase profits by 10 per cent. It all ends up on the bottom line and that is what counts.

Productivity targets expressed in financial terms, such as 'reduce costs per unit of output by 3 per cent', may be less immediate but they can usefully be incorporated in a set of cost-reduction targets as longer-term objectives. Increases in productivity can be obtained by reducing costs in relation to output, or by increasing output in relation to costs or, preferably, by both reducing costs and increasing output. The message must be got across that unit costs are there to be attacked at all times – after all, they aggregate into total costs. Get down to basics: the shop floor, the distribution centre, the retail unit or the general office. This is where the main costs are incurred. Keep it simple. Look at specific items. Don't accept excuses. Compare and contrast to identify areas where costs are excessive. Benchmark similar organizations to find out what their cost ratios are and what they are doing about optimizing them. You can learn a lot from the experiences of other people. Competitors are not going to cooperate, but comparable organizations that are broadly similar to yours in different manufacturing or retailing areas may do so. Employers' and trade associations can help with information.

Decide where to cut – typically, the most fruitful areas are in employment costs (reducing headcounts) and wasteful practices. It is remarkable how often departmental managers who scream with pain when they are told to cut their staff by, say, 10 per cent will cope quite well afterwards. People responsible for cost-reduction exercises will claim and prove that they can always cut staff numbers by 15 per cent or even more without reducing efficiency.

Decide how to cut – allocating responsibilities, drawing up the programme and implementing it.

Responsibility for the cost-reduction exercise

The most important thing to do is to appoint as senior an executive as possible, preferably a full-time member of the board, to direct the cost-reduction exercise. He or she should have drive, energy, determination and, most important, the authority and courage to implement measures, however unpleasant some of them may be.

The question of who is to assist this executive then arises. You may consider using management consultants to help and advise on specific problem areas. But do not ask consultants to carry out the main task. If your organization is not capable of taking action itself, however drastic, it does not deserve to survive. In any case, consultants are expensive and this is supposed to be a cost-cutting exercise.

Neither should you set up a committee to control the exercise. Committees are obstacles to action. You might establish a small (not more than three people) project team of senior executives, but do not let them function as a standing committee with agendas, minutes and so on. Better still, give complete authority to one director to control the exercise to use whom he or she wants when he or she wants and to call meetings as she or he thinks fit.

The director in charge of the exercise needs terms of reference by which to operate. They should take the form of a set of targets to be achieved by a certain date or sequence of dates. If there are any constraints (eg don't sack the chairman's son-in-law) they should be mentioned now. The director should then be told the extent of his or her authority to make decisions and when and in what circumstances to report back. She or he can them proceed to carry out an initial survey of the situation and scope for cuts, and then solicit opinions about what needs to be done, gather the facts to support or refute those opinions, define the problem areas, decide what to do and draw up a programme for doing it.

Approach to the exercise

Successful cost-reduction exercises use the most simple of questioning techniques:

- What is done?
- Why is it done?
- Does it need to be done at all?
- If it needs to be done, can it be simplified or carried out more cheaply?

The following principles can be applied:

- Top managers must accept a revision of the administrator's task. Top management may have imposed or supported countless rules and regulations to ensure that the systems and methods used in the business are foolproof. These may seem to have been written on the assumption that all employees fall into two categories: stupid or crooked. It has been said that if you cast the administrator in the role of bureaucrat he will do it superbly. The paraphernalia of administrative systems and routines drawn up under this type of regime can only be swept away by top management.

- The price of perfection is prohibitive: sensible approximation costs less. In Voltaire's words: 'the best is the enemy of the good.' Aim high but don't overstretch yourself in doing it. Productivity in administration means one person trying to reach 95 per cent efficiency and reaching it, rather than two people trying to reach 100 per cent and only reaching 90 per cent.

- Most employees can be trusted. If this principle is accepted, a wide range of checks and monitoring can be replaced by managers managing and team leaders leading. Thorough spot checks can be used to supplement day-to-day management and eliminate expensive and oppressive supervision.

- All staff can help to bring about the desired changes. Most people, if encouraged, will bring forward ideas to simplify and rationalize their work. Improvement groups can be formed to look at specific issues.

- Consider ways of cutting employment costs without compulsory redundancy. Discussions with employees and their union representatives can produce alternative ways such as part-time working for a temporary period.

- Staff can become too specialized. Too many specialists can produce unnecessary work and hinder flexibility. Specialists exist to serve and ease the running of the business, not to stifle initiative, become barriers to action or create yet another paper chain.

- Never legislate for every eventuality. Leave as much as possible to the common sense of those who are trusted in managerial positions.

- There is no substitute for personal probing into what is happening. You will find out more if you find out for yourself. Don't be afraid to conduct a sample first-hand investigation. A focused study can be more valuable than an all-embracing but superficial investigation.

11 How to be decisive

Good managers are decisive. They can quickly size up a situation and reach the right conclusion on what should be done about it.

To say someone 'is decisive' is praise indeed as long as it is understood that the decisions are effective. To be decisive it is first necessary to know something about the decision-making process as summarized below. You should also be familiar with the techniques of problem-solving, as explained in Chapter 45. Armed with this knowledge you can adopt the approaches described at the end of this chapter.

Characteristics of the decision-making process

Decision-making is about analysing a situation or problem, identifying possible courses of action, weighing them up and defining a course of action. Peter Drucker[1] says:

- A decision is a judgement. It is a choice between alternatives. It is rarely a choice between right and wrong. It is at best a choice between almost right and probably wrong – but much more often a choice between two courses of action neither of which is probably more nearly right than the other.
- You should not expect or even welcome a bland consensus view.
- The best decisions emerge from conflicting viewpoints. This is Drucker's first law of decision-making: 'One does not make a decision without disagreements.' You can benefit from a clash of opinion to prevent people falling into the trap of starting with the conclusion and then looking for the facts that support it.

Alfred P Sloan of General Motors knew this. At a meeting of one of his top committees he said 'Gentlemen, I take it we are all in agreement on the decision here.' Everyone around the table nodded assent. 'Then', continued Mr Sloan, 'I propose we postpone further discussion of the matter until our next meeting to give ourselves time to develop disagreement and perhaps gain some understanding of what the decision is all about.'

Ten approaches to being decisive

1 *Make decisions faster* – Jack Welch when heading General Electric used to say 'In today's lightning-paced environment, you don't have time to think about things. Don't sit on decisions. Empty that in-basket so that you are free to search out new opportunities... Don't sit still. Anybody sitting still, you are going to guarantee they're going to get their legs knocked from under them.'

2 *Avoid procrastination* – it is easy to put an e-mail demanding a decision into the 'too difficult' section of your actual or mental in-tray. Avoid the temptation to fill your time with trivial tasks so that the evil moment when you have to address the issue is postponed. Make a start. Once you have got going you can deal with the unpleasant task of making a decision in stages. A challenge often becomes easier once we have started dealing with it. Having spent five minutes on it we don't want to feel it was time wasted, so we carry on and complete the job.

3 *Expect the unexpected* – you are then in the frame of mind needed to respond decisively to a new situation.

4 *Think before you act* – this could be a recipe for delay, but decisive people use their analytical ability to come to swift conclusions about the nature of the situation and what should be done about it.

5 *Be careful about assumptions* – we have a tendency to leap to conclusions and seize on assumptions that support our case and ignore the facts that might contradict it.

6 *Learn from the past* – build on your experience in decision-making; what approaches work best. But don't rely too much on precedents. Situations change. The right decision last time could well be the wrong one now.

7 *Be systematic* – adopt a rigorous problem-solving approach as described in Chapter 45. This means specifying objectives – what you want to achieve – defining the criteria for judging whether they have been achieved, getting and analysing the facts, looking for causes rather than focusing on symptoms, developing and testing hypotheses and alternative solutions, and evaluating possible causes of action against the objectives and criteria.

8 *Talk it through* – before you make a significant decision talk it through with someone who is likely to disagree so that any challenge they make can be taken into account (but you have to canvass opinion swiftly).

9 *Leave time to think it over* – swift decision-making is highly desirable but you must avoid knee-jerk reactions. Pause, if only for a few minutes, to allow yourself time to think through the decision you propose to make. And confirm that it is logical and fully justified.

10 *Consider the potential consequences* – McKinsey calls this 'consequence management'. Every decision has a consequence, and you should consider very carefully what that might be and how you will manage it. When making a decision it is a good idea to start from where you mean to end – define the end result and then work out the steps needed to achieve it.

Note

1 Drucker, P (1967) *The Effective Executive*, Heinemann, London

How to delegate

12

Delegation is the process of allocating work for subordinates to do. You can't do everything yourself, so you have to delegate. At first sight delegation looks simple: just tell people what you want them to do and then let them do it. But there is more to it than that.

It may be that you would wish to delegate everything except what your subordinate cannot do. But you cannot then withdraw. You have arranged for someone else to do the job, but you have not passed on the responsibility for it. You are always accountable to your superior for what your subordinate does.

Hence, as is often said, you can't delegate responsibility.

Delegation is difficult. It is perhaps the hardest task that managers have to do. The problem is achieving the right balance between delegating too much or too little and between over- or under-supervision. When you give people a job to do you have to make sure that it is done. And you have to do that without breathing down their necks, wasting your time and theirs, and getting in the way. There has to be trust as well as guidance and supervision.

Advantages of delegation

- It relieves you of routine and less critical tasks, and it frees you for more important work.
- It extends your capacity to manage.
- It reduces delay in decision-making – as long as authority is delegated close to the point of action.
- It allows decisions to be taken at the level where the details are known.
- It develops the abilities and confidence of staff.

The process of delegation

Delegation is a process that can follow a sequence from total control (no freedom of action for the individual to whom work has been allocated) to full devolution (the individual is completely empowered to carry out the work), as illustrated in Figure 12.1.

FIGURE 12.1   The delegation sequence

Degree of control exercised by manager

Degree of freedom devolved to individual

| Manager allocates task but exercises total control | Manager gives specific instructions and checks constantly | Manager briefs individual and checks regularly | Manager gives general directions to individual and asks for feedback at the latter's discretion | Manager empowers individual to control own performance of task |

When to delegate

You should delegate when:

- You have more work than you can effectively carry out yourself.
- You cannot allocate sufficient time to your priority tasks.
- You want to develop your subordinate.
- The job can be done adequately by your subordinate.

How to delegate

When you delegate you have to decide:

- What to delegate.
- To whom you delegate – choosing who does the work.
- How to inform or brief your subordinate – giving out the work.
- How you will guide and develop your subordinate.
- How you will monitor his or her performance.

What to delegate

You delegate tasks that you don't need to do yourself. You are not just ridding yourself of the difficult, tedious or unrewarding tasks. Neither are you trying to win for yourself an easier life. Delegation will, in fact, make your life more difficult, but also more rewarding.

Clearly, you delegate routine and repetitive tasks that you cannot reasonably be expected to do yourself – as long as you use the time you have won productively.

You also delegate specialist tasks to those who have the skills and know-how to do them. You cannot do it all yourself. Nor can you be expected to know it all yourself. You have to know how to select and use expertise. There will be no problem as long as you make it clear what you want from the experts and ask – if necessary force – them to present it to you in a usable way. As a manager you must know what specialists can do for you and you should be knowledgeable enough about the subject to understand whether or not what they produce is worth having.

Choosing who does the work

Ideally, the person you choose to do the work should have the knowledge, skills, motivation and time needed to get it done to your complete satisfaction. Frequently, however, you will have to use someone who has less than ideal experience, knowledge or skills. In these cases you should try to select an individual who has intelligence, natural aptitude and, above all, willingness to learn how to do the job with help and guidance. This is how people develop, and the development of your staff should be your conscious aim whenever you delegate.

You are looking for someone you can trust. You don't want to over-supervise, so you have to believe that the person you select will get on with it and have the sense to come to you when stuck or before making a bad mistake.

How do you know whom you can trust? The best way is to try people out first on smaller and less important tasks, increasingly giving them more scope so that they learn how far they can go and you can observe how they do it. If they get on well, their sense of responsibility and powers of judgement will increase and improve and you will be able to trust them with more demanding and responsible tasks.

Giving out the work

When you delegate you should ensure that your subordinates understand:

- why the work needs to be done;
- what they are expected to do;

- the date by which they are expected to do it;
- the authority they have to make decisions;
- the problems they must refer back;
- the progress or completion reports they should submit;
- how you propose to guide and monitor them;
- the resources and help they will have to complete the work.

Subordinates may need guidance on how the work should be done. The extent to which you spell it out will clearly depend on how much they already know about how to do the work. You don't want to give directions in such laborious detail that you run the risk of stifling initiative. As long as you are sure they will do the job without breaking the law, exceeding the budget, embarrassing you or seriously upsetting people, let them get on with it. Follow Robert Heller's[1] golden rule: 'If you can't do something yourself, find someone who can – and then let him do it in his own sweet way.'

You can make a distinction between *hard* and *soft* delegation.

Hard delegation takes place when you tell someone exactly what to do, how to do it and when you want the results. You spell it out, confirm it in writing and make a note in your diary of the date when you expect the job to be completed. And then you follow up regularly.

Soft delegation takes place when you agree generally what has to be achieved and leave your subordinate to get on with it. You should still agree limits of authority, define the decisions to be referred to you, say what exception reports you want (see Chapter 8), and indicate when and how you will review progress. Then you sit back until the results are due and observe from afar, only coming closer for periodical progress meetings, or when the exception report suggests that something needs looking into, or when a problem or decision is referred to you.

You should always delegate by the results you expect. Even if you do not need to specify exactly how the results should be achieved, it is a good idea when delegating a problem to ask your subordinates how they propose to solve it. You then have the opportunity to provide guidance at the outset; guidance at a later stage may be seen as interference.

Guidance and development

Delegation not only helps you to get your work done; it can be used to improve your subordinates' performance and therefore your trust in their ability to carry out more responsible work. Instruction, training and development are part of the process of delegation.

Monitoring performance

At first you may have to monitor your subordinates' performance carefully. But the sooner you can relax and watch progress informally the better.

You will have set target dates, and you should keep a reminder of these in your diary so that you can ensure they are achieved. Don't allow your subordinates to become careless about meeting deadlines.

Without being oppressive, you should ensure that progress reports are made when required and that you discuss deviations from the original plan in good time. You will have clearly indicated to your subordinates the extent of their authority to act without further reference to you. They must therefore expect to be reprimanded if on any occasion they exceed their brief or fail to keep you informed. You don't want any surprises and your subordinates must understand that you will not tolerate being kept in the dark.

Try to restrain yourself from undue interference in the way the work is being done. It is, after all, the results that count. Of course, you must step in if there is any danger of things going off the rails. The Nelson touch is all right if your subordinate is a Nelson, but how many Nelsons have you got? Rash decisions, over-expenditure and ignoring defined and reasonable constraints and rules must be prevented.

There is a delicate balance to be achieved between hedging people around with restrictions that may appear petty and allowing them licence to do what they like. You must use your knowledge of your subordinates and the circumstances to decide where the balance should be struck. The best delegators are those who have a comprehensive understanding of the strengths and weaknesses of their staff and the situation in which they are working.

Above all, avoid 'river banking'. This happens when a boss gives a subordinate a task that is more or less impossible to do. As the subordinate is 'going down' for the third time the boss is observed in a remote and safe position on the river bank saying: 'It's easy really, all you need to do is to try a bit harder.'

The thoughts of some successful delegators

John H Johnson, editor and publisher of Johnson Publishing Company, chief executive officer of Supreme Life Insurance Company and a board member of many large US corporations, said of his delegation techniques: 'I want to be big and I want to be bigger and I can't do it all by myself. So I try to do only those things that I can't get anyone else to do.'

Franklin D Roosevelt used a particularly ruthless technique based on competition when he requested his aides to find some information. One of his aides told the story as follows:

He would call you in, and he'd ask you to get the story on some complicated business and you'd come back after a couple of days of hard labour and present the juicy morsel you'd uncovered under a stone somewhere and *then* you'd find out he knew all about it, along with something else you *didn't* know. Where he got this information from he wouldn't mention, usually, but after he had done this to you once or twice you got damn careful about your information.

Robert Townsend's approach to delegation when he was chairman of Avis was to emphasize the need to delegate 'as many important matters as you can because that creates a climate in which people grow'.

When he started, the head of a supermarket chain told his division managers: 'I don't know anything about the grocery business but you fellows do. From now on, you're running your division as if it were your own business. You don't take orders from anyone but me and I'm not going to give you orders. I'm going to hold you responsible.'

Franklin Moore related the following example of strong delegation: Ralf Cordiner, the head of General Electric in the United States for 10 years, had a vice president who wanted to see him urgently about a problem. The vice president explained his problem, and the choices he thought he had. 'Now, Mr Cordiner,' he said, 'what should I do?' 'Do?' Cordiner answered, 'You'd damn well better get on an airplane and get back to your office and decide. And if you can't decide we'd better get someone who can.'

Peter Drucker,[2] writing about responsibility, referred to a newspaper interview with a young American infantry captain in the Vietnam jungle. The reporter asked: 'How in this confused situation can you retain command?' The captain replied:

> Around here, I am the only guy who is responsible. If these men don't know what to do when they run into an enemy in the jungle, I'm too far away to tell them. My job is to make sure they know. What they do depends on the situation that only they can judge. The responsibility is always mine, but the decision lies with whoever is on the spot.

A case study

A group of researchers studying how managers delegate found that the following was happening in one of the companies they were studying:

In the situations in which the men we were interviewing found themselves, the boss was usually a hurried, and sometimes a harried, man. He gave out broad, briefly stated assignments, expecting his subordinates to make sense out of them. He also expected them to decide what information they needed, to obtain that information and then to go ahead and carry out their assignments. In the case of repetitive tasks, the typical boss assumed that after a few trials his subordinates would know for themselves when a job needed doing.

Frequently the boss wasn't sure himself about which issues needed attention in his department. And although he knew what eventually had to be accomplished, often he had less idea than his subordinates about the approaches to take. It wasn't unusual, therefore, for the boss to be vague or even impatient when approached with questions about the job while it was going on.

Usually he was much more assertive in describing what he wanted after a job was done than while it was in progress.

The production director came out of the board of directors' meeting where he had been roundly criticized for not getting the most out of his organization. He immediately called a meeting of his subordinates and told them: 'I don't intend to subject myself to such humiliation again. You men are paid to do your jobs; it's not up to me to do them for you. I don't know how you spend your time and I don't intend to try to find out. You know your responsibilities, and these figures bear out that you haven't discharged them properly. If the next report doesn't show a marked improvement, there will be some new faces around here.'

Notes

1 Heller, R (1972) *The Naked Manager*, Barrie & Jenkins, London
2 Drucker, P (1967) *The Effective Executive*, Heinemann, London

13 How to delight customers

A delighted customer is one that is completely satisfied with a product or service from the viewpoint of quality, value for money, reliability and the level of customer service provided. To delight customers you have to meet or exceed their expectations under each of these headings. A delighted customer will continue to purchase the goods or services you offer – repeat sales are very important. Loyal customers are worth nurturing. They buy more and buy more regularly. And the cost of selling to them is low, whereas finding new customers can be expensive. Satisfied customers will recommend products and services to others. It has been established that dissatisfied customers will complain to as many as 10 other customers and potential customers.

Factors influencing customer satisfaction

- *Quality* – the product or service meets customers' expectations on the degree of quality they require by delivering what was promised. For products this will refer to such criteria as fitness for purpose, reliability, durability and low maintenance. For services it will be concerned with the achievement of an acceptable level of provision, reliability and accessibility.
- *Value for money* – the product or service meets customers' requirements on value for money in the sense of giving them at least what they paid for and preferably more. Belief about whether value for money is provided will often be on a comparative basis, setting off one manufacturer or supplier against others.
- *Reliability* – customers are most likely to be satisfied when the manufacturer or supplier 'delivers the deal' by achieving a consistent level of performance and dependability.
- *Responsiveness* – increasingly, customers expect their supplier to be willing and ready to provide prompt service and help at the point of sale and afterwards. Individual attention, speed and flexibility are required.

- *Access* – customers must be able to gain access to the supplier or provider with the minimum of trouble. They have learnt to put up with mechanized answering services but hate endless delays in getting though while listening to the Four Seasons and to seemingly insincere assurances that their custom is valued. They like to talk to human beings who will respond to their query or complaint.

- *Courtesy* – customers require politeness, respect, consideration and friendliness from the people they contact over the counter, in a call centre or when faced with a service problem.

- *Communication* – it is essential to keep customers informed in language they can understand about the product or service and how they can make quick and easy contact if they have a problem. It should be obvious to them when they make contact that they are listened to so that their specific query is dealt with quickly.

- *Credibility* – customers are more likely to be satisfied if they find as a result of their experiences that the supplier or provider is trustworthy, believable and honest. This is based on the knowledge and courtesy displayed by staff and their ability to inspire trust and confidence.

When considering how to delight customers it should be remembered that their expectations tend to increase. They expect continually rising levels of service and more choice and will be dissatisfied if standards are only maintained at a level that they once found acceptable. Customers are changing the way in which they purchase, especially through the internet, which gives them more choice and enables them to compare product prices and attributes. It should also be noted that other organizations improve the services they offer and competitive edge will be lost if these are not matched or preferably exceeded.

Simply to seek satisfaction is not enough. It is necessary to go beyond satisfaction by exceeding expectations in anticipation of what customers will want in the future and what competitors will be doing.

Delighting customers

To delight customers it is necessary to create a culture that focuses on customer satisfaction and to ensure that anyone in contact with them behaves in a way that will create continuing satisfaction.

Ten steps to creating a customer-focused culture

- Articulate the core values for service excellence that will be adopted by the organization.
- Communicate those values to all staff.

- Live the values at top management level – how they lead is how others serve.
- Implement programmes of continuous improvement that provide for incremental but significant enhancements to service levels.
- Implement quality management programmes that provide for the achievement of high levels of product and service quality.
- Focus on internal as well as external customers.
- Define the behaviours expected of all those dealing with customers (see below for a list of appropriate behaviours).
- Select people with the right attitudes, train them in the customer service skills they need and empower them to have greater autonomy in relating to customers.
- Monitor performance by reference to core customer service values and expected behaviour.
- Recognize and reward high levels of customer service achieved by individuals and teams.

Behaviours that delight customers

- Be helpful, polite, friendly and positive with customers.
- When dealing with customers, smile, make eye contact and look and sound enthusiastic.
- Speak clearly.
- Show personal interest.
- Show sympathy with customers making complaints – listen to what the customer has to say, establish the facts, agree what needs to be done, keep the customer informed.
- Provide information immediately or let customers know when they can expect it.
- Keep promises.
- Answer telephones promptly.
- Reply to letters, faxes, e-mails and voicemail messages quickly.
- Concentrate on the needs of customers, not on what is easiest to sell.

Case study: customer service at Lands' End

At Lands' End, the highly successful mail-order clothing company, one of the key values is expressed as: 'Put the customer first. Achieve an even higher level of customer service through personal attention and new technology.' This is expanded by the following statement of 'what we believe in':

1 Satisfied customers and employees.

2 Integrity, honesty, friendliness, respect and trust.

3 The imperative to offer quality products and services at a fair price.

4 Lasting relationships with customers who appreciate our brand and its value.

5 Innovation in all we do.

The reason why the company wants to inspire staff is because it believes that the difference between doing something and doing it well comes down to the amount of effort people will put into their work. While individuals cannot be blamed for not taking an initiative or only working to their job description, their willingness to do that little bit extra is the difference between a good experience for customers and a poor one.

Lands' End staff are willing to make that extra effort because of their sense of pride in what the organization stands for: quality, service and value. Management believes that every employee wants to do a good job, and is motivated by doing so, but that being able to do this depends on the 'amount of space', in the sense of not being frantically busy the whole time, and the degree of responsibility that you give them. So, Lands' End ensures that staffing levels are such that employees have the time to offer a good level of service, which in turn creates greater pride and so on in a self-fulfilling cycle. The company takes a pride in its history of good service and publishes a book of 'great service stories' to help people understand how far they can go to help a customer.

Lands' End says that what front-line staff do has a far greater impact on customers than what the executive team does, which is why every staff member, including the managing director, works in a front-line job for four hours a week for the busy six weeks before Christmas. This reminds everyone of the importance of the front-line jobs and demonstrates to front-line staff that everyone else understands and values what they do.

Where jobs are repetitive or less challenging, Lands' End believes it is particularly important to provide some challenge and fun. And if it isn't possible to give people a choice as to the type of work they do, they can be given a choice as to how they do it. So, for example, in the Lands' End call centre, unlike many others, good performance is not primarily measured by the number of calls, call duration or the amount of time a person is available to take a call. If a customer wants a service assistant to go to the distribution centre, pick the item they want to buy, call them back and describe the feel of the garment then that is what they should do. The company invests more heavily in staff training and giving people more responsibility than in putting in controls.

14 How to develop people

Investing in people

The chairman of an advertising firm once said that his 'inventory goes up and down in the lift'. His prime resource – his working capital – was people. The same applies in any other sort of organization. Money matters, but the human beings who work there matter even more.

If you want to take a pragmatic view of people, regard them as an investment. They cost money to acquire and maintain and they should provide a return on that outlay; their value increases as they become more effective in their jobs and capable of taking on greater responsibility. In accounting terms, people may be treated like any other asset on the balance sheet, taking into account acquisition costs and their increasing value as they gain experience.

The manager's contribution to effective development

The following are 10 ways in which you can contribute to the effective development of your staff:

1 Determine the standards of performance required for each of the jobs you control.

2 Analyse the competences (what you expect people to know and to be able to do) relevant to the achievement of these standards. If necessary, seek help from specialized trainers to carry out this analysis.

3 Agree with the individuals concerned what these standards and competences are.

4 Review with these individuals their performance so that agreement can be reached on any gaps to be filled between what they can do and what they should be able to do.

5 Every time you give someone an instruction, treat it as a learning opportunity. Encourage individuals to tell you how they would do the job. If they get it wrong, help them to work out the best way for themselves, progressively giving them less guidance so they learn to stand on their own feet.

6 Allow for the learning curve. Don't expect too much, but do require learners to improve at a pace that matches their natural aptitudes. Only bear down hard on people if they are clearly not trying – without any excuse.

7 Train and develop by example. Give people the opportunity to learn from the way you do things. Remember the truth of the saying that managers learn best how to manage by managing under a good manager. This principle applies equally well to other categories of job holders.

8 Remember that the prime responsibility for training and developing your staff rests with you. Your results depend on their competence. You neglect your training responsibilities at your peril. And you must not rely on the training department to do it for you. It can provide advice and help but cannot replace your capacity to train on the job.

9 Plan the training for your staff in accordance with a regular review of their training needs.

10 Remember that one of the best ways in which you can develop your staff is by coaching them, as described below.

How to coach

Coaching is a personal (usually one-to-one), on-the-job approach that can be used by managers to help people develop their skills and levels of competence. As a manager, you are there to get results through people; this means that you have a personal responsibility for ensuring that they acquire and develop the skills they need. Other people in the shape of coaching, training and management development specialists may help, but because by far the best way of learning is on the job, the onus is mainly on you.

The need for coaching may arise from formal or informal performance reviews but opportunities for coaching will emerge during normal day-to-day activities. Every time you delegate a new task to someone, a coaching opportunity is created to help the individual learn any new skills or techniques that are needed to do the job. Every time you provide feedback to an individual after a task has been completed, there is an opportunity to help that individual do better next time.

Coaching can be carried out informally on the spot – it is not essential to set up special coaching sessions. Coaching should be regarded as a normal part of your job and accepted as such by the members of your team.

Aims

The aims of coaching are to:

- help people to become aware of how well they are doing, where they need to improve and what they need to learn;
- put controlled delegation into practice; in other words, managers can delegate new tasks or enlarged areas of work, provide guidance as necessary on how the tasks or work should be carried out and monitor performance in doing the work;
- get managers and individuals to use whatever situations arise as learning opportunities;
- enable guidance to be provided on how to carry out specific tasks as necessary, but always on the basis of helping people to learn rather than spoon-feeding them with instructions on what to do and how to do it.

The coaching sequence

Coaching can be carried out in the following stages:

1 Identify the areas of knowledge, skills or capabilities where learning needs to take place to qualify people to carry out the task, provide for continuous development, enhance transferable skills or improve performance.
2 Ensure that the person understands and accepts the need to learn.
3 Discuss with the person what needs to be learnt and the best way to undertake the learning.
4 Get the person to work out how they can manage their own learning while identifying where they will need help from you or someone else.
5 Provide encouragement and advice to the person in pursuing the self-learning programme.
6 Provide specific guidance as required where the person needs your help.
7 Agree how progress should be monitored and reviewed.

How to empower

15

Empowerment is the process of giving people more scope or 'power' to exercise control over and take responsibility for their work. It means giving people more autonomy, getting them to use their own judgement when carrying out their work – dealing with customers, planning their activities, meeting targets and deadlines, and solving problems. The purpose of empowerment is to free someone from rigorous control by instructions and orders and give them freedom to take responsibility for their ideas and actions, to release hidden resources that would otherwise remain inaccessible.

The case for empowerment

Empowerment gives greater 'space' for individuals to use their abilities by enabling and encouraging them to take decisions close to the point of impact. The rationale for empowering people is that those who are nearest to the problem are best able to judge its solution, providing they have a framework of values and rules within which to make their decisions. Empowerment can: speed up decision-making and reaction times; release the creative and innovative capacities of employees; provide for greater engagement and job satisfaction; enable employees to gain a greater sense of achievement from their work; and reduce operational costs by eliminating unnecessary layers of management, reducing the size of staff and support functions, and removing the necessity for tight quality control and checking procedures.

Assumptions about empowerment

Charles Handy[1] suggested that the assumptions behind the concept of empowerment are:

- *Competence* – the belief that individual employees can be expected to perform to the limit of their competence with the minimum of supervision.

- *Trust* – it is necessary not only to believe in people's competence but also trust them to get on with the job.
- *Teamwork* – few organizational problems can be solved by one person working alone. The sheer rate of change and turbulence means that as new challenges and problems appear, people must naturally group together in flexible teams without barriers of status or hierarchy to solve the problems within the framework of the organization's goals and values. The organization is held together by these values – by people who are committed to one another and to common goals.

The process of empowerment at organizational levels

Empowerment can be achieved by structural means (organizational and work group) and involving people in issues.

Structural empowerment – organizational

An empowered organization is likely to have a flat structure with the minimum number of management layers. A multi-layered structure filters the two-way flow of information and hinders decision-making from penetrating as far down the organization as it should.

Structural empowerment – work group

As suggested by Christian Schumacher,[2] of *Small is Beautiful* fame, empowerment can be achieved at the work group level by applying the following principles:

- Work should be organized around basic operations to form 'whole tasks'.
- The basic organizational unit should be the primary work group of 4–20 people.
- Each work group should include a designated leader.
- Each work group and leader should, as far as possible, plan and organize its own work.
- Each work group should be able fully to evaluate its performance against agreed standards of excellence.
- Jobs should be structured so that work group members can personally plan, execute and evaluate at least one operation in the process.
- All work group members should have the opportunity to participate in the group's processes of planning, problem-solving and evaluation.

Involving people in issues

Empowerment can be achieved by involving people in developing their own solutions to issues. This is done by expecting teams not simply to propose ways forward or to hope that someone else will do something, but actually to solve the problem in their part of the organization in accordance with the resources they have and the constraints within which they work.

When he was the CEO of General Electric Jack Welch arranged for employees at all levels to get together and work out how to improve the ways in which work was carried out. His aim was 'to give people a voice, give people a say, give them a chance to participate'. In describing these 'work outs' he said that:

> Ultimately, we're talking about redefining the relationship between boss and subordinate. I want to get to the point where people challenge their bosses every day: 'Why do you require me to do wasteful things?' 'Why don't you let me do things you shouldn't be doing so you can move on and create?' That's the job of the leader – to create not to control. Trust me to do my job and don't make me waste all my time trying to deal with you on control issues.'[3]

What you can do individually

As a manager or team leader you can play an important part in empowering your people. The following are 10 ways of doing so:

- Delegate more.
- Involve people in setting their targets and standards of performance and in deciding on performance measures.
- Allow individuals and teams more scope to plan, act and monitor their own performance.
- Involve people in developing their own solutions to problems.
- Create self-managed teams – ones that set their own objectives and standards and manage their own performance.
- Give people a voice in deciding what needs to be done.
- Help people to learn from their own mistakes.
- Encourage continuous development so that people can both grow in their roles and grow their roles.
- Share your vision and plans with members of your team.
- Trust people and treat them as adults.

Notes

1 Handy, C (1989) *The Age of Unreason*, Business Books, London

2 Schumacher, C (1976) Structuring work, *Industrial Participation*, Winter, pp 8–15

3 Welch, J, quoted in J Gabarro (ed) (1991) *Managing People and Organizations*, Harvard Business School Publications, Boston, MA

How to get on

16

Getting on is first about knowing who you are and what you can do – your strengths and weaknesses. Then you can decide what you want to do and set out to do it.

You can start in the right direction, therefore, by trying to analyse yourself and the situation that you are in.

Beyond that there are certain actions you can take that will help you to get on. Some are obvious, others less so. How you apply them must depend on your assessment of where you are and what you can do. With due acknowledgement to the two men who have written the most sense on this subject – Peter Drucker[1] and Robert Townsend[2] – the list of steps to take is set out below under five main headings:

● Develop self-awareness.
● Know what you want.
● Display the personal qualities and behave in the ways that will contribute to your success.
● Develop your emotional intelligence.
● Take steps to develop yourself.

Develop self-awareness

Self-awareness is about knowing yourself, so far as that is possible, and analysing your achievements, skills and knowledge, and managerial competences. The aim is to identify strengths and weaknesses in order to make the most of the former and do what you can to overcome the latter.

Knowing yourself

The question you have to answer is 'What sort of person am I?' This is the most difficult question to answer truthfully. Try answering the following self-analysis questionnaire (Figure 16.1), which is based on Cattell's[3] classification of primary personality factors. Consider each statement under the heading 'I think I am someone who is...' and indicate in the appropriate box the extent to which you agree or disagree with it. The outcome will be a profile that you can study to identify any personality characteristics that you might need to do something about.

FIGURE 16.1   Self-assessment questionnaire

Reserved – detached, critical, cool, introverted	1 2 3 4 5 6 7 8 9 10	Outgoing – easy-going, participating, extroverted
Rigid – conforming, staid, rule-bound	1 2 3 4 5 6 7 8 9 10	Flexible – innovative, adaptable
Sober – prudent, taciturn, serious	1 2 3 4 5 6 7 8 9 10	Enthusiastic – lively, happy-go-lucky, talkative
Emotionally unstable – easily upset	1 2 3 4 5 6 7 8 9 10	Emotionally stable – calm
Self-absorbed – not interested in other people	1 2 3 4 5 6 7 8 9 10	Easy to get on with – relates well with others
Suspicious – self-opinionated, distrustful	1 2 3 4 5 6 7 8 9 10	Trusting – free of suspicion or jealousy
A worrier – depressive, troubled	1 2 3 4 5 6 7 8 9 10	Confident – self-assured, serene
Tense – driven, overwrought, fretful	1 2 3 4 5 6 7 8 9 10	Relaxed – tranquil, unfrustrated, calm
Self-absorbed – does not take account of other people's feelings	1 2 3 4 5 6 7 8 9 10	Considerate – cares about other people's feelings
Autocratic – imposes decisions, manipulates people to gain compliance	1 2 3 4 5 6 7 8 9 10	Inspirational – empowers people, who respond with enthusiasm

This analysis will help you to think about how you behave. You can't really change your personality but, given what you know about the sort of person you are, you may be able to adjust your behaviour to make it more productive and acceptable to people. However, remember what Shakespeare advised: 'to your own self be true.' Also bear in mind what Browning wrote: 'Best be yourself, imperial plain and true.' Your behaviour must be genuine not assumed, otherwise people will see through you and the relationships will simply get worse.

An alternative questionnaire you might use is the 'Big Five Personality Test'. This is based on the 'big five' personality characteristics of openness, conscientiousness, extraversion, agreeableness and neuroticism. It can be downloaded from **www.outofservice.com/bigfive**.

Analysis of achievements, skills and knowledge

An analysis of your achievements, skills and knowledge can be conducted by answering the following questions:

- *What have I achieved so far?* Answer this question by looking back on your life and list the key events, happenings, incidents and turning points that have taken place. Whenever you have succeeded in doing something new or better than ever before, analyse the factors that contributed to that success. Was it initiative, hard work, determination, the correct application of skills and knowledge based on a searching analysis of the situation, the ability to work in a team, the exercise of leadership, the capacity to seize and exploit an opportunity (another and better term for luck), the ability to articulate a need and take action to satisfy it, the ability to make things happen – or any other factor you can think of?

- *When have I failed to achieve what I wanted?* You do not want to dwell too much on failure but it can be treated positively, as long as you analyse dispassionately where you went wrong and assess what you might have been able to do to put it right.

- *What am I good or not so good at doing?* What are your distinctive competences? Consider these in terms of professional, technical or managerial know-how as well as the exercise of such skills as communicating, decision-making, problem-solving, teamworking, exercising leadership, delegating, coordinating, meeting deadlines, managing time, planning, organizing and controlling work, dealing with crises.

- *What have been my significant learning experiences?* Recall events when you have learned something worthwhile and how you made use of it.

- *How well do I know my chosen area of expertise?* Have you got or are you getting the right qualifications? Have you acquired or are you acquiring the right know-how through study, training and relevant experience?

Assess your managerial competencies

The self-awareness questionnaire may help to produce an overall assessment of your behavioural strengths and weaknesses as a manager, but you need also to consider your specific basic managerial qualities and the competencies required to operate effectively.

In analysing your effectiveness as a manager it is useful to look at the criteria used by major organizations in measuring the competence of their managers at their assessment or development centres (two-to-three-day affairs where managers are subjected to a number of tests and undertake various exercises to demonstrate their skills).

The following are typical headings or criteria in an organization's competence framework:

- *Achievement/results orientation* – the desire to get things done well and the ability to set and meet challenging goals, create own measures of excellence and constantly seek ways of improving performance.
- *Business awareness* – the capacity continually to identify and explore business opportunities, understand the business opportunities and priorities of the organization and constantly to seek methods of ensuring that the organization becomes more businesslike.
- *Communication* – the ability to communicate clearly and persuasively, orally or in writing.
- *Customer focus* – the exercise of unceasing care in looking after the interests of external and internal customers to ensure that their wants, needs and expectations are met or exceeded.
- *Developing others* – the desire and capacity to foster the development of members of his or her team, providing feedback, support, encouragement and coaching.
- *Flexibility* – the ability to adapt to and work effectively in different situations and to carry out a variety of tasks.
- *Leadership* – the capacity to inspire individuals to give of their best to achieve a desired result and to maintain effective relationships with individuals and the team as a whole.
- *Planning* – the ability to decide on courses of action, ensuring that the resources required to implement the action will be available and scheduling the programme of work required to achieve a defined end result.
- *Problem-solving* – the capacity to analyse situations, diagnose problems, identify the key issues, establish and evaluate alternative courses of action and produce a logical, practical and acceptable solution.
- *Teamwork* – the ability to work cooperatively and flexibly with other members of the team with a full understanding of the role to be played as a team member.

You can assess your competence as a manager against these criteria, giving yourself marks between 1 and 10 for each item relating to a classification along these lines:

A = outstanding (9–10 points)
B = very effective (7–8 points)
C = satisfactory (5–6 points)
D = barely satisfactory (3–4 points)
E = unsatisfactory (0–2 points)

On completing this assessment, note the particularly high and low scores in each list and draw up a schedule of your strengths and weaknesses as a manager. You can complete this 'SWOT' (Strengths and Weaknesses, Opportunities and Threats) analysis by considering your opportunities for advancement in your present organization (or elsewhere) and assessing any threats that might prevent you from realizing your ambitions.

Know what you want

1 Find out what you are good at doing and then do it.

2 Analyse not only your strengths but also your weaknesses: 'there is nothing that helps a man in his conduct through life more than a knowledge of his own characteristic weaknesses' (William Hazlitt).

3 Decide what you want to do and then go for it. Believe that if you really want something you can get it, and act accordingly.

4 Set demanding targets and deadlines for yourself. 'People grow according to the demands they make on themselves' (Drucker[1]). But don't overcommit yourself. Be realistic about what you can achieve.

5 Pursue excellence. 'If you can't do it excellently don't do it at all' (Townsend[2]).

6 Focus on what you can contribute: 'to ask "what can I contribute?" is to look for the unused potential in a job' (Drucker).

7 Get your priorities right. Adapt Drucker's rules for identifying them:
   – pick the future as against the past;
   – focus on opportunities rather than on problems;
   – choose your own direction – rather than climb on the bandwagon;
   – aim high, aim for something that will make a difference rather than something that is 'safe' and easy to do.

8 Keep it simple. Concentrate. Consider all your tasks and eliminate the irrelevant ones. Slough off old activities before you start new ones. 'Concentration is the key to economic results... no other principle of effectiveness is violated as constantly today as the basic principle

of concentration... Our motto seems to be: "let's do a little bit of everything"' (Drucker[1]).

9 Take the broad view but don't ignore the significant detail: 'Ill can he rule the great, that cannot reach the small' (Spenser). It is sometimes necessary to penetrate beneath the surface to find out what is really happening – on the shop floor or in the field. But do this selectively.

10 Adapt to changing demands. 'the executive who keeps on doing what he has done successfully before is almost bound to fail' (Drucker[1]).

Personal qualities and behaviour

- Be enthusiastic and show it.

- Innovate and create – come up with new ideas and react positively to other people's ideas. Don't sulk if your ideas are not accepted. Try again another way.

- Show willing – there is nothing worse than the person who always moans when he is given something to do. Don't say: 'How can I possibly do that?' Instead, respond immediately with something like this: 'Right, this is what I propose to do – is that what you want?'

- Be positive – in the words of the old Bing Crosby song: 'accentuate the positive, eliminate the negative.'

- Work hard – people who get on are hard workers. But they don't work for work's sake. Effectiveness is never a function of how late you stay in the office. It's what you do while you are there that counts.

- Present yourself well – life is not all about making a good impression, but you might as well make sure that your achievements are known and appreciated. And if people are impressed by executives who are decisive, punctual and answer promptly, why not impress them that way? More good than harm will come of it.

- Be ambitious – 'A man's reach should exceed his grasp, or what's a heaven for?' (Robert Browning). But don't overdo it. Don't appear to be more concerned about your future status than about present effectiveness.

- Be courageous – take calculated risks, believe in what you are doing and stick to your guns.

- Be assertive but not aggressive.

- Put your points across firmly and succinctly.

- Don't talk too much. Never overcommit yourself. Save up what you want to say until the right moment. Keep your powder dry. Don't shoot your mouth off. 'Whereof one cannot speak, thereon one must remain silent' (Wittgenstein).

- Learn to cope with stress. You won't avoid it and you have to live with it. If problems are coming at you thick and fast, try to slow down. Relax. Take a little time off. Give yourself a chance to put the situation into perspective.
- If things go wrong, bounce back. Accept reverses calmly. Think about what you need to do and then get into action – fast. There is nothing like purposeful activity in these circumstances.
- Get people to trust you – you will do this if you never lie or even shade the truth, if you avoid playing politics and if you always deliver what you promise.
- Accept constructive criticism.
- 'Admit your own mistakes openly, even joyfully' (Townsend[2]). Never make an excuse. Accept the responsibility and the blame if you make a mistake.

Consider the extent to which you display emotional intelligence in carrying out your work, and do something about it if you are lacking in this essential requirement, as described below.

Develop your emotional intelligence

Emotional intelligence is what people have when they are good at managing themselves and relating to people because they understand their strengths and weaknesses and know that it is more productive to manage emotions rather than be led by them.

The significance of emotional intelligence

To succeed it is not enough to have technical ability and a high IQ (intelligence quotient); emotional intelligence is also required. It is a familiar situation. Someone with lots of technical, professional or specialist expertise is promoted to a managerial job and fails. This may be partly attributed to an inability to manage in the sense of planning, organizing and controlling the use of resources. But the main reason is probably a failure to manage personal relationships as a leader or a colleague, and this may be attributed to a lack of understanding of the individual's own emotions and an inability to appreciate the emotions of people with whom he or she is involved. In other words, an inadequate level of emotional intelligence.

The components of emotional intelligence

The four components of emotional intelligence identified by Daniel Goleman[4] are:

- *Self-management* – the ability to control or redirect disruptive impulses and moods and regulate one's own behaviour, coupled with a propensity to pursue goals with energy and persistence. The six competencies associated with this component are self-control, trustworthiness and integrity, initiative, adaptability – comfort with ambiguity – openness to change and strong desire to achieve.
- *Self-awareness* – the ability to recognize and understand your moods, emotions and drives as well as their effect on others. This is linked to three competencies: self-confidence, realistic self-assessment and emotional self-awareness.
- *Social awareness* – the ability to understand the emotional make-up of other people and skill in treating people according to their emotional reactions. This is linked to six competencies: empathy, expertise in building and retaining talent, organizational awareness, cross-cultural sensitivity, valuing diversity and service to clients and customers.
- *Social skills* – proficiency in managing relationships and building networks to get the desired result from others and reach personal goals, and the ability to find common ground and build rapport. The five competencies associated with this component are: leadership, effectiveness in leading change, conflict management, influence/ communication and expertise in building and leading teams.

Developing emotional intelligence: what organizations do

When organizations try to help people develop their emotional intelligence they take the following steps:

- Assess the requirements of jobs in terms of emotional skills.
- Assess individuals to identify their level of emotional intelligence – 360-degree feedback (ie getting feedback from colleagues, clients or customers and subordinates as well as one's boss) can be a powerful source of data; instruments such as the Bar-on Emotional Quotient Inventory can be used to measure levels of emotional intelligence.
- Gauge readiness – ensure that people are prepared to improve their level of emotional intelligence.
- Motivate people to believe that the learning experience will benefit them.
- Make change self-directed – encourage people to prepare a learning plan that fits their interests, resources and goals.
- Focus on clear manageable goals – the focus must be on immediate, manageable steps, bearing in mind that cultivating a new skill is gradual.

- Prevent relapse – show people how they can learn lessons from the inevitable relapses.
- Give performance feedback.
- Encourage practice, remembering that emotional competence cannot be improved overnight.
- Provide models of desired behaviours.
- Encourage and reinforce – create a climate that rewards self-improvement.
- Evaluate – establish sound outcome measures and then assess performance against them.

What you can do

Your organization can do much to help. But there is a lot you can do for yourself. Allowing for the nature of emotional intelligence, the following are 10 steps you can take:

1 Recognize that only you can improve the results you achieve.

2 Get to know yourself better by carrying out a formal self-assessment using the questionnaire set out earlier in this chapter on page 80. Obtain answers to questions such as: 'What aspects of my performance are going well?', 'What aspects of my performance do I need to improve?' and 'What do I need to do to improve my emotional intelligence skills (interacting with other people)?'

3 On the basis of this assessment take Goleman's four components of emotional intelligence listed above, and analyse your own behaviour and the impact it has made on other people. Obtain answers to the following questions: 'How good am I at self-management?', 'How self-aware am I?', 'How socially aware am I?' and 'How effective are my social skills?'

4 Seek feedback from your boss, your colleagues, your subordinates and your clients. Try to find out what impression you make on them and where they think you could do better.

5 Focus on those aspects of your behaviour where, first, there is the most room for improvement, and second, the likelihood of being able to change is reasonably high. Don't expect quick results. Changing behaviour can be a long haul.

6 Refer to specific aspects of behaviour rather than generalizations.

7 If possible, get help from a mentor, a counsellor or an executive coach. The latter can be particularly useful if they know their job.

8 Make the most of any training or development courses your organization provides on such matters as leadership, teamwork and interpersonal skills.

9 Use your imagination and be patient. You will not necessarily get easy answers to your quest for improvements. You will not change ingrained behavioural habits without being quite radical in your approach. And you have to recognize that it will take time.

10 Monitor progress by analysing your own behaviour and the impact it makes, and obtaining further feedback from others. Adjust your development programme as necessary in the light of this feedback.

Develop yourself

The best way to get on is to rely on yourself, while seeking and benefiting from any support you can get from your manager or the organization. Self-development takes place through self-managed or self-directed learning. This means that you take responsibility for satisfying your own learning needs to improve performance, to support the achievement of career aspirations, or to enhance your experience within and beyond your present organization. It can be based on processes that enable you to identify what you need to learn, by reflecting on your experience and analysing what you need to know and be able to do, so that you can perform better and progress your career.

The case for self-managed learning is that people learn and retain more if they find things out for themselves. But they may still need to be helped to identify what they should look for. Self-managed learning is about self-development, and this will be furthered by self-assessment, which leads to better self-understanding. Pedler *et al*[5] recommend the following four-stage approach:

● Self-assessment based on analysis by individuals of their work and life situation.

● Diagnosis derived from the analysis of learning needs and priorities.

● Action planning to identify objectives, helps and hindrances, resources required (including people) and timescales.

● Monitoring and review to assess progress in achieving action plans.

Identify development needs

You can use performance management processes as described in Chapter 30 to identify self-development needs on your own or in discussion with your boss. This will include reviewing performance against agreed plans, and assessing competence requirements and your capacity to achieve them. The analysis is therefore based on an understanding of what you are expected to do, the knowledge and skills you need to carry out your job effectively, what you have achieved, and what knowledge and skills you have. If there are any gaps between the knowledge and skills you need and those you have, then this defines a development need. The analysis is always related to work and the capacity to carry it out effectively.

By making your own assessment of your personal development needs as a basis for identifying the means of satisfying them and acting accordingly, you can get more satisfaction from your work, advance your career and increase your employability.

Define the means of satisfying development needs

When deciding how to satisfy the needs you should remember that it is not just about selecting suitable training courses. These may form part of your development plan, but only a minor part; other learning activities are much more important. Examples of development activities include: observing and analysing what others do (good practice); planned use of internal training media, including e-learning (use of electronic learning materials) and learning libraries; being coached; training courses; distance learning – learning in your own time from material prepared elsewhere, such as correspondence courses; guided reading; project work or special assignments; working with a mentor; involvement in other work areas; input to policy formulation; increased professionalism on the job; involvement in the community; coaching others.

Personal development plans

A personal development plan sets out the actions you propose to take to learn and to develop yourself. You take responsibility for formulating and implementing the plan, but you may receive support from the organization and your manager in doing so.

Personal development planning aims to promote learning and to provide you with knowledge and a portfolio of transferable skills that will help to progress your career.

A personal development action plan sets out what needs to be done and how it will be done under headings such as:

- development needs;
- outcomes expected (learning objectives);
- development activities to meet the needs;
- responsibility for development – what individuals will do and what support they will require from their manager, the HR department or other people;
- timing – when the learning activity is expected to start and be completed;
- outcome – what development activities have taken place and how effective they were.

Ten self-development steps

The following are 10 steps you can take to develop yourself.

1 *Create a development log* – record your plans and action.
2 *State your objectives* – the career path you want to follow and the skills you will need to proceed along that path.
3 *Develop a personal profile* – what sort of person you are, your likes and dislikes about work, your aspirations.
4 *List your strengths and weaknesses.*
5 *List your achievements* – what you have done well so far and why you believe these were worthwhile achievements.
6 *List significant learning experiences* – recall events when you have learnt something worthwhile (this can help you to understand your learning style).
7 *Ask other people* about your strengths and weaknesses and what you should do to develop yourself.
8 *Focus on the present* – what is happening to you now: your job, your current skills, your short-term development needs.
9 *Focus on the future* – where you want to be in the longer term and how you are going to get there (including a list of the skills and abilities you need to develop).
10 *Plan your self-development strategy* – how you are going to achieve your ambitions.

Notes

1 Drucker, P (1955) *The Practice of Management*, Heinemann, London
2 Townsend, R (1970) *Up the Organization*, Michael Joseph, London
3 Cattell, R B (1963) *The Sixteen Personality Factor Questionnaire*, Institute for Personality and Ability Training, Champaign, Ill
4 Goleman, D (1995) *Emotional Intelligence*, Bantam, New York
5 Pedler, M, Burgoyne J and Boydell, T (1994) *A Manager's Guide to Self Development*, McGraw-Hill, Maidenhead

How to handle people problems

17

We all have to deal with people problems from time to time; we come across difficult individuals and often have to deal with the negative behaviour of both colleagues and subordinates. If we don't handle them well the result is frustration, anger and other counterproductive activities. It is necessary to understand why people can be difficult, and to be able to anticipate problems so that they can be dealt with before they arise. We may also have to deal with people who are not performing well. This can be a difficult task and one that many managers fail to do properly.

Handling difficult people

Why people are difficult

When considering why people can be difficult it is worth remembering that they may be equally convinced that it is you who are being difficult, not them. People respond in kind. So when assessing the situation you have to ask yourself whether the problem is caused by your behaviour rather than theirs.

There are many reasons that people can be difficult (whether it is you or them). Here are some instances:

- a fundamental disagreement about policy;
- rivalry;
- different values about how things should be done;
- a real or imagined slight;
- arrogant behaviour – or behaviour perceived as arrogant;
- a feeling that they are not valued for their contribution or themselves;
- frustrated ambition – where the cause of frustration is attributed to you;

- not being given the attention they believe they deserve;
- not being able to get their own way;
- lack of trust;
- insecurity;
- concern about the impact of change;
- too much pressure – real or perceived.

In addition, there is the Dr Fell reason for being difficult:

> I do not love thee, Dr Fell,
> The reason why I cannot tell;
> But this I know, I know full well,
> I do not love thee, Dr Fell.

The last reason is, of course, the hardest to deal with. An attempt can be made to handle the other instances, although success will depend on how much effort you put into it, and will be limited or delayed if the causes of disagreement are deeply seated or are based more on prejudice than on reason (which is often the case).

Ten approaches to handling difficult people

1   Anticipate problems as far as possible. Look for the signs and take swift action in one or more of the ways described below.

2   If a difficulty arises or is anticipated, subject your own behaviour to close scrutiny. Is it caused by something you have done, or how you have been behaving? If so, what are you going to do about it? If you can anticipate a difficulty, you may be able to nip it in the bud by having an informal discussion with the individual. You are asking the essential questions: 'Is there a problem?', 'Why is there a problem?' and 'What can we do about it?' (emphasize the *we* – joint problem-solving approaches always produce the best results). A successful outcome of this approach in the shape of a resolution of the difficulties depends on creating rapport and a climate of trust. This will not be easy if things have gone too far, which is why it is advisable to anticipate problems as much as you can.

3   It may be difficult to anticipate difficult behaviour. It may simply happen. In this case you should try to analyse the cause or causes. Start by asking yourself whether or not you have created or contributed to the problem, and if so how. Go on to assess other possible causes by reference to the list given above. Be as specific as possible by identifying events that may have triggered the behaviour. The more instances you can produce, the more likely you are to reach a solution.

4 Where there are specific issues, discuss them with the individual. A joint problem-solving approach is best, when both parties spend some time in analysing the cause of the difficulty so that agreement can be reached on what they can both do about it. The aim should be to be constructive. It is not a matter of apportioning blame. It is much more about providing an answer to the question, 'What are we going to do about it?'

5 When dealing with aggressive people, stand your ground by being assertive (see Chapter 2). State your case, and ask questions to encourage the person to explain the cause of the problem and to discuss how it can be resolved.

6 Always be calm. Losing your temper with someone who is angry gets you nowhere.

7 Try to reason with the difficult person. But if he or she is too angry or upset to listen, it may be best to walk away, with words to the effect that time is needed to reflect on this situation, so 'Let's get together later to discuss what needs to be done.' It's best to end an acrimonious telephone conversation similarly. You could say something like 'Perhaps it's best if we resume this conversation later when we can discuss the issues more calmly.' Never hang up.

8 Use avoidance tactics only as a short-term solution. They will not address the real issues.

9 Think carefully about the words you use. Try to limit your contribution and let the other person have his or her say.

10 Always try to reach agreement that a problem exists. Use questioning to identify ways of dealing with it and agree an action plan.

How to handle negative behaviour

Managers and team leaders sometimes come across negative behaviour from a member of their team. This may take the form of lack of interest in the work, unwillingness to cooperate with you or other team members complaining about the work or working conditions, grumbling at being asked to carry out a perfectly reasonable task, objecting strongly to being asked to do something extra (or even refusing to do it) – 'it's not in my job description' – or, in extreme cases, insolence.

People exhibiting negative behaviour may be quietly resentful rather than openly disruptive. They are negative, mutter away in the background at meetings and lack enthusiasm.

As a manager you can tolerate a certain amount of negative behaviour as long as the individual works reasonably well and does not upset other team members. You have simply to say to yourself 'It takes all sorts...' and put up with it, although you might quietly say during a review meeting 'You're doing a good job but...' If, however, you do take this line, you have to be specific. You must cite actual instances. It is no good making generalized accusations that will either be openly denied or internalized by the receiver, making him or her even more resentful.

If the negative behaviour means that the individual's contribution is not acceptable or is disruptive, then you must take action. Negative people are often quiet but are usually angry about something; their negative behaviour is an easy way of expressing their anger. To deal with the problem it is necessary to find out what has made the person angry.

Causes of negative behaviour

The causes could include one or more of the following:

- a real or imagined slight from you or a colleague;
- a feeling of being put upon;
- a belief that the contribution made by the person is neither appreciated nor rewarded properly in terms of pay or promotion;
- resentment at what was perceived to be unfair criticism;
- anger directed at the company or you because what was considered to be a reasonable request, for example for leave or a transfer, was turned down, or because of an unfair accusation, such as over-claiming travel expenses.

Dealing with the problem

It is because there can be such a variety of real or imagined causes of negative behaviour that dealing with it becomes one of the most difficult tasks a manager has to undertake. If the action taken is crude or insensitive, the negative behaviour will only be intensified. This might end up with your invoking the disciplinary procedure, which should be your last resort.

In one sense, it is easier to deal with an actual example of negative behaviour. This can and should be handled on the spot. If the problem is one of general attitude rather than specific actions, it is more difficult to cope with. When individuals are accused of being, for example, generally unenthusiastic or uncooperative, they can simply go into denial, and accuse you of being prejudiced. Their negative behaviour may be reinforced.

If you have to deal with this sort of problem it is best to do it informally, either when it arises or at any point during the year when you feel that something has to be done about it. An annual formal appraisal meeting is not the right time, especially if it produces ratings that are linked to a pay increase. Raising the issue then will only put individuals on the defensive and a productive discussion will be impossible.

The discussion may be informal but it should have three clear objectives:

1 To discuss the situation with individuals, the aim being if possible to get them to recognize for themselves that they are behaving negatively. If this cannot be achieved, then the objective is to make them aware that you believe their behaviour is unacceptable in certain ways.

2 To establish the reasons for the individuals' negative behaviour so far as this is feasible.

3 To discuss and agree any actions individuals could take to behave more positively, or what you or the organization could do to remove the causes of the behaviour.

Discussing the problem

Start by asking generally how individuals feel about their work. Do they have any problems in carrying it out? Are they happy with the support they get from you or their colleagues? Are they satisfied that they are pulling their weight to the best of their ability?

You may find that this generalized start provides the basis for the next two stages – identifying the causes and remedies. It is best if individuals identify for themselves that there is a problem. But in many, if not the majority of cases, this is unlikely to happen. Individuals may not recognize that they are behaving negatively or will not be prepared to admit it.

You will then have to bring to their attention the problem as you see it. You should indicate truthfully that you are concerned because they seem to be unhappy and you wish to know if they feel that you or the organization is treating them unfairly so that you can try to put things right. Give them time to say their piece and then give a rational explanation, dealing with specific grievances. If they are not satisfied with your explanation you can say that they will be given the opportunity to discuss the problem with higher authority, thus indicating that you recognize that your judgement is not final.

If the response you get to these initial points does not bring out into the open the problem as you see it, then you have to explain how the individual's behaviour gives the impression of being negative. Be as specific as possible about the behaviour, bringing up actual instances. For example, a discussion could be based on the following questions: 'Do you recall yesterday's team meeting?' 'How did you think it went?' 'How helpful do you think you were in dealing with the problem?' 'Do you remember saying...?' 'How helpful do you think that remark was?' 'Would it surprise you to learn that I felt you had not been particularly helpful in the following ways...?'

Of course, even if this careful approach is adopted, there will be occasions when individuals refuse to admit that there is anything wrong with their behaviour. If you reach this impasse, then you have no alternative but to spell out to them your perceptions of where they have gone wrong. But do this in a positive way: 'Then I think that it is only fair for me to point out to you that your contribution (to the meeting) would have been more helpful if you had...'

Establishing causes

If the negative behaviour is because of a real or imagined grievance about what you or colleagues or the organization have done, then you have to get individuals to spell this out as precisely as possible. At this point, your job is to listen, not to judge. People can be just as angry about imaginary as about real slights. You have to find out how they perceive the problem before you can deal with it.

It may emerge during the discussion that the problem has nothing to do with you or the company. It may be family troubles or worries about health or finance. If this is the case, you can be sympathetic and may be able to suggest remedies in the form of counselling or practical advice from within or outside the organization.

If the perceived problem is you, colleagues or the organization, try to get chapter and verse on what it is so that you are in a position to take remedial action or to explain the real facts of the case.

Taking remedial action

If the problem rests with the individual, the objective is, of course, to get them to recognize for themselves that remedial action is necessary and to understand what they need to do about it – with your help as necessary. In this situation you might suggest counselling or recommend a source of advice. But be careful; you don't want to imply that there is something wrong with them. You should go no further than suggesting that individuals may find this helpful – they don't need it but they could benefit from it. You should be careful about offering counselling advice yourself. This is usually better done by professional counsellors.

If there is anything specific that the parties involved in the situation can do, then the line to take is that *we* can tackle this problem together: 'this is what I will do', 'this is what the company will do', 'What do you think you should do?' If there is no response to the last question, then this is the point where you have to spell out the action you think they need to take. Be as specific as possible and try to express your wishes as suggestions, not commands. A joint problem-solving approach is always best.

Ten approaches to managing negative behaviour

1 Define the type of negative behaviour that is being exhibited. Make notes of examples.
2 Discuss the behaviour with the individual as soon as possible, aiming to reach agreement about what it is and the impact it makes.

3 If agreement is not obtained, give actual examples of the behaviour and explain why you believe them to be negative.

4 Discuss and so far as possible agree reasons for the negative behaviour, including those attributed to the individual, yourself and the organization.

5 Discuss and agree possible remedies – actions on the part of the individual, yourself or the organization.

6 Monitor the actions taken and the results obtained.

7 If improvement is not achieved and the negative behaviour is significantly affecting the performance of the individual and the team, then invoke the disciplinary procedure.

8 Start with a verbal warning, indicating the ways in which behaviour must improve, and give a timescale and offers of further support and help as required.

9 If there is no improvement, issue a formal warning, setting out as specifically as possible what must be achieved over a defined period of time, indicating the disciplinary action that could be taken.

10 If the negative behaviour persists and continues seriously to affect performance, take the disciplinary action.

How to manage under-performers

Why poor performance occurs

Poor performance may arise because individuals lack the skills and/or the motivation to achieve the results expected of them. In such cases, as Stewart and Stewart[1] suggest: 'Managing poor performers falls into three parts: spotting that there is a problem, understanding the causes of the problem and attempting a remedy.'

Poor performance can result from poor leadership. It is the manager's responsibility to specify the results expected and the levels of skill and competence required.

Performance also depends on the system of work. The quality guru William Deming[2] states unequivocally that differences in performance are largely due to systems' variations. It is not necessary to accept that statement in its entirety, but it is essential to analyse the causes of poor performance in terms of influences beyond the individual's control.

The actions required to manage under-performance

Where the performance failure cannot be attributed to poor leadership or the system of work, the five basic actions required to manage under-performance are as follows:

1 *Identify and agree the problem.* Analyse the feedback and, as far as possible, obtain agreement from the individual on what the shortfall has been. Feedback may be provided by managers, but it can in a sense be built into the job. This takes place when individuals are aware of their targets and standards, know what performance measures will be used and either receive feedback/control information automatically or have easy access to it. They will then be in a position to measure and assess their own performance and, if they are well motivated and well trained, take their own corrective actions. In other words, a self-regulating feedback mechanism exists. This is a situation that managers should endeavour to create on the grounds that prevention is better than cure.

2 *Establish the reason(s) for the shortfall.* When seeking the reasons for any shortfalls, the manager should not crudely be trying to attach blame. The aim should be for the manager and the individual jointly to identify the facts that have contributed to the problem. It is on the basis of this factual analysis that decisions can be made on what to do about it by the individual, the manager or the two of them working together.

It is necessary first to identify any causes that are outside the control of the individual. These will include external pressures, changes in requirements, systems faults, inadequate resources (time, finance, equipment), jobs or tasks allocated to people who do not have the necessary experience or attributes, inadequate induction and continuation training, and poor leadership, guidance or support from the manager, team leader or colleagues. Any factors that are within the control of the individual and/or the manager can then be considered. What needs to be determined is the extent to which the reason for the problem is because the individual:

– did not receive adequate support or guidance from their manager;

– did not fully understand what they were expected to do;

– could not do it – ability;

– did not know how to do it – skill;

– would not do it – attitude.

3 *Decide and agree on the action required.* Action may be taken by the individual, the manager or both parties. This could include:

– Taking steps to improve skills – joint.

– Changing behaviour – this is up to individuals as long as they accept that their behaviour needs to be changed. The challenge for managers is that people will not change their behaviour simply because they are told to do so. They can only be helped to understand that certain changes to their behaviour could be beneficial not only to the organization but also to themselves.

– Changing attitudes – changing behaviour is easier than changing attitudes, which may be deep-rooted; the sequence is therefore to change behaviour first, so far as this is possible, and encourage attitude changes later.

- Providing more support or guidance from the manager.
- Jointly clarifying expectations.
- Jointly developing abilities and skills in the sense that individuals may be expected to take steps to develop themselves but managers may provide help in the form of coaching, additional experience or training.
- Redesigning the job.

Whatever action is agreed, both parties must understand how they will know that it has succeeded. Feedback arrangements can be made but individuals should be encouraged to monitor their own performance and take further action as required.

4 *Resource the action.* Provide the coaching, training, guidance, experience or facilities required to enable agreed actions to happen.

5 *Monitor and provide feedback.* Both managers and individuals monitor performance, ensure that feedback is provided or obtained and analysed, and agree on any further actions that may be necessary.

Handling disciplinary interviews

If poor performance persists, it may be necessary to invoke a disciplinary procedure. Make sure that you have got all the facts and then use the following approach:

1 Give employees notice that the interview is going to take place so that they can be prepared and can get a representative to accompany them.

2 Arrange for a colleague to be present to help conduct the interview and to take notes.

3 State the complaint to the employee, giving chapter and verse and giving supporting statements from other people involved where appropriate.

4 Allow employees to give their side of the story and call any supporting witnesses.

5 Question employees and their witnesses and allow them to do the same.

6 Allow time for a general discussion on the issues raised and any other relevant issues.

7 Give employees an opportunity to have a final say and mention any mitigating circumstances.

8 Sum up the points emerging from the meeting as you see them, but allow employees to comment on them and be prepared to amend your summary.

9 Adjourn the meeting so that you can consider your decision on the basis of what came out in the interview. It is best not to announce the decision during the initial meeting. The adjournment may be only half an hour or so in a straightforward case. It could be longer in a more complex case.

10 Reconvene the meeting and announce your decision.

11 Confirm your decision in writing.

Dismissing people

You should always try to help someone to improve, and if there are performance problems you should go conscientiously through each stage of the capability or disciplinary procedure.

Unfortunately, however, you may still find yourself unable to avoid having to dismiss a person because of a continuing failure to meet an acceptable standard. The following are the points to bear in mind if this happens:

1 Come straight to the point. Tell the person within 30 seconds of starting the interview that he or she has to go.

2 Be clear about shortcomings, quoting chapter and verse, but avoid 'badmouthing' the individual.

3 Don't apologize. If you are certain that this is the right course of action, you have nothing to apologize for.

4 Make it plain that as far as you are concerned, the decision is irrevocable but that the employee has the right to appeal.

5 Ensure that you have a witness in case there is an appeal or legal action.

6 Carry out the dismissal on a Friday.

7 Take steps to ensure that the individual does not have access to a computer or confidential information after dismissal. But do not arrange for him or her to be 'marched off the premises' as sometimes happens.

8 Be aware of the legal issues: the possibility of a claim for unfair dismissal if you have not followed the disciplinary procedure or do not have just cause for your action.

Ten steps to manage under-performers

1 Identify the areas of under-performance – be specific.

2 Establish the causes of poor performance – the individual, the manager, the system of work or any combination of these three.

3 Adopt a problem-solving approach to dealing with the situation – obtain agreement on the actions required by the individual and/or by the manager.

4 Ensure that the necessary resources are provided to enable the problem to be overcome.

5 Provide coaching.

6 Provide additional training.

7 Consider reallocation of duties.

8 Monitor progress and provide feedback.

9 Provide additional guidance as required.

10 As a last resort, invoke the capability or disciplinary procedure, starting with an informal warning.

Notes

1 Stewart, V and Stewart, A (1982) *Managing the Poor Performer*, Gower, Aldershot

2 Deming, W E (1986) *Out of the Crisis*, MIT Center for Advanced Engineering Study, Boston, MA

18

How to increase engagement

The term 'engagement' has come to the fore fairly recently. It is sometimes used very loosely as a powerful notion that embraces pretty well everything the organization is seeking with regard to the contribution and behaviour of its employees in terms of levels of job performance, willingness to do that much more and identification with the organization. More precisely, employee engagement can be defined as what takes place when people at work are interested in and positive, even excited, about their jobs, are prepared to go the extra mile to get them done to the best of their ability by exercising 'discretionary effort' – that is, doing more than is normally expected of them, things that are not in their job description – and are committed to the organization and its values.

Drivers of engagement

The following drivers of engagement were listed by MacLeod and Clarke:[1]

- leadership that ensures a strong, transparent and explicit organizational culture that gives employees a line of sight between their job and the vision and aims of the organization;
- engaging managers who offer clarity, appreciation of employees' effort and contribution, who treat their people as individuals and who ensure that work is organized efficiently and effectively so that employees feel they are valued, and equipped and supported to do their job;
- employees feeling they are able to voice their ideas and be listened to, both about how they do their job and in decision-making in their own department, with joint sharing of problems and challenges and a commitment to arrive at joint solutions;
- a belief among employees that the organization lives its values, and that espoused behavioural norms are adhered to, resulting in trust and a sense of integrity.

Engagement can be increased by actions at organizational level, but it is line managers and team leaders who can make the greatest contribution.

What organizations can do

It was suggested by David Guest[2] that engagement can be achieved:

> through effective leadership of a strong, positive culture that ensures the enactment of organizational values; through strong management that supports employees' work and well-being; through careful design of systems and jobs to enable employees to contribute through full use of their knowledge and skills; through effective employee voice; and through provision of appropriate resources, tools and information to perform effectively.

A basis for enhancing organizational engagement was established by the longitudinal research in 12 companies conducted by Professor John Purcell and his colleagues.[3] They found that the most successful companies had 'the big idea'. This meant that:

> they had a clear vision and a set of integrated values. They were concerned with sustaining performance and flexibility. Clear evidence existed between positive attitudes towards HR policies and practices, levels of satisfaction, motivation and commitment, and operational performance. Policy and practice implementation (not the number of HR practices adopted) is the vital ingredient in linking people management to business performance and this is primarily the task of line managers.

At Lands' End the thinking behind how the company inspires its staff is straightforward – employees' willingness to do that little bit extra arises from their sense of pride in what the organization stands for: quality, service and value. It makes the difference between a good experience for customers and a poor one.

Justin King, CEO of Sainsbury's,[4] has stressed that: 'In our business with almost 150,000 people, engagement is a key concern. In businesses of our scale, you don't even get started without engagement.' For anyone working in Sainsbury's, engagement was only possible if three conditions were met:

- They were clear about what they were expected to do.
- They had the skills to do it.
- They understood why they had to do it.

These three conditions can be satisfied through good job design, learning and development programmes, performance management, and improving the quality of leadership provided by line managers. In addition rewards in the broadest sense – non-financial as well as financial – can play an important part.

What you can do

Developing job engagement starts with how jobs are structured or designed. As a manager or team leader you will often have considerable influence on this. You can help to increase job engagement if you provide for:

- *Interest and challenge* – the degree to which the work is interesting in itself and creates demanding goals for people.
- *Variety* – the extent to which the activities in the job call for a selection of skills and abilities.
- *Autonomy* – the freedom and independence the job holder has, including discretion to make decisions, exercise choice, schedule the work and decide on the procedures to carry it out, and the job holder's personal responsibility for outcomes.
- *Task identity* – the degree to which the job requires completion of a whole and identifiable piece of work.
- *Task significance* – the extent to which the job contributes to a significant end result and has a substantial impact on the lives and work of other people.

All these factors are affected by the quality of leadership. This is vital. You can make a major contribution to achieving job engagement and therefore higher performance by the way in which you lead people, and this includes making an effort to ensure that their jobs have the characteristics set out above. All this depends more on the way in which you manage and lead job holders than on any formal process of job design. You often have considerable discretion on how you allocate work and the extent to which you delegate. You can provide feedback that recognizes the contribution of people, and you can spell out the significance of the work they do.

Notes

1 MacLeod, D and Clarke, N (2009) *Engaging for Success: Enhancing performance through employee engagement*, Department for Business Innovation and Skills, London

2 Guest, D (2009) *Review of Employee Engagement: Notes for a discussion* (unpublished), prepared specifically for the MacLeod and Clarke 2009 review of employee engagement

3 Purcell, J, Kinnie, K, Hutchinson, S, Rayton, B and Swart, J (2003) *People and Performance: How people management impacts on organizational performance*, CIPD, London

4 King, J (2009) Address to DBIS Employee Engagement Conference, 16 July, London

How to interview

19

The overall purpose of a selection interview

This chapter is about selection interviews, which provide the information required to assess candidates against a person specification. A selection interview should provide you with the answers to three fundamental questions:

1 Can the individual do the job? Is the person capable of doing the work to the standard required?
2 Will the individual do the job? Is the person well motivated?
3 How is the individual likely to fit into the team? Will I be able to work well with this person?

The nature of a selection interview

A selection interview should take the form of a conversation with a purpose. It is a conversation because candidates should be given the opportunity to talk freely about themselves and their careers. But the conversation has to be planned, directed and controlled to achieve your aims in the time available.

Your task as an interviewer is to draw candidates out to ensure that you get the information you want. Candidates should be encouraged to do most of the talking – one of the besetting sins of poor interviewers is that they talk too much. But you have to plan the structure of the interview to achieve its purpose and decide in advance the questions you need to ask – questions that will give you what you need to make an accurate assessment:

- *Content* – the information you want and the questions you ask to get it.
- *Contact* – your ability to make and maintain good contact with candidates; to establish the sort of rapport that will encourage them to talk freely, thus revealing their strengths and their weaknesses.
- *Control* – your ability to control the interview so that you get the information you want.

All this requires you to plan the interview thoroughly in terms of content, timing, structure and use of questions. But before doing all this you need to consider who is to conduct the interview and what arrangements need to be made for it.

Preparing for the interview

Initial preparations

Your first step in preparing for an interview should be to familiarize or refamiliarize yourself with the person specification, which defines the sort of individual you want in terms of qualifications, experience and personality. It is also advisable at this stage to prepare questions that you can put to all candidates so as to obtain the information you require. If you ask everyone some identical questions you will be able to compare the answers.

You should then read the candidates' CVs and application forms or letters. This will identify any special questions you should ask about their career or to fill in the gaps – 'What does this gap between jobs C and D signify?' (although you would not put the question as baldly as that; it would be better to say something like this: 'I see there was a gap of six months between when you left your job in C and started in D. Would you mind telling me what you were doing during this time?').

Timing

You should decide at this stage how long you want to spend on each interview. As a rule of thumb, 45 to 60 minutes is usually required for serious, professional or technical appointments.

Middle-ranking jobs need about 30 to 45 minutes. The more routine jobs can be covered in 20 to 30 minutes. But the time allowed depends on the job and you do not want to insult a candidate by conducting a superficial interview.

The content of an interview

The content of an interview can be analysed by dividing it into three sections: the interview's beginning, middle and end.

Beginning

At the start of the interview you should put candidates at their ease. You want them to talk freely in response to your questions. They won't do this if you plunge in too abruptly. At least welcome them and thank them for coming to the interview, expressing genuine pleasure about the meeting. But don't waste too much time talking about their journey or the weather.

Some interviewers start by describing the company and the job. Wherever possible it is best to eliminate this part of the interview by sending candidates a brief job description and something about the organization. If you are not careful you will spend far too much time at this stage, especially if the candidate turns out to be clearly unsuitable. A brief reference to the job should suffice and this can be elaborated on at the end of the interview.

Middle

The middle part of the interview is where you find out what you need to know about candidates. It should take at least 80 per cent of the time, leaving, say, 5 per cent at the beginning and 15 per cent at the end. This is when you ask questions designed to provide information on:

- the extent to which the knowledge, skills, capabilities and personal qualities of candidates meet the person specification;
- the career history and ambitions of candidates and, sometimes, certain aspects of their behaviour at work such as sickness and absenteeism.

End

At the end of the interview you should give candidates the opportunity to ask questions about the job and the company. The quality of these questions can often give you clues about the degree to which applicants are interested and their ability to ask pertinent questions.

You may want to expand a little on the job. If candidates are promising, some interviewers at this stage extol the attractive features of the job. This is fine as long as these are not exaggerated. To give a 'realistic preview' the possible downsides should be mentioned, for example the need to travel, or unsocial working hours. If candidates are clearly unsuitable you can tactfully help them to deselect themselves by referring to aspects of the work that may not appeal to them, or for which they are not really qualified. It is best not to spell out these points too strongly. It is often sufficient simply to put the question: 'This is a key requirement of the job; how do you feel about it?' You can follow up this general question by more specific questions: 'Do you feel you have the right sort of experience?' 'Are you happy about (this aspect of the job)?'

At this stage you should ask final questions about the availability of candidates, as long as they are promising. You can ask when they would be able to start and about any holiday arrangements to which they are committed.

You should also ask their permission to obtain references from their present and previous employers. They might not want you to approach their present employer, and in that case you should tell them that if they are made an offer of employment it would be conditional on a satisfactory reference from their employer. It is useful to ensure that you have the names of people you can approach.

Finally, you inform candidates of what happens next. If some time could elapse before they hear from you, they should be told that you will be writing as soon as possible but that there will be some delay (don't make a promise you will be unable to keep).

It is not normally good practice to inform candidates of your decision at the end of the interview. You should take time to reflect on their suitability and you don't want to give them the impression that you are making a snap judgement.

Planning the interview

When planning interviews you should give some thought to how you are going to sequence your questions, especially in the middle part. There are two basic approaches as described below.

Biographical approach

The biographical approach is probably the most popular because it is simple to use and appears to be logical. The interview can be sequenced chronologically, starting with the first job or even before that at school and, if appropriate, college or university.

The succeeding jobs, if any, are then dealt with in turn, ending with the present job, on which most time is spent if the candidate has been in it for a reasonable time. If you are not careful, however, using the chronological method for someone who has had a number of jobs can mean spending too much time on the earlier jobs, leaving insufficient time for the most important, recent experiences.

To overcome this problem, an alternative biographical approach is to start with the present job, which is discussed in some depth. The interviewer then works backwards, job by job, but only concentrating on particularly interesting or relevant experience in earlier jobs.

The problem with the biographical approach is that it is predictable. Experienced candidates are familiar with it and have their story ready, glossing over any weak points. It can also be unreliable. You can easily miss an important piece of information by concentrating on a succession of jobs rather than focusing on key aspects of the candidates' experience that illustrate their capabilities.

Criteria-based or targeted approach

This approach is based on an analysis of the person specification. From this you can select the criteria on which you will judge the suitability of the candidate, and this will put you in a position to 'target' these key criteria during the interview. You can decide on the questions you need to ask in order to draw out from candidates information about their knowledge, skills, capabilities and personal qualities, which can be compared with the criteria to assess the extent to which candidates meet the specification.

This is probably the best way of focusing your interview to ensure that you get all the information you require about candidates for comparison with the person specification.

Interviewing techniques

Questioning

The most important interviewing technique you need to acquire and practise is questioning. Asking pertinent questions that elicit informative responses is a skill that people do not necessarily possess, but it is one they can develop. To improve your questioning techniques it is a good idea at the end of an interview to ask yourself: 'Did I ask the right questions?' 'Did I put them to the candidate well?' 'Did I get candidates to respond freely?'

There are a number of different types of questions, as described below. By choosing the right ones you can get candidates to open up or you can pin them down to giving you specific information or to extending or clarifying a reply. The other skills you should possess are the ability to establish rapport, and listening, maintaining continuity, keeping eye contact and note-taking.

The main types of questions are described below.

Open questions

Open questions are the best ones to use to get candidates to talk – to draw them out. These are questions that cannot be answered by a yes or no and that encourage a full response. Single-word answers are seldom illuminating. It is a good idea to begin the interview with one or two open questions, thus helping candidates to settle in.

Open-ended questions or phrases inviting a response can be phrased as follows:

- 'I'd like you to tell me about the sort of work you are doing in your present job.'
- 'What do you know about...?'

- 'Could you give me some examples of...?'
- 'In what ways do you think your experience fits you to do the job for which you have applied?'

Probing questions

Probing questions are used to get further details or to ensure that you are getting all the facts. You ask them when answers have been too generalized or when you suspect that there may be some more relevant information that candidates have not disclosed. A candidate may claim to have done something and it may be useful to find out more about exactly what contribution was made. Poor interviewers tend to let general and uninformative answers pass by without probing for further details, simply because they are sticking rigidly to a predetermined list of open questions. Skilled interviewers are able to flex their approach to ensure they get the facts while still keeping control to ensure that the interview is completed on time.

The following are some examples of probing questions:

- 'You've informed me that you have had experience in... Could you tell me more about what you did?'
- 'Could you describe in more detail the equipment you use?'
- 'What training have you had to operate your machine/equipment/computer?'
- 'Why do you think that happened?'

Closed questions

Closed questions aim to clarify a point of fact. The expected reply will be an explicit single word or brief sentence. In a sense, a closed question acts as a probe but produces a succinct factual statement without going into detail. When you ask a closed question you intend to find out:

- What the candidate has or has not done – 'What did you do then?'
- Why something took place – 'Why did that happen?'
- When something took place – 'When did that happen?'
- How something happened – 'How did that situation arise?'
- Where something happened – 'Where were you at the time?'
- Who took part – 'Who else was involved?'

Capability questions

Capability questions aim to establish what candidates know, the skills they possess and use, and what they are capable of doing. They can be open, probing or closed but they will always be focused as precisely as possible on the contents of the person specification, referring to knowledge, skills and capabilities.

The sort of capability questions you can ask are:

- 'What do you know about...?'
- 'How did you gain this knowledge?'
- 'What are the key skills you are expected to use in your work?'
- 'How would your present employer rate the level of skill you have reached in...?'
- 'What do you use these skills to do?'
- 'How often do you use these skills?'
- 'What training have you received to develop these skills?'
- 'Could you please tell me exactly what sort and how much experience you have had in...?'
- 'Could you tell me more about what you have actually been doing in this aspect of your work?'
- 'Can you give me some examples of the sort of work you have done that would qualify you to do this job?'
- 'Could you tell me more about the machinery, equipment, processes or systems that you operate/for which you are responsible?' (The information could refer to such aspects as output or throughput, tolerances, use of computers or software, technical problems.)
- 'What are the most typical problems you have to deal with?'
- 'Would you tell me about any instances when you have had to deal with an unexpected problem or a crisis?'

Unhelpful questions

There are two types of questions that are unhelpful:

- *Multiple questions* such as 'What skills do you use most frequently in your job? Are they technical skills, leadership skills, teamworking skills or communicating skills?' will only confuse candidates. You will probably get a partial or misleading reply. Ask only one question at a time.
- *Leading questions* that indicate the reply you expect are also unhelpful. If you ask a question such as 'That's what you think, isn't it?', you will get the reply 'Yes, I do.' If you ask a question such as 'I take it that you don't really believe that...?', you will get the reply 'No, I don't.' Neither of these replies will get you anywhere.

Questions to be avoided

Avoid any questions that could be construed as being biased on the grounds of sex, race, disability or age.

Ten useful questions

The following are 10 useful questions from which you can select any that are particularly relevant in an interview you are conducting:

1 'What are the most important aspects of your present job?'

2 'What do you think have been your most notable achievements in your career to date?'

3 'What sort of problems have you successfully solved recently in your job?'

4 'What have you learnt from your present job?'

5 'What has been your experience in...?'

6 'What do you know about...?'

7 'What is your approach to handling...?'

8 'What particularly interests you in this job and why?'

9 'Now you have heard more about the job, would you please tell me which aspects of your experience are most relevant?'

10 'Is there anything else about your career that hasn't come out yet in this interview but you think I ought to hear?'

Assessing the data

If you have carried out a good interview, you should have the data to assess the extent to which candidates meet each of the key points in the person specification. You can summarize your assessments by marking candidates against each of the points – 'exceeds specification', 'fully meets specification', 'just meets the minimum specification', 'does not meet the minimum specification'.

You can assess motivation broadly as 'highly motivated', 'reasonably well motivated', 'not very well motivated'.

You should also draw some conclusions from the candidates' career history and the other information you have gained about their behaviour at work. Credit should be given for a career that has progressed steadily, even if there have been several job changes. But a lot of job-hopping for no good reason and without making progress can lead you to suspect that a candidate is not particularly stable. No blame should be attached to a single setback – it can happen to anyone. Redundancy is not a stigma – it is happening all the time. But if the pattern is repeated, you can reasonably be suspicious.

Finally, there is the delicate question of whether you think you will be able to work with the candidate, and whether you think he or she will fit into the team. You have to be very careful about making judgements about how you will get on with someone. But if you are absolutely certain that the chemistry will not work, then you have to take account of that feeling, as long as you ensure that you have reasonable grounds for it on the basis of the behaviour of the candidate at the interview. But be aware of the common mistakes that interviewers can make. These include:

- jumping to conclusions on a single piece of favourable evidence – the 'halo effect';
- jumping to conclusions on a single piece of unfavourable evidence – the 'horns effect';
- not weighing up the balance between the favourable and unfavourable evidence logically and objectively;
- coming to firm conclusions on the basis of inadequate evidence;
- making snap or hurried judgements;
- making prejudiced judgements on the grounds of sex, race, disability, religion, appearance, accent, class, or any aspect of the candidate's life history, circumstances or career that do not fit your preconceptions of what you are looking for.

Coming to a conclusion

Compare your assessment of each of the candidates against one another. If any candidate fails in an area that is critical to success, he or she should be rejected. You can't take a chance. Your choice should be made between the candidates who reach an acceptable standard against each of the criteria. You can then come to an overall judgement, by reference to their assessments under each heading and their career history, as to which one is most likely to succeed.

In the end, your decision between qualified candidates may well be judgemental. There may be one outstanding candidate, but quite often there are two or three. In these circumstances you have to come to a balanced view on which one is more likely to fit the job and the organization *and* have potential for a long-term career, if this is possible. Don't, however, settle for second-best in desperation. It is better to try again.

Remember to make and keep notes of the reasons for your choice and why candidates have been rejected. These, together with the applications, should be kept for at least six months just in case your decision is challenged as being discriminatory.

20 How to be interviewed

Just as there are skills in interviewing, as described in Chapter 19, there are skills in being interviewed – making the right impression and responding to questions in a way that convinces the interviewer that you are the right person for the job. This chapter provides advice on the basic approaches you can adopt when being interviewed that, while none will guarantee that you will get the job, will all help to improve your chances. These approaches are concerned with:

- preparing for the interview;
- creating the right impression;
- responding to questions;
- ending on a high note.

Preparing for the interview

The first thing to remember when preparing for the interview is that you would not have been asked to attend unless you at least matched the basic specification. This should give you the confidence to plan how best to build on that foundation. You need to answer the following questions:

- *What have I got to offer that is likely to put me in a strong position to get this job?* Answer this by studying what you know about the job from the advertisement or, ideally, a more detailed specification produced by the prospective employers. This should give you some idea of what they are looking for.
- *How should I present my qualifications for the job?* Answer this by preparing a brief 40 or 50-word statement that sums up what you have to offer, what your ambitions are and why you want this job. This can be your point of reference throughout the interview, and you can use it as the basis for more detailed descriptions of your achievements and experience, accompanied by explanations of why these are relevant. Such a statement might read like this:

I am an experienced project manager with a proven track record of delivering projects on time, to specification and within budget. My achievements in a company operating in broadly the same field as yours fit me for the senior management position we are discussing.

- *What answers might I give to some typical questions?* For example:
  - Why do you want this job?
  - Tell me about yourself.
  - What have been your major achievements in your present job?
  - What are your strengths?
  - What are your weaknesses?
  - What do you think you would bring to this job?
  - What interests you most in your work?
  - Tell me about a time when you successfully dealt with a major problem at work.
  - What are your ambitions for the future?
  - What are your interests outside work?

Some of the material for answers to these questions should be found outlined in your statement. You may have to think how you would elaborate on it, but don't try to learn answers by heart. You have to appear spontaneous and, in any case, you cannot be sure that these questions will be asked in the same form (although it would be an unusual interview if none of them appeared in one shape or another).

Creating the right impression

First impressions in interviews count. Interviewers tend (often wrongly) to allow their initial reaction to you to colour the whole interview. So you must try to present yourself well from the very start. The things you can do include:

- dressing the part – neat, not gaudy;
- walking confidently into the room;
- giving a firm handshake and making eye contact;
- providing non-verbal clues such as smiling (but not a foolish grin), responding to the interviewer by nodding your head, leaning forward while listening and replying;
- sitting as far back on the chair as you can, not slumping;
- looking at the interviewer, maintaining a high level of eye contact.

From the start you have to give the impression of self-confidence. This is what interviewers are always looking for. And throughout the interview the way you respond to questions should convey your confidence in your own ability and your suitability for the job. The more articulate you are, without being glib, the better.

Responding to questions

A good interviewer will ask you open questions that will encourage you to talk and reveal your strengths and weaknesses. Some people talk themselves out of a job, so be careful not to over-elaborate. Make your replies as concise, clear and self-confident as possible.

Use positive language and provide positive information. You have to present your case convincingly. If you prefix your answers with a phrase such as 'I feel', 'I think' or 'Perhaps' you weaken your position. However, there is a danger of appearing too boastful or egotistical if you constantly blow your own trumpet and use 'I' to start every sentence.

Although it may be more powerful to say 'I did' rather than 'We did', it is possible to reduce the impression of egotism by using phrases such as 'My experience shows that I...', 'Colleagues tell me that...', 'My boss once remarked that...' or 'the team I was leading were able to...'

One of the trickiest questions you may be asked is about your weaknesses. You cannot claim that you have none (no one will believe you). Remember that negative information carries more weight with interviewers than positive information. Although interviewers usually ask about weaknesses (plural), you should only ever admit to one.

The approach you should adopt is to respond to questions, not answer them, by which is meant that you should control the information you release about yourself. To illustrate this approach, the answer to a question about weaknesses should be along the following lines:

- Choose a trait about your character or personality that is obviously true.
- Extend that trait until it becomes a fault.
- Put it back in the distant past.
- Show how you have overcome it.
- Confirm that it is no longer a problem.

Ending on a high note

You will often be asked if you have any questions at the end of an interview. Do not bore the interviewer with trivial questions about the organization or the job. Instead ask positive questions that tacitly assume that the job is yours, such as 'What would be my priorities when (not if) I join you?' and 'What would you expect me to achieve in my first year?'

How to be
a better leader

21

Leadership is the process of setting the direction and ensuring that the members of the leader's organization or team give of their best to achieve the desired result. It is about getting people to go where you want them to go, gaining their commitment, and motivating them to achieve their goals.

What leadership involves

Leaders have three essential roles. They have to:

- *Define the task* – they make it quite clear what the group is expected to do.
- *Achieve the task* – that is why the group exists. Leaders ensure that the group's purpose is fulfilled. If it is not, the result is frustration, disharmony, criticism and, eventually, perhaps disintegration of the group.
- *Maintain effective relationships* – between themselves and the members of the group, and between the people within the group. These relationships are effective if they contribute to achieving the task. They can be divided into those concerned with the team and its morale and sense of common purpose, and those concerned with individuals and how they are motivated.

The roles can be described in a number of ways as discussed below.

The John Adair three circles model

John Adair,[1] the leading British expert on leadership, explained that demands on leaders are best expressed as three areas of need that they must satisfy. These are:

- *Task needs* – to get the job done.
- *Individual needs* – to harmonize the needs of the individual with the needs of the task and the group.
- *Group maintenance needs* – to build and maintain team spirit.

As shown in Figure 21.1, he modelled these demands as three interlocking circles.

FIGURE 21.1   Leadership needs

This model suggests that the task, individual and group needs are interdependent. Satisfying task needs will also satisfy group and individual needs. Task needs, however, cannot be met unless attention is paid to individual and group needs, and looking after individual needs will also contribute to satisfying group needs and vice versa. There is a danger in becoming so task orientated that you ignore individual and group or team needs. It is just as dangerous to be too people orientated, focusing on meeting individual or group needs at the expense of the task. The best leaders are those who keep these three needs satisfied and in balance according to the demands of the situation.

The path–goal model

The path–goal model states that leaders are there to define the path that should be followed by their team in order to achieve its goals. It is the leader's job to guide and help team members to select the best paths towards achieving their own goals and those of the group.

The Welch way

Jack Welch, former chief executive of General Electric, has his own prescription for leadership. He wrote:[2]

> Being a leader changes everything. Before you are a leader success is all about you – your performance, contributions and solutions. Once you become a leader, success is all about growing others. It's about making the people who

work for you smarter, bigger and bolder. Nothing you do as an individual matters, except how you nurture and support your team and increase their self-confidence. Your success as a leader will come not from what you do, but from the reflected glory of your team.

This is in line with the belief expressed by Charles Handy[3] that the post-heroic leader has come to the fore who 'asks how every problem can be solved in a way that develops other people's capacity to handle it'. The Welch way also draws attention to the well-known phenomenon of people who are excellent at their non-managerial job but fail when they are promoted, for example successful sales representatives who become unsuccessful sales managers.

Leaders and followers

Successful leaders depend on followers who want to feel that they are being led in the right direction. They need to know where they stand, where they are going and what is in it for them. They want to feel that it is all worthwhile.

Kelley[4] suggested that the role of the follower should be studied as carefully as that of the leader. Leaders need effective followers. Grint[5] pointed out that 'the trick of the leader is to develop followers who privately resolve the problems leaders have caused or cannot resolve, but publicly deny their intervention.'

Ulrich's leadership brand

Ulrich and Smallwood[6] emphasized that businesses are responsible for establishing a leadership brand as an organizational capability by introducing and maintaining processes that help leaders to grow and develop. Leadership brand is pervasive through all levels of leadership in the organization. It endures by not being tied to one person or a strategic era. Every leader must contribute to the creation of this leadership brand, which defines their identity as leaders, translates customer expectations into employee behaviours and outlasts them.

A leadership brand statement is necessary, which is developed by means of the following steps:

1 Start by defining the organization's strategy.
2 Translate the strategy into the firm's brand.
3 Identify desired outcomes for employees, customers and investors.
4 Define the desired leadership code.

5 Combine attributes and results into a leadership brand statement.

6 Create a set of expectations based on the leadership brand statement.

Leadership styles

There are many styles of leadership and no one style is necessarily better than the other in any situation. Leaders can be classified as:

- *Charismatic/non-charismatic* – charismatic leaders rely on their personality, their inspirational qualities and their 'aura'. They are visionary leaders who are achievement orientated, calculated risk takers and good communicators. Non-charismatic leaders rely mainly on their know-how (authority goes to the person who knows), their quiet confidence and their cool, analytical approach to dealing with problems.

- *Autocratic/democratic* – autocratic leaders impose their decisions, using their position to force people to do as they are told. Democratic leaders encourage people to participate and involve themselves in decision-taking.

- *Enabler/controller* – enablers inspire people with their vision of the future and empower them to accomplish team goals. Controllers command people to obtain their compliance.

- *Transactional/transformational* – transactional leaders trade money, jobs and security for compliance. Transformational leaders motivate people to strive for higher-level goals.

But there is no such thing as an ideal leadership style. The situation in which leaders and their teams function will influence the approaches that leaders adopt. It all depends. The factors affecting the degree to which a style is appropriate will be the type of organization, the nature of the task, the characteristics of the group and, importantly, the personality of the leader.

An *achievement-orientated* approach may be appropriate when expectations of the results the team has to produce are high and team members can be encouraged to rise to the occasion. A *task-orientated* approach (autocratic, controlling, directive) may be required in emergency or crisis situations. It can work, but not always well, when the leader has power, formal backing and a relatively well-structured task. In these circumstances some but not all groups may be more ready to be directed and told what to do, although a more democratic approach can work better. In less well-structured or ambiguous situations, where results depend on the group working well together with a common sense of purpose, leaders who are concerned with maintaining good relationships (democratic, participative or supportive) are more likely to obtain good results.

Good leaders are capable of flexing their style to meet the demands of the situation. Normally democratic or participative leaders may have to shift into a more directive mode when faced with a crisis, but they make clear what they are doing and why. Poor leaders change their style arbitrarily, so their team members are confused and do not know what to expect next.

Effective leaders may also flex their style when dealing with individual team members according to their characteristics. Some people need more positive directions than others. Others respond best if they are involved in decision-making with their boss. But there is a limit to the degree of flexibility that should be used. It is unwise to differentiate too much between the ways in which individuals are treated or to be inconsistent in one's approach.

The kind of leadership you exercise will indeed be related to the nature of the task and the people being led. But it also depends on the context and, of course, on the leaders themselves. If you have a natural leadership style and it works, you have to be careful about changing it arbitrarily or substantially: modification yes, to a degree; transformation, no. And you can learn how to improve it, as discussed towards the end of this chapter, so that it fits the demands of the situation.

What makes a good leader?

What makes a good leader? There is no universal answer to this question. But Lao-Tzu in the 6th century BC had a pretty good stab at it.

> A leader is best
> When people barely know that he exists.
> Not so good when people obey and acclaim him.
> Worst when they despise him.
> Fail to honour people, they fail to honour you.
> But a good leader who talks little,
> When his work is done, his aim fulfilled,
> They will all say 'We did this ourselves'.

More recent thinking about leadership has indicated that good leaders are confident and know where they want to go and what they want to do. They have the ability to take charge, convey their vision to their team, get their team members into action and ensure that they achieve their agreed goals. They are trustworthy, effective at influencing people and earn the respect of their team. They are aware of their own strengths and weaknesses and are skilled at understanding the needs, attitudes and perspective of team members. They appreciate the advantages of consulting and involving people in decision-making. They can switch flexibly from one leadership style to another to meet the demands of different situations and people.

Leadership and emotional intelligence

According to Goleman,[7] emotional intelligence as defined in Chapter 16 is a critical ingredient in leadership. He claimed that effective leaders are alike in one crucial way: they have a high degree of emotional intelligence that plays an increasingly important part at higher levels in organizations where differences in technical skills are of negligible importance. It is obvious that leaders have to be good at relating to people, and emotional intelligence is a convenient label to attach to the skills involved.

Developing leadership skills

It is often said that leaders are born not made. This is a rather discouraging statement for those who are not leaders by birthright. It may be true to the extent that some exceptional people seem to be visionaries, have built-in charisma and have a natural ability to impose their personality on others. However, even they have probably had to develop and hone these qualities when confronted with a situation demanding leadership.

Ordinary mortals need not despair. They too can build on their natural capacities and develop their leadership capabilities. A 10-point plan for doing this is given below, and is followed by three leadership checklists.

1 Understand what is meant by leadership.

2 Appreciate the different leadership styles available.

3 Assess what you believe to be your fundamental leadership style.

4 Get other people, colleagues and indeed your own team members to tell you what they think your leadership style is and how well it works.

5 In the light of this information, consider what you need to do and can do to modify your style, bearing in mind that you have to go on being the same person. In other words, your style should still be a natural one.

6 Think about the typical situations and problems with which you are confronted as a leader. Will your leadership style, modified as necessary, be appropriate for all of them? If not, can you think of any of those situations where a different style would have been better? If so, think about what you need to do to be able to flex your style as necessary without appearing inconsistent to your team.

7 Examine the various explanations of the qualities that make a good leader and assess your own performance using the checklists set out below. Decide what you need to do – what you can do – about any weaknesses.

8 Think about or observe any managers you know whom you have worked for or with.

9 Assess each of them in terms of the qualities using the checklist.

10 Consider what you can learn from them about effective and less-effective leadership behaviours. In the light of this, assess where you could usefully modify your own leadership behaviours.

Leadership checklists

Task

- What needs to be done and why?
- What results have to be achieved and by when?
- What problems have to be overcome?
- To what extent are these problems straightforward?
- Is there a crisis situation?
- What has to be done now to deal with the crisis?
- What are these priorities?
- What pressures are likely to be exerted?

Individuals

- What are their strengths and weaknesses?
- What are likely to be the best ways of motivating them?
- What tasks are they best at doing?
- Is there scope to increase flexibility by developing new skills?
- How well do they perform in achieving targets and performance standards?
- To what extent can they manage their own performance and development?
- Are there any areas where there is a need to develop skill or competence?
- How can I provide them with the sort of support and guidance that will improve their performance?

Teams

- How well is the team organized?
- Does the team work well together?

- How can the commitment and motivation of the team be achieved?
- What is the team good and not so good at doing?
- What can I do to improve the performance of the team?
- Are team members flexible – capable of carrying out different tasks?
- To what extent can the team manage its own performance?
- Is there scope to empower the team so that it can take on greater responsibility for setting standards, monitoring performance and taking corrective action?
- Can the team be encouraged to work together to produce ideas for improving performance?

Case studies

The following are descriptions of the leadership style deployed by three highly effective managers. In each case the style was influenced by three factors: the environment, the people involved and the personality of the manager.

Edward Smith

Ted Smith was the planning manager in a large engineering works. He had some 200 people working in the departments under his control who dealt with process planning, shop loading and production control. It was a very responsible job and his staff included highly qualified engineers as well as large numbers of clerks doing routine work.

Ted's job was to make sure that his departments ran like clockwork. Everyone had to know exactly what to do and when they had to do it. Close cooperation between the three areas under his control was essential. Charismatic-type leadership was out. He had to be cool, calm, measured and a little bit distant. Everyone in the department had to believe Ted knew what he was doing and what he wanted.

He therefore held regular meetings with all his subordinates at which he quickly and efficiently reviewed progress, gave instructions and, as and when necessary, discussed problems. At these meetings he was prepared to switch quickly from being someone who knew exactly what he wanted and who expected people to do exactly as they were told (because it was sensible and right for them to do so) to someone who was prepared to listen to different views, weigh them up and decide. Sometimes he would deliberately throw his managers a problem and tell them to go away and solve it, and let him know the outcome of their actions.

Ted also ensured that his managers transmitted the content of these meetings down to first-line supervisor level. And the supervisors were encouraged to meet their sections regularly. He emphasized throughout the need for teamwork and demonstrated his commitment by ensuring that at inter-departmental meetings, problems of lack of cooperation or poor communications were given priority. The only time he was ever seen to express anger was when work suffered because of feuds between departments.

Elwyn Jones

Elwyn Jones was the HR director of a large conglomerate in the food industry with over 80,000 employees. The firm had grown fast by acquisition and was highly decentralized. Staff were deliberately kept to a minimum at headquarters and Jones had only four executives responsible directly to him. He was, however, also responsible for the implementation of group personnel policies in each of the divisions, and on these matters the divisional personnel directors were responsible to him.

Jones was not in a position to dictate to divisions what he wanted them to do. He could only influence them, and he felt that he had to get genuine acceptance for new policies before they could be introduced. He therefore had to consult on any changes or innovations he wished to introduce and, in most cases, he had to solicit cooperation on the testing of new ideas.

With his headquarters staff, Jones adopted a highly informal, almost permissive approach. He gave them broad guidelines on how they should develop their ideas in the divisions but encouraged them to think and act for themselves. He never called a formal meeting. He was more likely to withdraw to the local pub where, under the watchful eyes of 'big fat Nellie' behind the bar, he consumed pink gins with his colleagues and discussed strategies on entirely equal terms. He adopted precisely the same approach with the divisional personnel directors, although once or twice a year they all got together in a country hotel (one recommended by the *Good Food Guide*, of course) and spent a pleasant couple of days talking generally about their mutual interests.

James Robinson

Jim Robinson was the managing director of a medium-sized business (1,000 employees) in the fast-moving consumer goods sector of industry. He had come up the hard way and his experience had always been in similar firms. Business was highly competitive and the pressures on maintaining, never mind increasing, market share were considerable. Tough decisions about products, markets and people had to be made often and quickly. There was a non-executive chairman and three outside non-executive directors on the board, but they let Robinson get on with it as long as he delivered the results they wanted – which he did.

Robinson was a despot, although a benevolent one. He knew much more about the business as a whole than any of the other four executive directors, and the chairman, and the key institutions (who were represented by the non-executive directors on the board) relied implicitly on his judgement.

Robinson's management style was rumbustious. He did not suffer fools gladly and he cracked down on any repeated inefficiencies or mistakes. He made the key decisions himself. At meetings of the executive directors he would sometimes say that he wanted the views of those present but stated quite clearly that he had already made up his mind and would need a lot of convincing to change it.

But his deep understanding of the business and his ability to think faster on his feet than anyone else meant that while his autocratic behaviour was sometimes resented at the time, those subjected to it would say on almost every occasion: 'You've got to give it to the old so-and-so – he knows his stuff and he's right.' He led, they followed. This was simply because they knew he could accomplish whatever was required in the volatile environment in which they worked.

Notes

1 Adair, J (1973) *The Action-Centred Leader*, McGraw-Hill, London

2 Welch, J (2007) Mindset of a leader, *Leadership Excellence*, 24 (1), pp 8–9

3 Handy, C (1994) *The Empty Raincoat*, Hutchinson, London; Industrial Society (1997)

4 Kelley, R E (1991) In praise of followers, in J J Gabarro (ed) *Managing People and Organizations*, Harvard Business School Press, Boston, MA

5 Grint, K (2005) *Leadership: Limits and possibilities*, Palgrave Macmillan, Basingstoke

6 Ulrich, D and Smallwood, N (2007) *Leadership Brand: Developing customer-focused leaders to drive performance and build lasting value*, Harvard Business School Press, Boston, MA

7 Goleman, D (2001) What makes a leader? In *What Makes a Leader*, Harvard Business School Press, Boston, MA

How to influence people and make a business case

22

Managers are constantly having to exert influence – on their bosses, their colleagues, their staff and their clients, customers and suppliers. They must know about persuading people and how to resolve problems when exerting influence. They must also know how to make and present a formal business case.

Persuading people

A manager's job is 60 per cent getting it right and 40 per cent putting it across. Managers spend a lot of time persuading other people to accept their ideas and suggestions. Persuasion is just another word for selling. You may feel that good ideas should sell themselves, but life is not like that. Everyone resists change and anything new is certain to be treated with suspicion. So it's worth learning a few simple rules that will help you to sell your ideas more effectively.

Ten rules for effective persuasion

1 Define the problem. Determine whether the problem is a misunderstanding (a failure to understand each other accurately) or a true disagreement (a failure to agree even when both parties understand one another). It is not necessarily possible to resolve a true disagreement by understanding each other better. People generally believe that an argument is a battle to understand who is correct. More often, it is a battle to decide who is more stubborn.

2 Define your objective and get the facts. Decide what you want to achieve and why. Assemble all the facts you need to support your case. Eliminate emotional arguments so that you and others can judge the proposition on the facts alone.

3 Find out what the other party wants. The key to all persuasion is to see your proposition from the other person's point of view. Find out how he or she looks at things. Establish what he or she needs and wants.

4 Accentuate the benefits. Present your case in a way that highlights the benefits to the other party, or at least reduces any objections or fears.

5 Predict the other person's response. Everything we say should be focused on that likely response. Anticipate objections by asking yourself how the other party might react negatively to your proposition and thinking up ways of responding to him or her.

6 Create the other person's next move. It is not a question of deciding what we want to do but what we want the other person to do. Your goal is to get results.

7 Convince people by reference to their own perceptions. People decide on what to do on the basis of their own perceptions, not yours.

8 Prepare a simple and attractive proposition. Make it as straightforward as possible. Present the case 'sunny side up', emphasizing its benefits. Break the problem into manageable pieces and deal with them one step at a time.

9 Make the other person a party to your ideas. Get him or her to contribute. Find some common ground so that you can start with agreement. Don't try to defeat the other person in an argument – you will only antagonize him or her.

10 Clinch and take action. Choose the right moment to clinch the proposal – don't prolong the discussion and risk losing it. But follow up promptly.

How to make a business case

A business case sets out the reasons why a proposed course of action will benefit the business, how it will provide that benefit and how much it will cost. The case should be made either in added value terms (ie the income generated by the proposal will significantly exceed the cost of implementing it), or on the basis of the return on investment (ie the cost of the investment, say in training, is justified by the financial returns in such areas as increased productivity).

The basis for a business case

Clearly, a business case is more convincing when it is accompanied by realistic projections of the return on investment. The case for capital expenditure can be made by an analysis of the cash flows associated with the investment and appraisals of the benefits that are likely to arise from them. The object is to demonstrate that in return for paying out a given amount of cash today, a larger amount will be received over a period of time. There are a number of investment appraisal techniques available such as payback, the accounting rate of return, discounted cash flow and net present value. The case for a new product idea can be based on answers to the following questions:

1 Does it meet a well-defined consumer need?
2 In what segment of the market can this product be sold?
3 In what way does this product provide more value to customers than existing products with which it would compete?
4 Can it be differentiated adequately from alternative products?
5 How well does it fit in with the existing product range?
6 Does it exploit the company's existing skills and resources?
7 What investment is required in developing and marketing the new product?
8 What is the likely return on that investment?

Making the business case can be more difficult in areas where it is hard to generate convincing estimates of future income, for example, when justifying investment in training. But an attempt should be made. In this example, training investment was justified because it would:

● improve individual, team and corporate performance in terms of output, quality, speed and overall productivity;
● attract high-quality employees by offering them learning and development opportunities, increasing their levels of competence and enhancing their skills, thus enabling them to obtain more job satisfaction, to gain higher rewards and to progress within the organization;
● improve operational flexibility by extending the range of skills possessed by employees (multiskilling);
● increase the commitment of employees by encouraging them to identify with the mission and objectives of the organization;
● help to manage change by increasing understanding of the reasons for change and providing people with the knowledge and skills they need to adjust to new situations;
● provide line managers with the skills required to manage and develop their people;

- help to develop a positive culture in the organization – one, for example, which is orientated towards performance improvement;
- provide higher levels of service to customers;
- minimize learning costs (reduce the length of learning curves).

Enhancing the business case

A business case will be enhanced if:

- It can be shown convincingly that the return on investment meets or exceeds the amount required by company policy and that the immediate costs are not going have detrimental effects on cash flow.
- Data are made available on the impact the proposal is likely to make on key areas of the organization's operations, such as customer service levels, quality, shareholder value, productivity, income generation, innovation, skills development, talent management.
- It can be shown that the proposal will increase the business's competitive edge, for example ensuring that it can achieve competitive advantage through innovation and/or reducing time-to-market.
- There is proof that the innovation has already worked well within the organization (perhaps as a pilot scheme) or represents 'good practice' that is likely to be transferable to the organization.
- It can be implemented without too much trouble, for example not taking up a lot of managers' time.
- It will add to the reputation of the company by showing that it is a 'world class' organization: that what it does is as good as, if not better than, the world leaders in the sector in which the business operates (a promise that publicity will be achieved through articles in professional journals, press releases and conference presentations will help).
- The proposal is brief, to the point and well argued – it should take no more than five minutes to present orally and should be summarized in writing on the proverbial one side of one sheet of paper (supplementary details can be included in appendices).

Case presentation

As a manager, you may have to make out your case in a presentation to follow up a written business case or on its own. You have to persuade people to believe in your views and accept your recommendations. To do this, you must have a clear idea of what you want, and you have to show that you believe in it yourself. Above all, the effectiveness of your presentation will depend upon the care with which you have prepared it.

Preparation

Thorough preparation is vital. You must think through not only what should be done and why, but also how people will react. Only then can you decide how to make your case: stressing the benefits without underestimating the costs, and anticipating objections.

You should think of the questions your audience is likely to raise, and answer them in advance, or at least have your answers ready. The most likely questions are:

- What
  - is the proposal?
  - will be the benefit?
  - will it cost?
  - are the facts, figures, forecasts and assumptions upon which the proposal is based?
  - are the alternatives?
- Why
  - should we change what we are doing now?
  - is this proposal or solution better than the alternatives?
- How
  - is the change to be made?
  - are the snags to be overcome?
  - have the alternatives been examined?
  - am I affected by the change?
- Who
  - will be affected by the change and what will be their reaction?
  - is likely to have the strongest views for or against the change, and why?
  - will implement the proposal?
- When
  - should this be done?

To make your case you have to do three things:

1 Show that it is based on a thorough analysis of the facts and that the alternatives were properly evaluated before the conclusion was reached. If you have made assumptions, you must demonstrate that these are reasonable on the basis of relevant experience and justifiable projections that allow for the unexpected. Bear in mind Robert Heller's words[1] that 'a proposal is only as strong as its weakest assumption.'

2 Spell out the benefits – to the company and the individuals to whom the case is being made. Present your case 'sunny side up'. Wherever possible, express benefits in financial terms. Abstract benefits, such as customer satisfaction or workers' morale, are difficult to sell. But don't produce 'funny numbers' – financial justification that will not stand up to examination.

3 Reveal costs. Don't try to disguise them in any way. And be realistic. Your proposition will be destroyed if anyone can show that you have underestimated the costs.

Remember, boards want to know in precise terms what they will get for their money. Most boards are cautious, being unwilling and often unable to take much risk. For this reason, it is difficult to make a case for experiments or pilot schemes unless the board, committee or individual can see what the benefits and the ultimate bill will be.

Presentation

Your proposal will often be made in two stages: a written report followed by an oral presentation. The quality of the latter will often tip the balance in your favour (or against you). Effective speaking and writing reports are dealt with in Chapters 44 and 50 respectively, but it is appropriate to note at this stage some special points you should bear in mind when making a case orally in front of an audience:

- Your presentation should not just consist of a repetition of the facts in a written case. It should be used to put across the main points of the argument, leaving out the detail.

- Do not assume that your audience has read the written report or understood it. While you are talking, try to avoid referring to the report. This may switch people's attention from what you are saying. Use visual aids, preferably a flip chart, to emphasize the main points. But don't overdo this – it is possible to be too slick. The audience will be convinced by you, not by your elegant visual aids.

- Make sure your opening secures people's attention. They must be immediately interested in your presentation. Begin by outlining your plan, its benefits and its costs, and let the audience know how you are going to develop your case.

- Bring out the disadvantages and the alternative courses of action so that you are not suspected of concealing or missing something.

- Avoid being drawn into too much detail. Be succinct and to the point.

- An emphatic summing up is imperative. It should convey with complete clarity what you want the board, committee or individual to do.

The effectiveness of your presentation will be largely dependent on how well you have prepared – not only putting your facts, figures and arguments clearly down on paper but also deciding what you are going to say at the meeting and how you are going to say it. The more important the case, the more carefully you should rehearse the presentation.

Checklist

1 Do you know exactly what you want?
2 Do you really believe in your case?
3 Have you obtained and checked all the facts that support your case?
4 What are the strongest arguments for your case?
5 Why must the present situation be changed?
6 Who else will be affected? Unions, other divisions or departments?
7 What are the arguments against your plan?
8 What alternatives are there to your plan?
9 To whom are you presenting your plan? Have you done any lobbying?
10 Have you discussed the finances with the experts?
11 Do you know who are your probable allies and who are likely to be your opponents?
12 Have you prepared handouts of any complicated figures?
13 Have you discussed the best time to present your case?
14 Your ideas were good when you first thought of them, but are they still as good?

Note

1 Heller, R (1982) *The Business of Success*, Sidgwick & Jackson, London

23 How to listen

There are many good writers and speakers but few good listeners. Most of us filter the spoken words addressed to us so that we absorb only some of them – frequently those we want to hear. Listening is an art that not many people cultivate. But it is a very necessary one, because a good listener will gather more information and achieve better rapport with the other person. And both these effects of good listening are essential to good communication.

People don't listen effectively because they are:

- unable to concentrate, for whatever reason;
- too preoccupied with themselves;
- over-concerned with what they are going to say next;
- uncertain about what they are listening to or why they are listening to it;
- unable to follow the points or arguments made by the speaker;
- simply not interested in what is being said.

Effective listeners:

- concentrate on the speaker, following not only words but also body language, which, through the use of eyes or gestures, often underlines meaning and gives life to the message;
- respond quickly to points made by the speaker, if only in the shape of encouraging grunts;
- ask questions frequently to elucidate meaning and to give the speaker an opportunity to rephrase or underline a point;
- comment on the points made by the speaker, without interrupting the flow, in order to test understanding and demonstrate that the speaker and listener are still on the same wavelength. These comments may reflect back or summarize something the speaker has said, thus giving an opportunity for him or her to reconsider or elucidate the point made;
- make notes on the key points – even if the notes are not referred to later they will help to concentrate the mind;

- are continuously evaluating the messages being delivered to check that they are understood and relevant to the purpose of the meeting;
- are alert at all times to the nuances of what the speaker is saying;
- do not slump in their chair – they lean forward, show interest and maintain contact through their oral responses and by means of body language;
- are prepared to let the speaker go on with the minimum of interruption.

How to make things happen

Making things happen, getting things done, achieving results – this is what management is all about.

It can be said that there are three sorts of managers: those who make things happen, those who watch things happening, and those who don't know what is happening. Before finding out how to get into the first category, there are three questions to answer:

- Is getting things done simply a matter of personality – characteristics like drive, decisiveness, leadership, ambition – which some people have and others haven't?

- And if you haven't got the drive, decisiveness and so forth that it takes, is there anything you can do about it?

- To what extent is an ability to make things happen a matter of using techniques that can be learnt and developed?

Personality is important. Unless you have willpower and drive, nothing will get done. But remember that your personality is a function of both nature and nurture. You are born with certain characteristics. Upbringing, education, training and, above all, experience, develop you into the person you are.

We may not be able to change our personality, which, according to Freud, is formed in the first few years of life. But we can develop and adapt it by consciously learning from our own experience and by observing and analysing other people's behaviour.

Techniques for achieving results, such as planning, organizing, delegating, communicating, motivating and controlling, can be learnt. These are dealt with in this book. But these techniques are only as effective as the person who uses them. They must be applied in the right way and in the right circumstances. And you still have to use your experience to select the right technique and your personality to make it work.

To become a person who makes things happen, you therefore have to develop skills and capacities by a process of understanding, observation, analysis and learning. The four actions you should take are:

- Understand what makes achievers tick – the personality characteristics they display in getting things done.
- Observe what achievers do – how they operate, what techniques they use.
- Analyse your own behaviour (behaviour, not personality), compare it with that of high achievers, and think how to improve your effectiveness.
- Learn as much as you can about the management techniques available.

What makes achievers tick?

David McClelland[1] of Harvard University carried out extensive research into what motivates managers. He interviewed, observed and analysed numbers of managers at their place of work and recorded findings before producing his theory. And before you dismiss anything that comes under the heading of theory, remember what Douglas McGregor[2] of the Massachusetts Institute of Technology said: 'there is nothing as practical as a good theory.'

McClelland identified three needs that he believes are key factors in motivating managers. These are:

- the need for achievement;
- the need for power (having control and influence over people);
- the need for affiliation (to be accepted by others).

All effective managers have these needs to a certain degree, but by far the most important one is achievement.

Achievement is what counts and achievers, according to McClelland, have these characteristics:

- They set themselves realistic but achievable goals with some 'stretch' built in.
- They prefer situations that they themselves can influence rather than those on which chance has a large influence.
- They are more concerned with knowing they have done well than with the rewards that success brings.
- They get their rewards from their accomplishment rather than from money or praise. This does not mean that high achievers reject money, which does in fact motivate them as long as it is seen as a realistic measure of performance.
- High achievers are most effective in situations where they are allowed to get ahead by their own efforts.

What do achievers do?

High achievers do some, if not all, of the following:

- They define to themselves precisely what they want to do.
- They set demanding but not unattainable timescales in which to do it.
- They convey clearly what they want done and by when.
- They are prepared to discuss how things should be done and will listen to and take advice. But once the course of action has been agreed they stick to it unless events dictate a change of direction.
- They are single-minded about getting where they want to go, showing perseverance and determination in the face of adversity.
- They demand high performance from themselves and are somewhat callous in expecting equally high performance from everyone else.
- They work hard and work well under pressure; in fact, it brings out the best in them.
- They tend to be dissatisfied with the status quo.
- They are never completely satisfied with their own performance and continually question themselves.
- They will take calculated risks.
- They snap out of setbacks without being personally shattered and quickly regroup their forces and their ideas.
- They are enthusiastic about the task and convey their enthusiasm to others.
- They are decisive in the sense that they are able quickly to sum up situations, define alternative courses of action, determine the preferred course, and convey to their subordinates what needs to be done.
- They continually monitor their own and their subordinates' performance so that any deviation can be corrected in good time.

How to analyse your own behaviour

It is no good trying to analyse your own behaviour unless you have criteria against which you can measure your performance. You have to set standards for yourself, and if you don't meet them, ask yourself why. The answer should tell you what to do next time.

The basic questions you should ask yourself are:

- What did I set out to do?
- Did I get it done?
- If I did, why and how did I succeed?
- If not, why not?

The aim is to make effective use of your experience.

Use the list of what high achievers do to check your own behaviour and actions. If your performance has not been up to scratch under any of these headings, ask yourself specifically what went wrong and decide how you are going to overcome this difficulty next time. This is not always easy. It is hard to admit to yourself, for example, that you have not been sufficiently enthusiastic. It may be even harder to decide what to do about it. You don't want to enthuse all over the place, indiscriminately. But you can consider whether there are better ways of displaying and conveying your enthusiasm to others in order to carry them with you.

Learning

There are a number of management skills and techniques that you need to know about. These techniques are discussed in other chapters in this book. The ones you should be particularly interested in are:

- communicating;
- controlling;
- coordinating;
- decision-making;
- delegating;
- leadership;
- motivating;
- planning and prioritizing;
- project management.

Conclusion

This process of observation, analysis and learning will help you to become an achiever. But remember, achieving results is ultimately about making promises – to others and to yourself – and keeping them. Robert Townsend,[3] in his book *Up the Organization*, has some excellent advice: 'Promises: keep. If asked when you can deliver something ask for time to think. Build in a margin of safety. Name a date. Then deliver it earlier than you promised.'

Notes

1 McClelland, D (1975) *Power: The inner experience*, Irvington, New York

2 McGregor, D (1960) *The Human Side of Enterprise*, McGraw-Hill, New York

3 Townsend, R (1970) *Up the Organization*, Michael Joseph, London

25 How to manage your boss

If you want to achieve results, innovate and get on, you have to learn how to manage your boss. The word 'manage' is defined in the *Oxford English Dictionary* as:

- to conduct affairs;
- to control; cause to submit to one's rule;
- to bring (a person) to consent to one's wishes by artifice, flattery, or judicious suggestion of motives;
- to operate upon, manipulate for a purpose;
- to bring to pass by contrivance;
- to succeed in accomplishing;
- to deal with or treat carefully.

Although such concepts as artifice, flattery and manipulation would not normally play any part, all these definitions provide clues to the various aspects of managing one's boss.

If you really believe that something needs to be done and you cannot do it without the consent of your boss, you have to work out how you are going to manage him or her. And it is worth careful and continuous thought. It is too easy to neglect this essential part of the art of management.

To manage your boss you need to know how to:

- Get agreement from him or her on what you want to do.
- Deal with him or her over problems.
- Impress him or her, so that they are more likely to accept your proposals and to place their trust in you.

Getting agreement

Getting agreement from bosses is in many ways like getting agreement from anyone else. You need to be good at case presentation and at persuasion. More specifically you need to do the following things:

- Find out what they expect.

- Learn about their likes and dislikes, their quirks and their prejudices.

- Establish how they like things presented to them. Do they like long, carefully worked out, written reports? Or do they prefer a succinct proposal on one side of one sheet of paper? Perhaps they are more likely to be persuaded if they are introduced gradually to a proposal – a softening-up process, as it were. It is often advisable to test the water before plunging straight in. Some people prefer to start by talking all the way around a problem before getting down to its essential elements. They don't like surprises.

- Get to know how they like things done – by observation and by asking other people. If something goes wrong, choose the right moment and ask their advice on how to do it better next time (most people love being asked for their advice).

- Find out the right time to approach them. Some people are at their best first thing. Others take time to warm up. It is obviously inadvisable to spring surprises on someone at the end of a long, hard day. Check on their mood in advance. Secretaries or PAs can help, and it is always worthwhile having these people on your side. PAs can be good friends but bad enemies.

- Work out the best circumstances in which to tackle them: alone in the office, or over lunch, or driving at speed along a motorway (there is a lot to be said for a captive audience). Getting away from the office may be an advantage: there will be no interruptions and your boss is less likely to call in the henchman, so you will not have to persuade two people at once. (Picking them off one at a time is much more likely to be successful.) Beware of the 'abominable no-man'. Most organizations have at least one – often the head of finance. They no doubt perform a useful role, but keep them out of your way if you can.

- Decide whether you want support. You may be able to make a better case on a one-to-one basis. There is a lot to be said for standing firmly on your own two feet.

- Don't go in for open confrontation if you cannot get your own way at first. Get agreement on the points your boss is prepared to agree, and then turn to the problem areas. Impress upon your boss that you want the two of you to cover every possible angle. Emphasize joint responsibility.

- Leave them an escape route – a way open to consent without their having to climb down. Don't beat them into the ground – you might win this one but what about the next time?

- Don't overwhelm them with your ideas. Don't expect to achieve everything at once. Tackle one important thing at a time. Keep it simple. If you come up against a strong objection, don't fight it for too long.

Survive to fight another day. This does not mean that you should not argue your case strongly, but that you should avoid giving the impression of being pig-headed.

- Keep in reserve alternative proposals or modifications to your original idea to use if you are getting nowhere.

- If your boss comes up with a better idea than yours, recognize and accept it. Everybody likes recognition. There is no need to flatter them. You are only reacting to them the way you would like them to react to you.

- If you can't convince your boss first time, remember who is the boss. Bosses make the ultimate decisions. If they say 'That's the way it's going to be', you may have to accept it. In the end your boss could say to you 'We're in a two-horse race and only one can win, and that's going to be me.' But you don't have to give up completely. Watch for any signs that your boss might be prepared to change his or her mind – given time and a revision to your argument or proposal.

- Don't nag. If you press too hard they will become stubborn and begin to think you are challenging their authority and position. Retire in good order and re-open your campaign at the right moment.

Dealing with problems

Things are going wrong. You've made a mistake. You need your boss's help in sorting out a problem. How do you tackle him or her? You should adopt the following approach:

- Keep your boss informed. Never let them be taken by surprise. Prepare them in advance for the bad news. If 'troubles come not in single spies but in battalions', don't let them have it all at once. Let them down as gently as possible. Don't use the 'first the good news, then the bad news' line too crudely, but don't be too gloomy. Give them hope.

- If something has gone wrong, explain what has happened, why it has happened (no excuses) and what you would like to do about it. Don't dump the problem in their lap in a 'take it or leave it' spirit.

- Emphasize that you are seeking their views on what you propose, as well as their agreement.

- If you think your boss is to blame, never say 'I told you so.' If you do, you will make an enemy for life.

- If you admit responsibility, try to stop your boss keeping on at you. Steer him or her away from recriminations into a positive attitude on what you can jointly do to solve the problem.

Impressing your boss

Your purpose as a manager is not solely to impress the bosses. Nor is it to make them like you. But you will get more done and get on better if you impress them. And why make an enemy of your boss when you can have him or her as a friend?

Your boss needs to trust you, to rely upon you and to believe in your capacity to come up with good ideas and to make things happen. He or she doesn't want to wet-nurse you or to spend time correcting your mistakes or covering up.

To succeed in impressing your boss without really trying – it's fatal to push too much – you should:

- Always be frank and open. Admit mistakes. Never lie or even shade the truth. If there is the faintest suspicion that you are not perfectly straightforward, your boss will never trust you again.

- Aim to help your boss to be right. This does not mean being subservient or time-serving. Recognize, however, that you exist to give him or her support – in the right direction.

- Respond fast to requests on a can do/will do basis.

- Don't trouble him or her unnecessarily with your problems.

- Provide him or her with protection where required. Loyalty is an old-fashioned virtue, but you owe it to your boss. If you cannot be loyal then you should get out from under as quick as you can.

- Provide your boss with what the army calls 'completed staff work'. This means that if you are asked to do something you should do it thoroughly. Come up with solutions, not problems.

Test your ideas in draft form if you like, but, having done so, present a complete proposal with whatever supporting arguments or evidence you need. Avoid half-baked suggestions. Your boss wants answers, not questions. When you have finished your report and studied your conclusions and recommendations, ask yourself the question: 'If I were my boss would I stake my reputation on this piece of work and put my name to it?' If the answer is 'No', tear up your report and do it again. It's not completed staff work.

26 How to manage change

Change is the only constant process that exists in organizations. An effective organization is one that takes deliberate steps to manage change smoothly. It will not always succeed – change can be a traumatic process – but at least it will try, and attempts to manage change will have the minimum objective of mitigating its effects on the organization and its employees.

The approach to the management of change will recognize that the key to success lies not only in a transformational leader supported by powerful change mechanisms, but also in understanding that change is implemented by people and that it is their behaviour and support that count. The most important aim of change management is to achieve commitment to change.

Successful change management requires an understanding of:

- the main types of change;
- how change affects individuals;
- the process of change;
- how to build commitment to change.

Types of change

There are two main types of change: strategic and operational.

Strategic change

Strategic change is concerned with broad, long-term and organization-wide issues. It is about moving to a future state that has been defined generally in terms of strategic vision and scope. It will cover the purpose and mission of the organization, its corporate philosophy on such matters as growth, quality, innovation and values concerning people, the customer needs served and the technologies employed. This overall definition leads to specifications of competitive positioning and strategic goals for achieving and maintaining competitive advantage and for product market development. These goals are supported by policies concerning marketing, sales, manufacturing, product and process development, finance and human resource management.

Strategic change takes place within the context of the external competitive, economic and social environment, and the organization's internal resources, capabilities, culture, structure and systems. Its successful implementation requires thorough analysis and understanding of these factors in the formulation and planning stages.

Operational change

Operational change relates to new systems, procedures, structures or technology that will have an immediate effect on working arrangements within a part of the organization. But the impact of such changes on people can be more significant than broader strategic change and they have to be handled just as carefully.

How people change

The ways in which people change are best explained by reference to the following assumptions developed by Bandura:[1]

- People make conscious choices about their behaviour.
- The information people use to make their choices comes from their environment.
- Their choices are based upon:
  - the things that are important to them;
  - the views they have about their own abilities to behave in certain ways;
  - the consequences they think will accrue from whatever behaviour they decide to engage in.

For those concerned in change management, the implications of this theory are that:

- The tighter the link between a particular behaviour and a particular outcome, the more likely it is that we will engage in that behaviour.
- The more desirable the outcome, the more likely it is that we will engage in behaviour that we believe will lead to it.
- The more confident we are that we can actually assume a new behaviour, the more likely we are to try it.

To change people's behaviour, therefore, we have first to change the environment within which they work; second, to convince them that the new behaviour is something they can accomplish (training is important); and third, to persuade them that it will lead to an outcome that they will value. None of these steps is easy. To achieve them, it helps to know more about the process of change.

The process of change

Change, as Rosabeth Moss Kanter[2] puts it, is the process of analysing 'the past to elicit the present actions required for the future'. It involves moving from a present state, through a transitional state, to a future desired state.

The process starts with an awareness of the need for change. An analysis of the present state and the factors that have created it leads to a diagnosis of the distinctive characteristics of the situation and an indication of the direction in which action needs to be taken. Possible courses of action can then be identified and evaluated and a choice made of the preferred action.

It is then necessary to decide how to get from here to there. Managing the change process in this transitional state is a critical phase in the change process. It is here that the problems of introducing change emerge and have to be managed. These problems can include resistance to change, low stability, high levels of stress, misdirected energy, conflict and loss of momentum. Hence the need to do everything possible to anticipate reactions and likely impediments to the introduction of change.

The installation stage can also be painful. When planning change there is a tendency for people to think that it will be an entirely logical and linear process of going from A to B. It is not like that at all. As described by Pettigrew and Whipp,[3] the implementation of change is an 'iterative, cumulative and reformulation-in-use process'.

The approach to change management

Michael Beer and his colleagues suggested in a seminal *Harvard Business Review* article, 'Why change programs don't produce change',[4] that most such programmes are guided by a theory of change that is fundamentally flawed. This theory states that changes in attitude lead to changes in behaviour. 'According to this model, change is like a conversion experience. Once people "get religion", changes in their behaviour will surely follow.'

They believe that this theory gets the change process exactly backwards:

> In fact, individual behaviour is powerfully shaped by the organizational roles people play. The most effective way to change behaviour, therefore, is to put people into a new organizational context, which imposes new roles, responsibilities and relationships on them. This creates a situation that in a sense 'forces' new attitudes and behaviour on people.

They prescribe six steps to effective change that concentrate on what they call 'task alignment' – reorganizing employees' roles, responsibilities and relationships to solve specific business problems in small units where goals and tasks can be clearly defined.

The aim of following the overlapping steps is to build a self-reinforcing cycle of commitment, coordination and competence. The steps are:

1 Mobilize commitment to change through the joint analysis of problems.
2 Develop a shared vision of how to organize and manage to achieve goals such as competitiveness.
3 Foster consensus for the new vision, competence to enact it, and cohesion to move it along.
4 Spread revitalization to all departments without pushing it from the top – don't force the issue, let each department find its own way to the new organization.
5 Institutionalize revitalization through formal policies, systems and structures.
6 Monitor and adjust strategies in response to problems in the revitalization process.

The approach suggested by Michael Beer and his colleagues is fundamental to the effective management of change. It can, however, be associated with a number of other guidelines as set out below.

Guidelines on how to facilitate change have been produced by General Electric. These are to ensure that:

- Employees see the reason for change.
- Employees understand why change is important and see how it will help them and the business in the long and short term.
- The people who need to be committed to the change to make it happen are recognized.
- A coalition of support is built for the change.
- The support of key individuals in the organization is enlisted.
- The link between the change and other HR systems such as staffing, training, appraisal, rewards, structure and communication is understood.
- The systems implications of the change are recognized.
- A means of measuring the success of the change is identified.
- Plans are made to monitor progress in the implementation of change.
- The first steps in getting change started are recognized.
- Plans are made to keep attention focused on the change.
- The likely need to adapt the change over time is recognized and plans can readily be made and implemented for such adaptations.

Guidelines for change management

- The achievement of sustainable change requires strong commitment and visionary leadership from the top.

- Understanding is necessary of the culture of the organization and the levers for change most likely to be effective therein.

- Those concerned with managing change at all levels should have the temperament and leadership skills appropriate to the circumstances of the organization and its change strategies.

- It is important to build a working environment that is conducive to change. This means developing the firm as a 'learning organization'.

- Although there may be an overall strategy for change, it is best tackled incrementally (except in crisis conditions). The change programme should be broken down into actionable segments for which people can be held accountable.

- The reward system should encourage innovation and recognize success in achieving change.

- Change implies streams of activity across time and 'may require the enduring of abortive efforts or the build up of slow incremental phases of adjustment which then allow short bursts of incremental action to take place' – Pettigrew and Whipp[3].

- Change will always involve failure as well as success. The failures must be expected and learned from.

- Hard evidence and data on the need for change are the most powerful tools for its achievement, but establishing the need for change is easier than deciding how to satisfy it.

- It is easier to change behaviour by changing processes, structures and systems than to change attitudes or the corporate culture.

- There are always people in organizations who welcome the challenges and opportunities that change can provide. They are the ones to be chosen as change agents.

- Resistance to change is inevitable if the individuals concerned feel that they are going to be worse off – implicitly or explicitly. The inept management of change will produce that reaction.

- In an age of global competition, technological innovation, turbulence, discontinuity, even chaos, change is inevitable and necessary. The organization must do all it can to explain why change is essential and how it will affect everyone Moreover, every effort must be made to protect the interests of those affected by change.

Gaining commitment to change

These guidelines point in one direction: having decided why changes are necessary, what the goals are and how they are to be achieved, the most important task is to gain the commitment of all concerned to the proposed change.

A strategy for gaining commitment to change should cover the following phases:

1 *Preparation* – in this phase, the person or persons likely to be affected by the proposed change are contacted in order to be made aware of it.

2 *Acceptance* – in the second phase, information is provided on the purpose of the change, how it is proposed to implement it and what effect it will have on those concerned. The aim is to achieve understanding of what the change means and to obtain a positive reaction. This is more likely if:

- the change is perceived to be consistent with the mission and values of the organization;
- the change is not thought to be threatening;
- the change seems likely to meet the needs of those concerned;
- there is a compelling and fully understood reason for change;
- those concerned are involved in planning and implementing the change programme on the principle that people support what they help to create;
- it is understood that steps will be taken to mitigate any detrimental effects of the change.

It may be difficult, even impossible to meet these requirements. That is why the problems of gaining commitment to change should not be underestimated.

During this phase, the extent to which reactions are positive or negative can be noted and action taken accordingly. It is at this stage that original plans may have to be modified to cater for legitimate reservations or second thoughts.

3 *Commitment* – during the third phase, the change is implemented and becomes operational. The change process and people's reaction to it need to be monitored. There will inevitably be delays, setbacks, unforeseen problems and negative reactions from those faced with the reality of change. A response to these reactions is essential so that valid criticisms can be acted upon or reasons given as to why the change should proceed as planned.

Following implementation, the aim is to have the change adopted, as with use its worth becomes evident. The decision is made at this stage whether to continue with the change or to modify or even abort it. Account should again be taken of the views of those involved.

Finally, and after further modifications as required, the change is institutionalized and becomes an inherent part of the organization's culture and operations.

Notes

1 Bandura, A (1986) *Social Boundaries of Thought and Action*, Prentice-Hall, Englewood Cliffs, NJ

2 Kanter, R M (1984) *The Change Masters*, Allen & Unwin, London

3 Pettigrew, A and Whipp, R (1991) *Managing Change for Competitive Success*, Blackwell, Oxford

4 Beer, M, Eisenstat, R and Specter, B (1990) Why change programs don't produce change, *Harvard Business Review*, November–December

How to manage conflict 27

Conflict is inevitable in organizations because the objectives, values and needs of groups and individuals do not always coincide. Conflict may be a sign of a healthy organization. Bland agreement on everything would be unnatural and enervating. There should be clashes of ideas about tasks and projects, and disagreements should not be suppressed. They should come out into the open because that is the only way to ensure that the issues are explored and conflicts are resolved.

There is such a thing as creative conflict – new or modified ideas, insights, approaches and solutions can be generated by a joint re-examination of the different points of view as long as this is based on an objective and rational exchange of information and ideas. But conflict becomes counterproductive when it is based on personality clashes, or when it is treated as an unseemly mess to be hurriedly cleared away, rather than as a problem to be worked through.

Conflict resolution can be concerned with conflict between groups or between individuals.

Handling inter-group conflict

There are three principal ways of resolving inter-group conflict: peaceful coexistence, compromise and problem-solving.

Peaceful coexistence

The aim here is to smooth out differences and emphasize the common ground. People are encouraged to learn to live together; there is a good deal of information, contact and exchange of views, and individuals move freely between groups (for example, between headquarters and the field, or between sales and manufacturing).

This is a pleasant ideal, but it may not be practicable in many situations. There is much evidence that conflict is not necessarily resolved by bringing people together. Improved communications and techniques such as briefing groups may appear to be good ideas but are useless if management has nothing to say that people want to hear. There is also the danger that the real issues, submerged for the moment in an atmosphere of superficial bonhomie, will surface again later.

Compromise

The issue is resolved by negotiation or bargaining and neither party wins or loses. This concept of splitting the difference is essentially pessimistic. The hallmark of this approach is that there is no 'right' or 'best' answer. Agreements only accommodate differences. Real issues are not likely to be solved.

Problem-solving

An attempt is made to find a genuine solution to the problem rather than just accommodating different points of view. This is where the apparent paradox of 'creative conflict' comes in. Conflict situations can be used to advantage to create better solutions.

If solutions are to be developed by problem-solving, they have to be generated by those who share the responsibility for seeing that the solutions work. The sequence of actions is: first, those concerned work to define the problem and agree on the objectives to be attained in reaching a solution; second, the group develops alternative solutions and debates their merits; third, agreement is reached on the preferred course of action and how it should be implemented.

Handling conflict between individuals

Handling interpersonal conflict can be even more difficult than resolving conflicts between groups. Whether the conflict is openly hostile or subtly covert, strong personal feelings may be involved. Yet, as James Ware and Louis Barnes[1] say:

> The ability to productively manage such conflict is critical to managerial success. Interpersonal differences often become sharpest when the organizational stakes seem to be high, but almost all organizations include their share of small issues blown into major conflicts. The manager's problem is to build on human differences of opinion while not letting them jeopardize overall performance, satisfaction and growth.

Ware and Barnes go on to say that interpersonal conflict, like intergroup conflict, is an organizational reality that is neither good nor bad. It can be destructive, but it can also play a productive role. 'Problems usually arise when potential conflict is artificially suppressed, or when it escalates beyond the control of the adversaries or third-party intermediaries.'

The reaction to interpersonal conflict may be the withdrawal of either party, leaving the other one to hold the field. This is the classic win–lose situation. The problem has been resolved by force, but this may not be the best solution if it represents one person's point of view that has ignored counter-arguments, and has, in fact, steamrollered over them. The winner may be triumphant but the loser will be aggrieved and either demotivated or resolved to fight again another day. There will have been a lull in, but not an end to, the conflict.

Another approach is to smooth over differences and pretend that the conflict does not exist, although no attempt has been made to tackle the root causes. Again, this is an unsatisfactory approach. The issue is likely to re-emerge and the battle will recommence.

Yet another approach is bargaining to reach a compromise.

This means that both sides are prepared to lose as well as win some points and the aim is to reach a solution acceptable to both sides. Bargaining, however, involves all sorts of tactical and often counterproductive games, and the parties are often more anxious to seek acceptable compromises than to achieve sound solutions.

Ware and Barnes identify two other approaches to managing interpersonal conflict: controlling, and constructive confrontation.

Controlling conflict

Controlling conflict can involve preventing interaction, or structuring the forms of interaction or reducing or changing external pressures.

- *Preventing interaction* is a strategy for use when emotions are high. Conflict is controlled by keeping the conflicting parties apart in the hope that, although the differences still exist, the people involved will have time to cool down and consider more constructive approaches. But this may only be a temporary expedient and the eventual confrontation could be even more explosive.

- *Structuring the forms of interaction* is a strategy that can be used when it is not possible to separate the parties. In these cases, ground rules can be developed to deal with the conflict concerning such behaviours as communicating information or dealing with specific issues. However, this may also be a temporary strategy if the strong underlying feelings are only suppressed rather than resolved.

- *Personal counselling* is an approach that does not address the conflict itself but focuses on how the two people are reacting. Personal counselling gives people a chance to release pent-up tensions and may encourage them to think about new ways of resolving the conflict. But it does not address the essential nature of the conflict, which is the relationship between two people.

Thus, constructive confrontation offers the best hope of a long-term solution.

Constructive confrontation

Constructive confrontation is a method of bringing the individuals in conflict together, ideally with a third party whose function is to help build an exploratory and cooperative climate.

Constructive confrontation aims to get the parties involved to understand and explore each other's perceptions and feelings. It is a process of developing mutual understanding to produce a win–win situation. The issues will be confronted but on the basis of a joint analysis, with the help of the third party, of facts relating to the situation and the actual behaviour of those involved. Feelings will be expressed but they will be analysed by reference to specific events and behaviours rather than inferences or speculations about motives.

Third parties have a key role in this process, and it is not an easy one. They have to get agreement to the ground rules for discussions aimed at bringing out the facts and minimizing hostile behaviour. They must monitor the ways in which negative feelings are expressed and encourage the parties to produce new definitions of the problem and its cause or causes and new motives to reach a common solution. Third parties must avoid the temptation to support or appear to support either of those in contention. They should adopt a counselling approach, as follows:

- listen actively;
- observe as well as listen;
- help people to understand and define the problem by asking pertinent, open-ended questions;
- recognize feelings and allow them to be expressed;
- help people to define problems for themselves;
- encourage people to explore alternative solutions;
- get people to develop their own implementation plans but provide advice and help if asked.

Conclusion

Conflict, as has been said, is in itself not to be deplored: it is an inevitable concomitant of progress and change. What is regrettable is the failure to use conflict constructively. Effective problem-solving and constructive confrontation both resolve conflicts and open up channels of discussion and cooperative action.

Many years ago one of the pioneering writers on management, Mary Parker Follett,[2] wrote something on managing conflict that is as valid today as it was then: 'Differences can be made to contribute to the common cause if they are resolved by integration rather than domination or compromise.'

Notes

1 Ware, J and Barnes, L (1991) Managing interpersonal conflict, in *Managing People and Organizations*, ed J Gabarro, Harvard Business School Publications, Boston, MA

2 Follett, M P (1924) *Creative Experience*, Longmans Green, New York

28 How to manage a crisis

What is crisis management?

The phrase 'crisis management' was coined by Robert McNamara at the time of the Cuban missile crisis when he said: 'There is no longer any such thing as strategy, only crisis management.'

Crisis management situations happen in any organization where the pressure of events – external or internal – forces management into making urgent decisions. These arise because a crisis is a turning point or a time of danger and suspense, and, in this turbulent age, turning points and dangerous moments are always with us.

Crisis management can be defined as:

The process of dealing with a pressurized situation in a way that plans, organizes, directs and controls a number of interrelated operations and guides the decision-making process of those in charge to a rapid but unhurried resolution of the acute problem faced by the organization.

Causes of crises

Crises are caused either by the actions of human beings or by natural disasters – fire, flood, earthquake and the like. If people are at the root of the crisis, they may be deliberately inflicting harm on the organization from outside or, also externally, they may have taken actions that indirectly create a major problem. Internally, crises can be caused deliberately by people attempting to enforce their point of view, accidentally by some colossal misjudgement or by a long history of compounded errors.

Crises may, however, be no more than sudden, unforeseen events that perhaps could have been anticipated. To dismiss strategy, as McNamara did, is perhaps going too far, but Robert Burns did suggest that 'the best laid schemes o' mice an' men gang aft a-gley,' and this is as true today as when he wrote it in the 18th century.

In an ideal world, crises would not happen. You would know where you want to go and you would get there, with only minor deviations along the way. Problems would have been foreseen and contingency plans made to deal with them. This, of course, is not the way things are in real life. Murphy's law is always ready to strike again – if anything can go wrong it will.

Crises may appear to come suddenly, but this does not mean that they are unforeseeable. The Garcia Márquez novella *Chronicle of a Death Foretold* was written about a crisis, the murder of a young man; as the title implies, everyone knew it was going to happen only no one seemed able to stop it. Prior to a crisis there are often warning signs that disaster is about to strike. Even a volcanic explosion can be predicted.

There is a phenomenon that can be described as 'crisis slide'. Gradually, imperceptibly but inevitably, there is a build-up of events. Rain falls in ever-increasing volumes; the overflowing river is joined by equally overflowing streams, and the pressure increases. The force becomes progressively more irresistible until, under overwhelming pressure, the dam breaks. The crisis management process should, of course, have started as soon as observers had noticed the unusually heavy rainfall. Human error, however, creeps in and dams burst.

Steady slides down the slippery slope to an outright crisis can also happen, not because of human error, but because of human cussedness. If crisis management techniques are used coolly to assess potentially dangerous situations and bring the parties together in good time to discuss how to resolve the problems before they become critical, the dire effects of cussedness can be avoided. This can happen on the international scene as well as within organizations. Before the Cuban missile crisis, President Kennedy had been made aware of 60 nuclear near-disasters, including the launching of two missiles with nuclear warheads. He took steps not only to improve the US system of accident proofing but also to exchange information with the Russians. The Falklands crisis, however, was a sad story of a complete failure of the British both to understand how strongly the Argentines felt about the Malvinas and to appreciate that President Galtieri was liable to go off the rails.

Management crises

In management all sorts of crises can happen: a takeover bid, a collapse in the foreign exchange rate, a drug that has disastrous side-effects, a competitive product that suddenly appears on the market and wipes the floor with a market-leader brand, an innovation that renders a product obsolete, a sudden damaging strike, a dishonest senior executive who gets the company into the headlines, a fire or a flood, the departure of key members of the management team to competitors, and so on. The list is endless.

Tolstoy said of marriages: 'All happy families resemble one another, but each unhappy family is unhappy in its own way.' The same can be said of crises. Each crisis is a unique event and has to be dealt with accordingly. However, there are certain types of behaviour that are appropriate in all critical situations, and there are some general principles that can be followed in crises involving negotiation or conflict. There are also a number of crisis management techniques that are generally applicable, subject to modification to suit particular circumstances.

Crisis management behaviour

The most important thing to do in a crisis is to keep cool. As Kipling put it:

If you can keep your head when all about you
Are losing theirs and blaming it on you...
Yours is the Earth and everything that's in it
And – which is more – you'll be a Man, my son.

Perhaps the best exponent of this approach was Harold Macmillan who said at London Airport of a political crisis in his cabinet: 'I thought the best thing to do was to settle up these little local difficulties, and then turn to the wider vision of the Commonwealth.'

Statesmen, of course, have to give the impression of playing it cool. Henry Kissinger, who spent his whole diplomatic career in crisis management, said once: 'There cannot be a crisis next week. My schedule is already full.' But managers should play it cool too.

One of the arts of dealing with a crisis is to maintain the confidence of everyone around that you are managing it. Insouciance like Macmillan's is one way of doing this. Another way is deliberately to give the impression that you are taking it easy – relaxing almost – when in actual fact you are working at top speed. Good crisis managers, in situations where all hell is let loose, people and pieces of paper are being thrown about in all directions and three telephones are ringing at once, will, from time to time, lean back in their chair, sip a cup of coffee and idly gossip about last night's football game. They then resume work with redoubled energy. Robert Townsend[1] described this approach well in *Up the Organization* when he wrote: 'There is a time for engagement and a time for withdrawal. A time to contemplate it, and a time just to laugh at it.'

And in *The Right Stuff*, Tom Wolfe, describing how Chuck Yeager (the man who broke the sound barrier for the first time with two broken ribs) influenced the crisis management style of airline pilots, wrote this about their approach:

Anyone who travels very much on airlines in the United States soon gets to know the voice of the airline pilot... coming over the intercom... with a particular drawl, a particular folksiness, a particular down-home calmness that is so exaggerated it begins to parody itself (nevertheless! – it's reassuring)... the voice that tells you, as the airliner is caught in thunderheads and goes bolting up and down a thousand feet at a single gulp, to check your seat belt because 'it might get a little choppy.'

Negotiating situations

Crises concerning takeovers, industrial relations, legal disputes and other problems where the crunch has come because two sides have radically different views, will often involve negotiations. The normal negotiating tactics described in Chapter 37 will apply, although they may have to be speeded up.

In tense situations, special ploys may have to be used. For example, you can use the 'Trollope' ploy, which is the acceptance of an offer that has not been made in order to induce the adversary to accept the acceptance. Robert Kennedy coined this term, naming it after those Victorian heroines in the novels of Anthony Trollope who interpret a squeeze of the hand on the hero's part as a proposal of marriage and succeed in making this interpretation stick. It was used in the Cuban missile crisis where the ambiguity arose in communications from Mr Krushchev. He sent two letters, one implying a hard line about the American blockade, the other a mild and even yielding one. To deepen the confusion, it was not clear whether the 'hawklike' letter (which was received second) had been written before or after the 'dovelike' one. The American decision (the Trollope ploy) was to treat the dovelike letter as the true communication, ignoring the other hawklike one, which was probably written second as the Russian's final position. As reported by Robert Kennedy, it was this creative use of ambiguity that enabled the settlement to be reached.

In negotiations it can indeed be said that a shadow of ambiguity over a situation may be as effective as real strength. It gives you more room to manoeuvre and more scope to vary your tactics.

When to fight

In a crisis, the decision about when and how hard to fight is a matter of judgement. You can go in for aggressive brinkmanship or progressive appeasement, but either of these approaches will be inadequate if taken to an extreme.

At this stage it might be a good idea to remember Krushchev's message to Kennedy during the Cuban missile crisis: 'If people do not show wisdom, then in the final analysis they will come to a clash, like blind moles, and then reciprocal extermination will begin.'

The decision on tactics is never an easy one. It was said by Clausewitz that 'War is nothing but the continuation of politics with the admixture of other means,' and you should normally wait to launch an attack until you are certain that the normal process of peaceful negotiation is not going to get you anywhere.

The decision will also be affected by your ability to understand your opponent's strategy and tactics so that you can take pre-emptive action. Crisis management is very much about analysing other people's motives, intentions and ploys, and responding accordingly. Another adage from Clausewitz is worth bearing in mind: 'Despise the enemy strategically, respect him tactically.' In other words, you may be quite certain that in the longer term your opponent will come to grief, but in the short term he may fight hard and you may have to fight back equally hard. Losing one battle may not lose the war, but a succession of defeats must prejudice your chances, however just your cause and however superior your strategy.

Thomas Schelling,[2] a leading commentator on crisis management, commented wisely on the fight or flight decision as follows:

> What is in dispute is usually not the momentary right of way, but everyone's expectations about how a participant will behave in the future. To yield is a signal that one can be expected to yield. To yield often or continuously may communicate an acknowledgement that that is one's role. To yield readily up to some limit, and then say 'enough', may guarantee that the first show of obduracy loses the game for both sides.

Crisis management may or may not take place within a well-defined strategy, but, whatever happens, the tactics have got to be worked out on the basis of a complete understanding of the situation, especially those aspects of it that concern other people's intentions. If you yield, then, as Schelling says, take care to ensure that, because you have misunderstood or underestimated your opponent, he will not take advantage of it. Be aware also of the possibility that both of you might lose in the end.

If you decide to fight, remember the following precepts of St Augustine and St Thomas Aquinas on what is a just war:

1 A just cause.

2 A right intention.

3 A reasonable chance of success.

4 If successful, a better situation than would prevail in the absence of action.

5 Force used (or threatened) should be proportional to the objective sought (or the evil repressed).

6 The intention should be to spare non-combatants or at least have a reasonable prospect of doing so.

Crisis management techniques

In *The Conventions of Crisis*, Coral Bell[3] wrote:

> Looking back over the history of the post-war crisis as a whole, one is struck by a sense of how often the decision-makers seem to have been 'playing it off the cuff', acting on the promptings of intuition or temperament rather than plan or logic.

This highlights the biggest pitfall crisis managers can walk into in industry and commerce as well as in international affairs. All too easily they feel that instant and decisive action is required. Under acute pressure they do not look before they leap and they fall into the elephant trap.

Crisis management starts with avoiding action, keeping your finger on the pulse so that as soon as the pace hots up – at the first signs of the beginning of a crisis slide – you can take pre-emptive action. At this stage you have time to think, to consider contingency plans and to put them into effect.

If, however, in spite of all your efforts, you are faced with a crisis, the following is a checklist of the 10 steps you should take:

1 Sit back as coolly as you can and assess the situation. You may have to go through the analytical and thinking process five times as fast as usual, but do it. You need to establish:
   - what exactly is happening;
   - why it is happening;
   - what is likely to happen unless something is done about it;
   - how quickly you have to act to prevent further damage;
   - who else is involved;
   - who is likely to be involved;
   - what resources you have – people, equipment, finance, back-up from other organizations, access to people with influence.

2 Draw up your preliminary plan of action – set it out step by step and prepare other contingency plans to deal with eventualities.

3 Line up a crisis management team to deal with the situation. Allocate roles and tasks and authorities to act (you may have to give emergency authority to some people).

4 Set up a crisis management centre (your office, the board room).

5 Set up a communications system so that you receive instant intelligence on what is happening and can put your messages across to the members of your team and anyone else whom you want to take action.

6 'Load shed' when you can, on the principle of the electrical system that sheds part of the load when the total load rises above a certain point.

This means getting rid of any peripheral problems as quickly as possible.

7 Put items on the 'back burner'; in other words, relegate problems to a non-crisis area where they can be dealt with at leisure.

8 Prepare your detailed plans, which will include:
   - timescales – act now or later;
   - scope for a cooling-off period;
   - longer-term solutions to be prepared and implemented at the right time;
   - contingency plans to deal with new developments or emergencies.

9 Monitor continuously exactly what is happening. Ensure that you get the information you need fast so that you can react quickly but without panicking.

10 Evaluate actions and reactions continuously so that you can modify the plan and swiftly take corrective or pre-emptive steps.

Qualities of a crisis manager

Good crisis managers are decisive. They can react swiftly but their great skill is in being able to speed up the decision-making process. They will not miss out any steps in the standard problem-solving, decision-making sequence:

- Define the situation.
- Specify objectives.
- Develop hypotheses.
- Gather the facts.
- Analyse the facts.
- Consider possible courses of action.
- Evaluate possible courses of action.
- Decide and implement.
- Monitor implementation.

Effective crisis managers will get through these stages more quickly, using their own experience and intelligence and that of their team.

Crisis managers buy time by putting issues on the back burner, but, like all good managers, they can make things happen fast when they want to. They are good leaders – providing inspiration to their team, encouraging their efforts and giving them confidence in the successful outcome of the crisis management process.

Finally, and most important, they keep cool. They do not panic, they do not over-react, they do not lose their head. In fact, they deliberately slow down the pace, when they can, to give the impression that everything is under control and it is all going according to plan.

To sum up, crisis management is no more than good management under pressure. The adrenalin may flow faster but this concentrates the mind wonderfully. Good managers thrive under pressure and they are the good crisis managers.

Crisis management techniques: organizations

From an organizational viewpoint, crisis management is not a quick-fix solution. It entails identifying, studying and forecasting crisis issues and setting forth specific ways that would enable the organization to prevent or cope with a crisis. This is a long-term commitment. A systematic, orderly procedure is required to manage a crisis and many crises can be prevented – or at least coped with effectively – through early detection.

A crisis audit is a useful approach to adopt. It means identifying potential issues, assessing the probability that they will occur and estimating their likely impact. On the basis of this audit a contingency plan can be developed that sets out the main steps that should be taken to deal with the crisis and who will be involved in managing it.

Notes

1 Townsend, R (1970) *Up the Organization*, Michael Joseph, London
2 Schelling, T (1960) *Strategy of Conflict*, Harvard University Press, Boston, MA
3 Bell, C (1971) *The Conventions of Crisis*, Oxford University Press, Oxford

29

How to manage culture

Organizational culture is sometimes described as 'the way we do things around here'. More specifically, organizational or corporate culture is the pattern of values, norms, beliefs, attitudes and assumptions that may not have been articulated but shape the ways in which people in organizations behave and things get done. Values refer to what is believed to be important about how people and organizations behave. Norms are the unwritten rules of behaviour.

The culture of an organization has a significant influence on people's behaviour. It therefore needs to be managed as far as that is possible. One of the problems of managing an organization's culture is that it has been developed over time and is therefore deeply embedded. It may be difficult to change. But if it is dysfunctional or new demands are being made on the existing culture, a programme of cultural change may be required.

Supporting and changing cultures

Embedded cultures exert considerable influence on organizational behaviour and therefore performance. If there is an appropriate and effective culture, it would be desirable to take steps to support or reinforce it through culture management. If the culture is inappropriate, attempts should be made to determine what needs to be changed and to develop and implement plans for change.

Culture management programmes

Culture management programmes aim to preserve and underpin what is good and functional about the present culture. The most powerful primary mechanisms for culture embedding and reinforcement are: the way leaders behave – their management style; what leaders pay attention to, measure and control; their reactions to critical incidents and crises; criteria for allocation of rewards and status; and criteria for recruitment, selection and promotion and commitment.

Analysing the culture

The first step is to analyse the existing culture. This can be done through questionnaires, surveys and discussions in focus groups or workshops. It is often helpful to involve people in analysing the outcome of surveys, getting them to produce a diagnosis of the cultural issues facing the organization and participate in the development and implementation of plans and programmes to deal with any issues. Groups can analyse the culture through the use of measurement instruments. Extra dimensions can be established by the use of group exercises such as 'rules of the club' (participants brainstorm the 'rules' or norms that govern behaviour) or 'shield' (participants design a shield, often quartered, which illustrates major cultural features of the organization). Joint exercises like this can lead to discussions on appropriate values that are much more likely to be 'owned' by people if they have helped to create them rather than having them imposed from above.

Operationalizing the culture

An understanding of the culture forms the basis for underpinning it through various programmes and activities that will enable it to operate effectively: for example, financial and non-financial rewards that recognize behaviour that supports the organization's values. The values identified during the analysis can be articulated to create a 'value set', the headings of which can be used when reviewing individual and team performance – emphasizing that people are expected to uphold the values. Induction programmes and further learning and development activities can cover core values and how people are expected to achieve them

Culture change

The analysis of the existing culture may indicate that substantial changes are required. But, as mentioned earlier, culture is deeply embedded and changing it can be a long and difficult haul.

A comprehensive change programme may be a fundamental part of an organizational transformation programme. But culture change programmes can focus on particular aspects of the culture, for example performance, quality, customer service or teamwork. In each case the underpinning values would need to be defined. It would probably be necessary to prioritize by deciding which areas need the most urgent attention. There is a limit to how much can be done at once except in crisis conditions.

Levers for change

Having identified what needs to be done and the priorities, the next step is to consider what levers for change exist and how they can be used. The levers could include, as appropriate:

- *Performance* – performance-related or contribution-related pay schemes; performance management processes; gainsharing; leadership training, skills development.
- *Engagement* – communication, participation and involvement programmes; developing a climate of cooperation and trust; taking a hard look at the design of jobs to ensure that they provide interest, challenge, autonomy and the opportunity to develop; leadership development programmes designed to help managers and team leaders in their crucial task of enhancing the levels of engagement of their staff.
- *Quality* – total quality programmes.
- *Customer service* – customer care programmes.
- *Teamwork* – team-building; team performance management; team rewards.
- *Values* – gaining understanding, acceptance and commitment through involvement in defining values, performance management processes and employee development interventions.

How you can help

As a manager or team leader you have considerable influence on how culture can be managed or changed. You can do this by:

- ensuring that you understand the values of the organization in the key areas of performance, quality, customer care, teamwork, treating people fairly and social responsibility;
- 'living the values' – acting as a role model for your team;
- playing your part in developing and implementing culture management or change programmes in such areas as quality and customer care;
- impressing on the members of your team the behaviour that you expect from them to support the reinforcement of the organization's values so that they become 'values in use' rather than values that are simply 'espoused': that is, ones that are given lip service only.

How to manage performance

30

Managers get things done through people. To do this well they must manage and improve the performance of people. This involves three key activities, as described in this chapter:

- defining expectations;
- monitoring and managing performance throughout the year;
- reviewing performance formally at periodic intervals, for example once or twice a year.

This is the performance management cycle as illustrated in Figure 30.1. This model illustrates that performance management is a continuous process – it proceeds from planning (defining expectations) to monitoring (managing performance throughout the year) to reviewing performance against expectations, and on the basis of that review reformulating the plan.

FIGURE 30.1   The performance management cycle

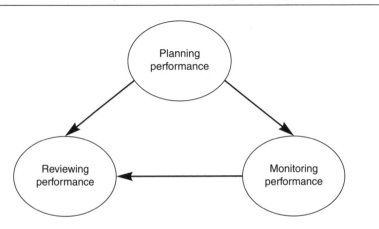

Planning performance

Performance planning is carried out jointly by you and the individual members of your team. The aim is to reach an agreement (often called a performance and development agreement) on what needs to be done by both parties. The starting point for the plan is a role profile that defines the results, knowledge and skills, and behaviours required. This should be agreed as the basis for deciding on objectives and performance measures as described in the next section of this chapter. Performance development plans are derived from an analysis of role requirements and performance in meeting them.

Setting objectives

One of your most important tasks as a manager is to make sure that the members of your team understand what is expected of them. Each individual and the team as a whole must know what they have to do and achieve. This is the 'management of expectations' aspect of your role.

Your task is to ensure that performance requirements expressed as objectives are defined and agreed. You will then be in a position to review achievements in relation to agreed objectives.

What are objectives?

An objective describes something that has to be accomplished – a point to be aimed at. Objectives or goals (the terms are interchangeable) define what organizations, functions, departments, teams and individuals are expected to achieve.

There are two main types of objective: work and personal.

Work objectives

Work or operational objectives refer to the results to be achieved or the contribution to be made to the accomplishment of team, departmental and corporate objectives. At *corporate level* they are related to the organization's mission, core values and strategic plans. At *departmental or functional level* they are related to corporate objectives, spelling out the specific mission, targets and purposes to be achieved by a function or department. At *team level* they will again be related specifically to the purpose of the team and the contribution it is expected to make to achieving departmental and corporate goals. At *individual level* they are job related, referring to the principal accountabilities, main activity areas or key tasks that constitute the individual's job. They focus on the results individuals are expected to achieve and how they contribute to the attainment of team, departmental and corporate goals and to upholding the organization's core values.

Personal objectives

Personal or learning objectives are concerned with what individuals should do and learn to improve their performance (performance improvement plans) and/or their knowledge, skills and overall level of competency (training and personal development plans).

How are individual work objectives expressed?

Individual objectives define the results to be achieved and the basis upon which performance in attaining these results can be measured. They can take the form of target or project-related objectives or standing objectives.

Target or project-related objectives

Individual objectives can be expressed as quantified output or improvement targets (open 24 new accounts by 31 December, reduce cost per unit of output by 2.5 per cent by 30 June) or in terms of projects to be completed (open distribution depot in Northampton by 31 October). Targets may be reset regularly, say once a year or every six months, or be subject to frequent amendments to meet new requirements or changed circumstances.

Standing objectives

Objectives for some aspects of a job (or for all aspects of some jobs) can be what might be described as 'standing objectives'. These are concerned with the permanent or continuing features of a job. They incorporate or lead to defined standards of performance, which may be expressed in quantified terms such as the requirement to ensure that all deliveries are made within three days of receiving an order. Alternatively, they may have to be defined as qualitative standards such as:

- Performance will be up to standard if requests for information are dealt with promptly and helpfully on a can do/will do basis and are delivered in the form required by the user.
- Qualitative standing objectives may also be defined for behaviour that will contribute to upholding the core values of the organization. For example, if one of the core values relates to the development of the skills and competences of employees, a performance standard for employee development could be one of the objectives agreed for all managers and team leaders.

What is a good work objective?

A good objective is 'SMART': that is, objective:

S = stretching
M = measurable
A = agreed
R = realistic
T = time-related.

Defining work objectives

The process of agreeing objectives need not be unduly complicated. It must start from an agreed list of the principal accountabilities or main tasks of the job. It is then simply a matter of jointly examining each area and agreeing targets and standards of performance as appropriate. Agreement can also be reached on any projects to be undertaken, which might be linked to a specific accountability, or may be more general projects that fall broadly within the remit of the jobholder.

Define targets

The first step is to identify the key result areas of the job from the list of accountabilities or main tasks to which targets can be attached. Targets are quantified and time based – they always define specific and measurable outputs and when they have to be reached. The target may be to achieve a specified level of output or to improve performance in some way. Targets may be expressed in financial terms such as profits to be made, income to be generated, costs to be reduced or budgets to be worked within. Or they may be expressed in numerical terms as a specified number of units to be processed, responses to be obtained or clients or customers to be contacted over a period of time.

Output targets are expressed in financial or unitary terms, for example:

- Achieve sales of £1.6 million by 30 June.
- Maintain inventory levels at no more than £12 million.
- Maintain throughput at the rate of 800 units a day.

Performance improvement targets may be expressed in terms such as:

- Increase sales turnover for the year by 8 per cent in real terms.
- Reduce the overhead-to-sales ratio from 22.6 to 20 per cent over the next 12 months.
- Increase the ratio of successful conversions (enquiries to sales) from 40 to 50 per cent.

Define performance standards

The next stage is to define performance standards for any area (accountability or main task) to which specific, time-based targets cannot be attached. These are sometimes described as standing or continuing objectives because, as explained earlier in this chapter, their essential nature may not change significantly from one review period to the next if the key task remains unaltered, although they may be modified if new circumstances arise.

Performance standards should preferably be quantified as key performance indicators (KPIs) in terms, for example, of level of service or speed of response. Where the standard cannot be quantified, a more qualitative approach may have to be adopted, in which case the standard of performance

definition would in effect state: 'this job or task will have been well done if...
(the following things happen)'. Junior or more routine jobs are likely to
have a higher proportion of standing objectives to which performance
standards are attached than senior and more flexible or output-orientated
jobs.

The following are some examples of performance standards that spell out
the end results required in quantitative terms:

- Prepare and distribute management accounts to managers within three
  working days of the end of the accounting period.

- Deal with 90 per cent of customer complaints within 24 hours – the
  remainder to be acknowledged the same day and answered within five
  working days.

- Hear job evaluation appeals within five working days.

It may not always be possible to quantify performance standards. In the
examples given above, the end results required may have to be defined in
qualitative terms.

It is often assumed that qualitative performance standards are difficult to
define. But all managers make judgements about the standards of performance they expect and obtain from their staff, and most people have some
idea of whether or not they are doing a good job. The problem is that these
views are often subjective and are seldom articulated. Even if, as often
happens, the final definition of a performance standard is somewhat bland
and unspecific, the discipline of working through the requirements in itself
will lead to greater mutual understanding of performance expectations.

A performance standard definition should take the form of a statement
that performance will be up to standard if a desirable, specified and observ-
able result happens. The following are some examples of qualitative performance standards:

- Performance will be up to standard if line managers receive guidance
  on the interpretation and implementation of inventory policies that is
  acted upon and makes a significant contribution to the achievement of
  inventory targets.

- Performance will be up to standard when callers are dealt with
  courteously at all times, even when they are being difficult.

- Performance will be up to standard if proposals for new product
  development are fully supported by data provided from properly
  conducted product research, market research and product testing
  programmes, and are justified by meeting return on investment
  criteria policies.

Define projects

Projects may already have been defined as part of a team, departmental or
functional plan, and when setting individual objectives it is simply necessary

to agree on the part that the individual will play and the contribution he or she is expected to make. Alternatively, projects may be linked to one or more specific accountabilities or they may be related generally to the overall purpose of the job.

Objective setting for projects will specify the required outcome of the project (results to be achieved), its budget and its timescale.

When a number of projects have to be undertaken by the jobholder, agreement should be reached on priorities.

Project or task achievement objectives may be expressed in terms such as:

- Introduce new stock control system by 30 November.
- All employees to have received training on the implementation of equal opportunities policies by 1 June.
- New distribution centre to be operational by 1 March.
- Reorganization of finance department to be completed by 1 October.

For each project or task it would also be necessary to set out the success criteria; for example:

- Introduce a new stock control system by 30 November to provide more accurate, comprehensive and immediate information on stock and thus enable inventory targets to be achieved without prejudicing production flows or customer service levels.

Monitoring performance

Remember that performance is what managers do. It is an integral part of the continuing process of management. You should therefore be ready, willing and able to deal with performance issues as they arise. It should not be left to the annual performance review. The process of continuing assessment should be carried out by reference to agreed objectives and to work, development and improvement plans. Progress reviews can take place informally or through an existing system of team meetings. But there should be more formal interim reviews at predetermined points in the year, for example quarterly. For some teams or individual jobs these points could be related to 'milestones' contained in project and work plans. Deciding when such meetings should take place would be up to individual managers in consultation with their staff and would not be a laid-down part of a 'system'.

Managers would be encouraged to consider how to accommodate the need for regular dialogue within the established pattern of briefings, team or group meetings or project review meetings.

In addition to the collective meetings, managers may have regular one-to-one meetings with their staff. If performance management is to be effective, there needs to be a continuing agenda through these regular meetings to ensure that good progress is being made towards achieving the objectives agreed for each key result area.

Reviewing performance

Although performance management is a continuous process, it is still necessary to have a formal review once or twice a year. This acts as a focal point for the consideration of key performance and development issues, provides an opportunity to take stock and forms the basis for performance and development planning.

Many managers are extraordinarily reluctant to conduct such meetings at all or at best their reviews are perfunctory. All sorts of reasons are given for this:

1 'I haven't got enough time.'

2 'It's not necessary – I am already reviewing performance on a day-to-day basis.'

3 'I don't like sitting down and making formal criticisms of someone.'

The answers to these objections are simple:

1 'Surely you can spare an hour or so to spend quality time with your staff if only to show that you are interested in their progress and prepared to give them your support.'

2 'That may well be so, but isn't it a good idea to carry out a systematic review of progress so that both parties are in a better position to plan for the future?'

3 'Performance reviews are not just about criticizing people. They are opportunities to recognize achievements as well as agreeing any areas where improvement is required and planning how this should take place.'

The performance review meeting is the means through which the five primary performance management elements of agreement, measurement, feedback, positive reinforcement and dialogue can be put to good use.

The review should be rooted in the reality of the employee's performance. It is concrete, not abstract and it allows managers and individuals to take a positive look together at how performance can become better in the future and how any problems in meeting performance standards and achieving objectives can be resolved. Individuals should be encouraged to assess their own performance and become active agents for change in improving their results. You are there to adopt your proper enabling role: coaching and providing support and guidance.

There should be no surprises in a formal review if performance issues have been dealt with as they should have been – as they arise during the year.

Traditional appraisals are often no more than an analysis of where those involved are now, and where they have come from. This static and historical approach is not what performance management is about. The true role of performance management is to look forward to what needs to be done by people to achieve the purpose of the job, to meet new challenges, to make even better use of their knowledge, skills and abilities, to develop their capabilities by establishing a self-managed learning agenda and to reach agreement on any areas where performance needs to be improved and how that improvement should take place. This process also helps managers to improve their ability to lead, guide and develop the individuals and teams for whom they are responsible.

Conducting a performance review meeting

There are 10 golden rules for conducting performance review meetings:

1 Be prepared. Managers should prepare by referring to a list of agreed objectives and their notes on performance throughout the year.

2 Work to a clear structure. The meeting should be planned to cover all the points identified during preparation.

3 Create the right atmosphere. A successful meeting depends on creating an informal environment in which a full, frank but friendly exchange of views can take place. It is best to start with a fairly general discussion before getting into any detail.

4 Provide good feedback. Individuals need to know how they are getting on. Feedback needs to based on factual evidence, and careful thought should be given to what is said and how it is said so that it motivates rather than demotivates people. The following are guidelines on providing feedback:

  – Build feedback into the job – to be effective, feedback should be built into the job or provided soon after the activity has taken place.

  – Provide feedback on actual events or observed behaviour – it should be related to specific items of behaviour and backed up by evidence.

  – Describe, don't judge – the feedback should be presented as a description of what has happened; it should not be accompanied by a judgement.

  – Ask questions rather than make statements.

  – Select key issues and restrict yourself to them – there is a limit to how much criticism anyone can take.

  – Focus on aspects of performance the individual can improve. It is a waste of time to concentrate on areas that the individual can do little or nothing about.

  – Provide positive feedback on the things that the individual did well in addition to areas for improvement.

5 Let the interviewees do most of the talking. This enables them to get things off their chest and helps them to feel that they are getting a fair hearing. Use open-ended questions (ie questions that invite the individual to think about what to say rather than indicating the expected answer). This is to encourage people to expand.

6 Use praise. If possible, managers should begin with praise for some specific achievement, but this should be sincere and deserved. Praise helps people to relax – everyone needs encouragement and appreciation.

7 Invite self-assessment. This is to see how things look from the individual's point of view and to provide a basis for discussion – many people underestimate themselves.

8 Discuss performance, not personality. Discussions on performance should be based on factual evidence, not opinion. Always refer to actual events or behaviour and to results compared with agreed performance measures. Individuals should be given plenty of scope to explain why something did or did not happen. Don't deliver unexpected criticisms – there should be no surprises. The discussion should only be concerned with events or behaviours that have been noted at the time they took place. Feedback on performance should be immediate. It should not wait until the end of the year.

9 Encourage analysis of performance. Don't just hand out praise or blame. Analyse jointly and objectively why things went well or badly and what can be done to maintain a high standard or to avoid problems in the future.

10 Agree measurable objectives and a plan of action. The aim should be to end the review meeting on a positive note.

31 How to manage projects

Project management is the planning, supervision and control of any activity or set of activities that leads to a defined outcome at a predetermined time and in accordance with specified performance or quality standards at a budgeted cost. It is concerned with *deliverables* – getting things done as required or promised. While delivering results on time is important, it is equally important to deliver them to meet the specification and within the projected cost.

Project management involves action planning – deciding *what* work is to be done, *why* the work needs to be done, *who* will do the work, *how much* it will cost, *when* it has to be completed (totally or stage by stage) and *where* it will be carried out.

The three main project management activities are project planning, setting up the project and project control.

Project planning

Initiation

Project planning starts with a definition of the objectives of the project. A business case has to be made. This means answering two basic questions:

- Why is this project needed?
- What benefits are expected from the project?

The answers to these questions should be quantified. The requirement could be spelt out in such terms as new systems or facilities to meet defined business needs, new plant required for new products, or improvements in productivity or quality. The benefits are expressed as revenues generated, productivity, quality or performance improvements, costs saved and return on investment.

Assessment

Projects involve investing resources – money and people. Investment appraisal techniques are used to ensure that the company's criteria on return on investment are satisfied. Cost–benefit analysis may be used to assess the degree to which the benefits justify the costs, time and number of people required by the project. This may mean identifying opportunity costs that establish whether a greater benefit would be obtained by investing the money or deploying the people on other projects or activities.

Performance specification

This sets out what the project is expected to do – how it should perform – and describes the details of the project's configuration or method of operation.

Project plan

The project plan sets out:

- the major operations in sequence – the main stages of the project;
- a breakdown where appropriate of each major operation into a sequence of subsidiary tasks;
- an analysis of the interrelationships and interdependencies of major and subsidiary tasks;
- an estimate of the time required to complete each major operation or stage;
- a procurement plan to obtain the necessary materials, systems and equipment;
- a human resource plan that defines how many people will be allocated to the project with different skills at each stage, and who is to be responsible for controlling the project as a whole and at each of the major stages or operations.

Setting up the project

Setting up the project involves:

- obtaining and allocating resources;
- selecting and briefing the project management team;
- finalizing the project programme – defining each stage;
- defining and establishing control systems and reporting procedures (format and timing of progress reports);

● identifying key dates, stage by stage, for the project (milestones) and providing for milestone meetings to review progress and decide on any actions required.

Controlling the project

The three most important things to control are:

● *Time* – achievement of project plan as programme.
● *Quality* – achievement of project specifications.
● *Cost* – containment of costs within budget.

Project control is based on progress reports showing what is being achieved against the plan. The planned completion date, actual achievement and forecast completion date for each stage or operation are provided. The likelihood of delays, overruns or bottlenecks is thus established so that corrective action can be taken in good time. Control can be achieved by the use of Gantt or bar charts and by reference to network plans or critical path analyses.

Progress meetings should be held at predetermined intervals. These can be treated as 'milestone' meetings when they are timed to coincide with the key stages of the project.

Ten steps to effective project management

1 Specify objectives and deliverables.
2 Carry out cost–benefit analysis or investment appraisal to justify project.
3 Determine:
 – what should be done;
 – who does what;
 – when it should be done (broken down into stages);
 – how much it should cost.
4 Define resource requirements (people, money, materials, systems, equipment, etc).
5 Prepare programme – identify stages.
6 Define methods of control – charts, network analysis, progress reports, progress (milestone) meetings.
7 Ensure that everyone knows what is expected of them and has the resources required.

8 Monitor progress continuously against the plan as well as at formal meetings.

9 Take corrective action as required; for example, reallocating resources.

10 Evaluate the end result against the objectives and deliverables.

32 How to manage risk

Risk management is concerned with avoiding unacceptable risks and managing existing risks in order to minimize any harmful impact they may make. Research carried out by the Economist Intelligence Unit amongst 3,000 executives showed that only 5 per cent of them were absolutely confident that their risk control systems were successfully identifying, evaluating, minimizing and managing all the potential significant risks affecting their business.

Risks may be purely financial – what is the chance of an investment paying off? But the risks that destroyed Arthur Anderson, Barings and Enron arose because of faults in management control, inadequate systems and staff negligence as well as unacceptable behaviour. An organization may sustain losses by failing to hedge its positions in the futures market. This may be because an inexperienced manager was given responsibility for the task and the company did not exercise reasonable supervision of that manager's activities. Public utilities may face regulatory notices and risks arising from political decisions, and these must be anticipated. Auditors must be aware of the risks they take when, if they are negligent, their audit report does not represent 'a full and fair view'. Overseas sales may be affected by political risks and a software firm has to be prepared for the risk that a competitor will produce a better product. A company that is a market leader may run the risk of being threatened by competitors – to what extent does the company monitor the competition, regularly assess customer requirements and seek improvements in the product or level of service to maintain competitive edge? A business may rely on one customer for 80 per cent of its sales. What happens if this customer looks elsewhere? How big is this risk? What can be done to lessen it?

These situations and the questions that arise from them are all matters that should be dealt with by a systematic approach to risk management.

Categories of risk

The categories of risk are:

- *Commercial risk* – increased competition, better products or services available elsewhere, price cutting by competition, problems with suppliers, key customers failing or switching their business elsewhere.
- *Economic risk* – recession in the United Kingdom or overseas markets, adverse exchange movements, worldwide decline in prices.
- *Political risk* – adverse political decisions (eg legislation, tax changes, regulatory changes, Office of Fair Trading investigations).
- *Technological development* – new developments making the company's products or services obsolescent.
- *Health and safety* – the risk of illness, accidents or injuries at work.
- *Natural disasters* – fire, flood, riots, etc.
- *Crime* – embezzlement, fraud, computer crime, industrial espionage.
- *Legal* – the risk of successful actions against the company causing loss of money and reputation.
- *Fashion* – changes in fashion affecting demand.

Minimizing risk

The main ways to minimize risk are:

- Institute financial controls to prevent fraud.
- Set up compliance arrangements to ensure that regulations are adhered to.
- Monitor key transactions or those above a certain value and the people that make them to ensure that they are carried out in accordance with policies and procedures and do not entail undue risk.
- Insure against such risks as a major customer becoming insolvent, natural disasters or a country to which the company is exporting imposing currency restrictions that prevent payment.
- Diversify into products or services that have a different risk profile; avoid relying too much on one supplier.
- Hedge – take action that will provide compensation if risk occurs. The most typical area where hedging takes place is foreign currency transactions, which might involve buying the currency in advance. If the business is vulnerable to a sudden fall in the stock market, an option can be bought to provide funds if this happens. If the business is vulnerable to one set of factors, it can buy or acquire an interest in a business that would prosper from such factors.

Managing risk

The approaches to managing risk are:

- Recognize that risk assessment is a continuous activity – you cannot take the risk of not assessing risk.
- Make risk assessment and management a major concern of the board and top management.
- Ensure that everyone in the organization knows that they are in the business of identifying, reporting on and managing risks.
- Focus on the avoidance of unacceptable business risks, followed by the management of other business risks to reduce them to an acceptable level.
- Formulate a business risk controls policy and ensure that everyone knows and understands it.
- Anticipate business risk at the source and monitor risk controls continuously.
- Remember that the primary source of business risk is ineffective processes and controls rather than ineffective people.

How to manage stress

You become stressed when you experience more pressure, frustration, or a higher level of emotional demand than you can handle. An acceptable degree of pressure can be a good thing. It can stimulate and motivate you. Some people thrive on it. They respond to challenges that others would find hard to bear.

Pressures include: achieving performance expectations; meeting deadlines; coping with an excessive workload; dealing with difficult bosses, colleagues, clients, customers or subordinates, including bullying; problems of achieving a satisfactory work–life balance (reconciling the demands of work with family responsibilities or outside interests); and role ambiguity (lack of understanding of what is expected).

Pressure is fine as long as it does not build up to too high a level. Up to a point it will motivate and improve performance but it then turns into stress and results in a decline in performance as illustrated in Figure 33.1.

FIGURE 33.1   How pressure becomes stress

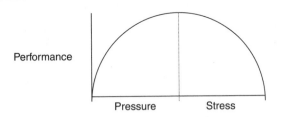

The important thing to remember is that the ability to withstand pressure varies: one person's stimulating amount of pressure is another person's stress. But this suggests that although some people may temperamentally be more prone to suffer from stress, there is some scope to manage or limit stress, bearing in mind that it is often self-imposed.

Symptoms of stress

The symptoms of stress that you can observe in others or yourself include inability to cope with the demands of the job (which creates more stress), tiredness, lethargy, lack of enthusiasm and bad temper.

Managing stress in others: what the organization can do

Organizations can manage stress by developing processes and policies that can be implemented by line managers and specialist staff. These include:

- clarifying roles to reduce role ambiguity and give people more autonomy;
- setting reasonable and achievable performance standards;
- establishing performance management processes that encourage a dialogue about work and its pressures between managers and their staff;
- giving individuals the opportunity to obtain professional counselling;
- developing anti-bullying policies;
- developing work–life balance policies that take account of the pressures on employees as parents, partners or carers, and that can include provisions such as special leave or flexible working hours.

Managing stress in others: what you can do

To manage stress in others you need to do the following:

- Be aware of organizational policies and procedures as set out above, and be prepared to implement them for your own staff.
- Tailor your demands on people according to their capacities – it is a good idea to agree stretching targets but they must be achievable (with effort but without undue stress) by the individual concerned.
- Look out for symptoms of stress and try to establish the cause as the basis for alleviating them.
- If an individual is under stress because of undue pressure, try to adjust demands to a more reasonable level, possibly by redesigning the job or transferring duties to someone else.
- Be prepared to listen and respond to individuals who complain of being over-stressed – you don't have to accept what they say but you should certainly hear them out.

Managing your own stress

If you feel that you are unduly stressed, here are 10 things you can do:

- Try to establish why you are stressed – are there any specific causes or is it a general feeling that the work is getting on top of you?
- Talk to someone about it – your boss (if likely to be sympathetic), colleagues, HR, friends, your partner.
- If the stress is serious, ask if the organization can provide advice from a professional counsellor.
- Discuss your workloads and deadlines with your boss to see if they can be alleviated in any way.
- Consider whether there is any scope to delegate more work to your staff.
- Decide what is beyond your control and put it firmly to one side. Focus on what is within your sphere of influence and get on with it.
- Take time off during the day – relax (switch off) for a few minutes over a cup of coffee with your colleagues.
- Don't work excessive hours.
- Don't take work home.
- Take regular exercise.

34 How to manage time

I wasted time, and now doth time waste me (*Richard II*).

If you were told by your chairman that you were needed for a special assignment that would mean working directly under him, give you the opportunity to deal with strategic issues, broaden your experience and provide you with excellent promotion prospects, would you take it? The answer would, of course, be yes. If, however, you were told that you would spend one day a week on this assignment and carry out your present duties in the remaining four days, would you still accept the job? Of course you would. But you would be admitting that you could, if you organized yourself better, do your existing work in four-fifths of the time you spend on it at the moment.

To recover that one-fifth or more, you need to think systematically about how you use your time. You can then take steps to organize yourself better and to get other people to help or at least not to hinder you.

Analysis

The first thing to do is to find out where there is scope for improving your use of time.

Your job

Start with your job – the tasks you have to carry out and the objectives you are there to achieve. Try to establish an order of priority between your tasks and among your objectives.

It is more difficult to do this if you have a number of potentially conflicting areas of responsibility. A good example of this was a director of administration who had a ragbag of responsibilities including property, office services and staff. He had perpetual problems with conflicting priorities and, all too frequently, at the end of the day he would say to himself: 'I have wasted my time, I have achieved next to nothing.'

He took a day off to think things through and realized that he had to take a broad view before getting into detail. He felt that if he could sort out the relative importance of his objectives he would be in a better position to attach priorities to his tasks.

Having done this, he could rely on preventive maintenance to reduce problems. But when a crisis did occur – which was inevitable in his area – he could concentrate on fire-fighting in one place without having to worry about what was going on elsewhere.

His second objective, therefore, was to give himself sufficient free time to concentrate on major problems so that he could react swiftly to them. He then classified the sort of issues that could arise and decided which could safely be delegated to others and which he should deal with himself. He was thus prepared to allocate priorities as the problems landed on his desk and to select the serious ones to deal with himself, knowing that the administrative system would go on without interruption.

How you spend your time

Having sorted out your main priorities you should analyse in more detail how you spend your time. This will identify time-consuming activities and indicate where there are problems as well as possible solutions to them.

The best way to analyse time is to keep a diary. You can do this electronically using Microsoft Outlook organizing software. Do this for a week, or preferably two or three, as one week may not provide a typical picture. Divide the day into 15-minute sections and note down what you did in each period. Against each space, summarize how effectively you spent your time by writing V for valuable, D for doubtful and U for useless. If you want to make more refined judgements give your ratings pluses or minuses.

For example:

Time	Task	Rating
9.00–9.30	Dealt with new e-mails	V
	and incoming mail	V
9.30–9.45	Discussed admin problem	D
9.45–10.00	Discussed admin problem	D
10.00–10.15	Deputized at meeting	U
10.15–10.30	Deputized at meeting	U
10.30–10.45	Deputized at meeting	U
10.45–11.00	Deputized at meeting	U

At the end of the week analyse your time under the following headings:

- Reading.
- Writing.
- Dictating.
- Sending and receiving e-mails.
- Telephoning.
- Dealing with people (individuals or groups).
- Attending meetings.
- Travelling.
- Other (specify).

Analyse also the VDU ratings of the worth of each activity under each heading. This analysis will provide you with the information you need to spot any weaknesses in the way in which you manage time.

Use the time-consumer's checklist at the end of this chapter to identify problems and possible remedies.

Organizing yourself

Such an analysis will usually throw up weaknesses in the way you plan your work and establish your priorities. You have to fit the tasks you must complete into the time available to complete them, and get them done in order of importance.

Some people find it difficult, if not impossible, to plan their work ahead. They find that they work best if they have to achieve almost impossible deadlines. Working under pressure concentrates the mind wonderfully, they say. Journalists are a case in point.

But ordinary mortals, who work under a variety of conflicting pressures, cannot rely upon crisis action to get them out of logjams of work. For most of us it is better to try to minimize the need to work under exceptional pressure by a little attention to the organization of our week or day. At the very least you should use your diary for long-range planning, organize your weekly activities in broad outline and plan each day in some detail.

Use the diary

Attempt to leave at least one day a week free of meetings and avoid filling any day with appointments. In other words leave blocks of unallocated time for planning, thinking, reading, writing and dealing with the unexpected.

Weekly organizer

Sit down at the beginning of each week with your diary and plan how you are going to spend your time. Assess each of your projects or tasks and work out priorities. Leave blocks of time for dealing with e-mails and other correspondence and for seeing people. Try to preserve one free day, or at least half a day, if it is at all possible.

If it helps you to put everything down on paper, draw up a simple weekly organizer form and record what you intend to do each morning, afternoon and, if it's work, evening.

Daily organizer

At the beginning of each day, consult your diary to check on your plans and commitments. Refer to the previous day's organizer to find out what is outstanding. Inspect your pending tray, in-tray and incoming e-mails to check on what remains and what has just arrived.

Then write down the things to do:

1 Meetings or interviews.
2 Respond to e-mails.
3 Telephone calls.
4 Tasks in order of priority:
   - A – must be done today;
   - B – ideally should be done today but could be left till tomorrow.
   - C – can be dealt with later.

Plan broadly when you are going to fit your A and B priority tasks into the day. Tick off your tasks as they have been completed. Retain the list to consult next day.

You can use your electronic organizer for this purpose. Many successful time managers only use a blank sheet of paper, but a simple form that you can use is shown below.

FIGURE 34.1   Example of a daily organizer

DAILY ORGANIZER   Date...................

Meetings and appointments

Committee/person	Where	When

To telephone/e-mail

Person	About what	When

To do

Tasks (in order of priority)	Priority rating* A, B or C	Approximate timing

*A = must be done today. B = ideally done today. C = later.

Organizing other people

Your first task is to organize yourself, but other people can help if you can guide and encourage them. They include your PA, boss, colleagues, subordinates and outside contacts.

Your PA

A PA can be a great help: sorting incoming mail into what needs immediate attention and what can be looked at later; managing appointments within your guidelines; keeping unwanted callers at bay; intercepting telephone calls; dealing with routine or even semi-routine correspondence; sorting and arranging your papers and the filing system for easy accessibility; getting people on the telephone for you, and so on. The list is almost endless. Every efficient boss will recognize that he or she depends a lot on an efficient PA.

Your boss

Your boss can waste your time with over-long meetings, needless interruptions, trivial requests and general nitpicking. Maybe there is nothing you can do about this. But you can learn how to avoid doing the same to your own staff.

On your own behalf you can cultivate the polite art of cutting short tedious discussions. Such formulas as 'I hope you feel we have cleared up this problem – I'll get out of your hair now and get things moving' are useful. And you might be able, subtly, to indicate that your boss is going to get better performance from you if he leaves you alone. It's difficult but it's worth trying.

Your colleagues

Try to educate them to avoid unnecessary interruptions. Don't anger them by shutting them out when they have something urgent to discuss. But if it can wait, get them to agree to meet you later at a fixed time. Try to avoid indulging in too many pleasantries over the telephone. Be brisk but not brusque. Try to persuade them not to deluge you with unnecessary e-mails.

Your subordinates

You will save a lot of time with your subordinates if you systematically decide what work you can delegate to them. You save even more time if you delegate clearly and spell out how and when you want them to report back.

An 'open door' policy is fine in theory but time-wasting in practice. Learn to say no to subordinates who want to see you when you are engaged on more important business. But always give them a time when they can see you – and stick to it.

Talking generally to your staff about their job and outside interests can be time well spent if it helps to increase mutual understanding and respect. Allow for this in your schedule and be prepared to extend business discussions into broader matters when the opportunity arises. But don't overdo it.

Outside contacts

The same rules apply to outside contacts. Prevent them from seeing you without an appointment. Ask your PA to block unwanted telephone calls. Brief your contacts on what you expect from them and when meetings should be arranged.

Time-consumer's checklist

Problem	Possible remedies
TASKS	
1 Work piling up	• Set priorities • Set deadlines • Make realistic time estimates – most people underestimate; add 20 per cent to your first guess.
2 Trying to do too much at once	• Set priorities • Do one thing at a time • Learn to say no to yourself as well as other people.
3 Getting involved in too much detail	• Delegate more.
4 Postponing unpleasant tasks	• Set a timetable and stick to it • Get unpleasant tasks over with quickly – you will feel better afterwards.
5 Insufficient time to think	• Reserve blocks of time – part of a day or week – for thinking. No paperwork, no interruptions.
PEOPLE	
6 Constant interruptions from people calling into your office	• Use PA to keep unwanted visitors out • Make appointments and see that people stick to them • Reserve block times when you are not to be interrupted.
7 Constant telephone interruptions	• Get your PA to intercept and, where appropriate, divert calls • State firmly that you will call back when convenient.
8 Too much time spent in conversation	• Decide in advance what you want to achieve when you meet someone, and keep pleasantries to a minimum at the beginning and end • Concentrate on keeping yourself and the other person to the point – it is too easy to divert or be diverted • Learn how to end meetings quickly but not too brusquely.

Problem	Possible remedies
PAPERWORK	
9 Flooded with incoming paper	• Get your PA to sort it into three folders: action now, action later, information • Take yourself off the circulation list of useless information • Only ask for written memos and reports when you really need them • Encourage people to present information and reports clearly and succinctly • Ask for summaries rather than the whole report • Take a course in rapid reading.
10 Too many e-mails to deal with	• If it really matters go and talk to them • Rediscover the power of a phone call • Use handwritten notes • Get yourself off distribution lists • Use Out of the Office Auto-reply more • Check your inbox only once or twice a day • Practise sending a succinct reply – 'yes/no/let's talk'.
11 Too many letters/ memos to write or dictate	• Use the telephone or e-mail more • Avoid individually typed acknowledgements.
12 Paperwork piling up	• Do it now • Set aside the first half hour or so in the day to deal with urgent correspondence • Leave a period at the end of the day for less urgent reading • Aim to clear at least 90 per cent of the paper on your desk or messages in your inbox every day.
13 Lost or mislaid papers	• Arrange, or get your PA to organize, papers on current projects in separate, easily accessible folders • Don't hang on to papers in your pending tray – clear it daily • Set up a filing and retrieval system which will enable you to get at papers easily • Ensure that your PA keeps a day book of correspondence as a last resort method of turning up papers • Keep a tidy desk.

Problem	Possible remedies
MEETINGS	
14 Too much time spent in meetings	• If you set up the meeting: avoid regular meetings when there is nothing that needs saying regularly, review all the meetings you hold and eliminate as many as you can • Get yourself taken off committees if your presence is not essential or it someone else is more appropriate • As chairperson: set limits for the duration of meetings and keep to them, cut out waffle and repetition, allow discussion but insist on making progress, have a logical agenda and stick to it • As a member: don't waffle, don't talk for the sake of talking, don't waste time scoring points or boosting your ego.
TRAVELLING	
15 Too much time spent on travelling	• Use the phone or post • Send someone else • Ask yourself, every time you plan to go anywhere, 'is my journey really necessary?' • Plan the quickest way – air, rail or car.

How to motivate

35

Motivating people is the process of getting people to move in the direction you want them to go.

The organization as a whole can provide the context within which high levels of motivation can be achieved through reward systems and the provision of opportunities for learning and development. But individual managers still have a major part to play in deploying their own motivating skills so as to get individual members of their team to give of their best, and to make good use of the motivational systems and processes provided by the company.

To do this it is necessary to understand:

- the process of motivation;
- the different types of motivation;
- the basic concepts of motivation;
- the implications of motivation theory;
- approaches to motivation;
- the role of financial and non-financial rewards as motivators.

The process of motivation

Motivation is concerned with goal-directed behaviour. People are motivated to do something if they think it will be worth their while.

The process of motivation is initiated by someone recognizing an un-satisfied need. A goal is then established that, it is thought, will satisfy that need, and a course of action is determined that is expected to lead towards the attainment of that goal.

Basically, therefore, management and managers motivate people by providing means for them to satisfy their unsatisfied needs. This can be done by offering incentives and rewards for achievement and effort. But the needs of individuals and the goals associated with them vary so widely that it is difficult, if not impossible, to predict precisely how a particular incentive or reward will affect individual behaviour.

Types of motivation

Motivation at work can take two forms. First, people can motivate themselves by seeking, finding and carrying out work that satisfies their needs or at least leads them to expect that their goals will be achieved. Second, people can be motivated by management through such methods as pay, promotion, praise, etc.

These two types of motivation are described as:

- *Intrinsic motivation* – the self-generated factors that influence people to behave in a particular way or to move in a particular direction. These factors include responsibility (feeling the work is important and having control over one's own resources), freedom to act, scope to use and develop skills and abilities, interesting and challenging work, and opportunities for advancement.
- *Extrinsic motivation* – what is done to or for people to motivate them. This includes rewards such as increased pay, praise or promotion, and punishments such as disciplinary action, withholding pay or criticism.

The extrinsic motivators can have an immediate and powerful effect, but this will not necessarily last for long. The intrinsic motivators, which are concerned with the quality of working life, are likely to have a deeper and longer-term effect because they are inherent in individuals and not imposed from outside.

Basic concepts of motivation

The basic concepts of motivation are concerned with needs, goals, reinforcement and expectations (expectancy theory).

Needs

Needs theory states that behaviour is motivated by unsatisfied needs. The key needs associated with work are those for achievement, recognition, responsibility, influence and personal growth.

Goals

Goal theory states that motivation will be increased if goal-setting techniques are used with the following characteristics:

- The goals should be specific.
- They should be challenging but reachable.
- They should be seen as fair and reasonable.

- Individuals should participate fully in setting goals.
- Feedback ensures that people feel pride and satisfaction from the experience of achieving a challenging but fair goal.
- Feedback is used to gain commitment to even higher goals.

Reinforcement

Reinforcement theory suggests that success in achieving goals and rewards acts as a positive incentive and reinforces the successful behaviour, which is repeated the next time a similar need arises.

Expectancy theory

Expectancy theory states that motivation only happens when individuals:

- feel able to change their behaviour;
- feel confident that a change in their behaviour will produce a reward;
- value the reward sufficiently to justify the change in behaviour.

The theory indicates that motivation is only likely when a clearly perceived relationship exists between performance and outcome, and the outcome is seen as a means of satisfying needs. This applies just as much to non-financial as to financial rewards. For example, if people want personal growth they will only be motivated by the opportunities available to them if they know what those opportunities are, if they know what they need to do to benefit from them (and can do it) and if the opportunities are worth striving for.

Expectancy theory explains why extrinsic motivation – for example, an incentive or bonus scheme – works only if the link between effort and reward is clear and the value of the reward is worth the effort. Such schemes should provide a clear line of sight between effort and reward. It also explains why intrinsic motivation arising from the work itself can sometimes be more powerful than extrinsic motivation. Intrinsic motivation outcomes are more under the control of individuals, who can place greater reliance on their past experiences to indicate the extent to which positive and advantageous results are likely to be obtained by their behaviour.

Implications of motivation theory

Motivation theory conveys two important messages. First, there are no simplistic solutions to increasing motivation. No single lever such as performance-related pay exists that is guaranteed to act as an effective motivator. This is because motivation is a complex process. It depends on:

- individual needs and aspirations, which are almost infinitely variable;
- both intrinsic and extrinsic motivating factors, and it is impossible to generalize on what the best mix of these is likely to be;
- expectations about rewards, which will vary greatly among individuals according to their previous experiences and perceptions of the reward system;
- the social context, where the influences of the organization culture, managers and co-workers can produce a wide variety of motivational forces that are difficult to predict and therefore to manage.

The second key message provided by motivation theory is the significance of expectations, goal-setting, feedback and reinforcement as motivating factors.

The implications of these messages are considered below.

Approaches to motivation

Creating the right climate

It is necessary, in general, to create a climate that will enable high motivation to flourish. This is a matter of managing the culture. The aims would be, first, to reinforce values concerning performance and competence; second, to emphasize norms (accepted ways of behaviour) relating to the ways in which people are managed and rewarded; and third, to demonstrate the organization's belief in empowerment – providing people with the scope and 'space' to exercise responsibility and use their abilities to the full. Without the right climate, quick fixes designed to improve motivation, such as performance-related pay, are unlikely to have much of an impact on overall organizational effectiveness, although they may work with some individuals.

Goal-setting, feedback and reinforcement

Goal-setting, feedback and reinforcement can all contribute to high motivation, and they are all within your control.

Managing expectations

It is necessary to manage expectations. No reward offered through an incentive, bonus or performance-related pay scheme will be effective as a motivator unless individuals believe it is worthwhile and can reasonably expect to obtain it through their own efforts. Similarly, people are more likely to be motivated if they know that their achievements will be recognized.

The implications of these approaches as they affect financial and non-financial reward policies and practices are set out below.

Financial rewards

Financial rewards need to be considered from three points of view:

- the effectiveness of money as a motivator;
- the reasons why people are satisfied or dissatisfied with their rewards;
- the criteria that should be used when developing a financial reward system.

Money and motivation

Money is important to people because it is instrumental in satisfying a number of their most pressing needs. It is significant not only because of what people can buy with it but also as a highly tangible method of recognizing their worth, thus improving their self-esteem and gaining the esteem of others.

Pay is the key to attracting people to join an organization, although job interest, career opportunities and the reputation of the organization will also be factors. Satisfaction with pay among existing employees is mainly related to feelings about equity and fairness. External and internal comparisons will form the basis of these feelings, which will influence their desire to stay with the organization.

Pay can motivate. As a tangible means of recognizing achievement, pay can reinforce desirable behaviour. Pay can also deliver messages on what the organization believes to be important. But to be effective, a pay-for-performance system has to meet the following stringent conditions:

- There must be a clear link between performance and reward.
- The methods used to measure performance should be perceived to be fair and consistent.
- The reward should be worth striving for.
- Individuals should expect to receive a worthwhile reward if they behave appropriately.

As a manager you can make sure that the company's reward system is applied in your part of the organization in accordance with these principles.

Non-financial rewards

Non-financial rewards can be focused on the needs most people have, in varying degrees, for achievement, recognition, responsibility, influence and personal growth. You will be in a position to provide or withhold these rewards for those of your staff who are doing well or badly.

Achievement

The need for achievement is defined as the need for competitive success measured against a personal standard of excellence.

Achievement motivation can take place by providing people with the opportunity to perform and the scope in their jobs to use their skills and abilities.

Recognition

Recognition is one of the most powerful motivators. People need to know not only how well they have achieved their objectives or carried out their work but also that their achievements are appreciated.

Praise, however, should be given judiciously – it must be related to real achievements. And it is not the only form of recognition. Financial rewards, especially achievement bonuses awarded immediately after the event, are clear symbols of recognition to which tangible benefits are attached, and this is an important way in which mutually reinforcing processes of financial and non-financial rewards can operate. There are other forms of recognition such as long-service awards, status symbols of one kind or another, sabbaticals and trips abroad, all of which can be part of the total reward process.

Recognition is also provided by managers who listen to and act upon the suggestions of their team members and, importantly, acknowledge their contribution. Other actions that provide recognition include promotion, allocation to a high-profile project, enlargement of the job to provide scope for more interesting and rewarding work, and various forms of status or esteem symbols.

Responsibility

People can be motivated by being given more responsibility for their own work. This is essentially what empowerment is about and is in line with the concept of intrinsic motivation based on the content of the job. It is also related to the fundamental concept that individuals are motivated when they are provided with the means to achieve their goals.

The characteristics required in jobs if they are to be intrinsically motivating are that: first, individuals must receive meaningful feedback about their performance, preferably by evaluating their own performance and defining the feedback they require; second, the job must be perceived by individuals as requiring them to use abilities they value in order to perform the job effectively; and third, individuals must feel that they have a high degree of autonomy or self-control over setting their own goals and defining the paths to these goals.

Influence

People can be motivated by the drive to exert influence or to exercise power. David McClelland's[1] research established that, alongside the need for achievement, the need for power is a prime motivating force for managers, although the need for 'affiliation' – that is, warm, friendly relationships with others – is always present. The organization, through its policies for involvement, can provide motivation by putting people into situations where their views can be expressed, listened to and acted upon. This is another aspect of empowerment.

Personal growth

In Maslow's[2] hierarchy of needs, self-fulfilment or self-actualization is the highest need of all and is therefore the ultimate motivator. Maslow defines self-fulfilment as 'the need to develop potentialities and skills, to become what one believes one is capable of becoming'.

Ambitious and determined people will seek and find these opportunities for themselves, although the organization needs to clarify the scope for growth and development it can provide (if it does not, they will go away and grow elsewhere).

Increasingly, however, individuals at all levels in organizations, whether or not they are eaten up by ambition, recognize the importance of continually upgrading their skills and of progressively developing their careers. Many people now regard access to training as a key element in the overall reward package.

The availability of learning opportunities, the selection of individuals for high-prestige training courses and programmes, and the emphasis placed by the organization on the acquisition of new skills as well as the enhancement of existing ones, can all act as powerful motivators.

Ten steps to achieving high levels of motivation

The following 10 steps need to be taken if you wish to achieve higher levels of motivation:

- Set and agree demanding but achievable goals.
- Provide feedback on performance.
- Create expectations that certain behaviours and outputs will produce worthwhile rewards when people succeed but will result in penalties if they fail.
- Design jobs that enable people to feel a sense of accomplishment, to express and use their abilities and to exercise their own decision-making powers.
- Provide appropriate financial incentives and rewards for achievement (pay-for-performance).
- Provide appropriate non-financial rewards such as recognition and praise for work well done.
- Communicate to individuals and publicize generally the link between performance and reward – thus enhancing expectations.
- Select and train team leaders who will exercise effective leadership and have the required motivating skills.
- Give people guidance and training that will develop the knowledge, skills and competencies they need to improve their performance.
- Show individuals what they have to do to develop their careers.

Notes

1 McClelland, D (1975) *Power: The inner experience*, Irvington, New York
2 Maslow, A (1954) *Motivation and Personality*, Harper & Row, New York

How to run and participate in effective meetings

36

Down with meetings

Meetings Bloody Meetings, the title of a training film, strikes a familiar chord with us all. When you think how many committees exist and how many meetings are held in any organization, it is remarkable how hard it is to find anyone who has a good word to say about them.

It has been said that committees are made up of the unfit appointed by the incompetent to do the unnecessary, and that a camel is a horse designed by a committee. Experience of badly organized and pointless meetings is so widespread that, for many people, these cynical comments come very close to the truth.

What's wrong with meetings?

Meetings are criticized because they:

- Waste time – too many people talk too much.
- Fail to produce decisions and can be slow, exasperating and frustrating – they legitimize procrastination and indecisiveness.
- Tend to be dominated by a few people with strong personalities.
- Make lowest common denominator recommendations.
- Encourage political decisions where vested interests can prevail by means of lobbying and pressure.
- Dilute responsibility.

- Are costly in time and money.
- Concentrate on trivialities they can grasp rather than big issues beyond their scope. Northcote Parkinson cited as an example of this a committee that approved a £10 million capital development project (which it couldn't properly understand) in 10 minutes flat yet spent two hours arguing about a new cycle shed costing £2,000.

What's right with meetings?

Meetings tend to incite such criticism because they are not properly organized. Many of the criticisms levelled at meetings are really criticisms of their misuse, not their proper use. A well-organized meeting held at the right time for the right reasons can bring a number of benefits. It can:

- ensure that important matters receive proper consideration from all involved;
- clarify thinking, in that members have to justify their positions before the others present;
- ensure that different viewpoints are aired;
- act as a medium for the exchange of information;
- save time by getting a number of people together;
- promote coordination;
- create something as a group that the individuals could not have achieved working separately – this is the process of synergy, where the whole is greater than the parts.

To make meetings work there are three things that must happen:

- They should be set up properly.
- There should be a good chairperson.
- The members should be able to participate effectively.

DOS AND DON'TS OF MEETINGS

DO	DON'T
Use a meeting if the information or the judgement is too great for one person.	Use a meeting if one person can do the job better.
Set up committees only when it is essential to assemble people with different viewpoints in one place at one time.	Set up a committee if you want sharp, clear responsibility.
Appoint a chairperson who is going to be able to control the meeting and get the best out of it.	Use a committee to administrate anything.
Put people with different backgrounds who can contribute ideas on the committee.	Use a meeting or committee if you need speedy action.
Tell committees what they are to do and what their authority is.	Appoint a bigger committee than you need – over 10 people can become unwieldy.
Be explicit about when you want the meeting to report back.	Hold unnecessary meetings – it may be good to meet regularly on the first Friday of every month but it may be even better to meet only when you have something to discuss.
Use meetings where they work best – reviewing or developing policies, coordinating decisions, ensuring that all concerned with a programme are consulted and kept informed.	
Wind up committees as soon as they have served their purpose.	

Chairing meetings

The success or failure of a meeting largely depends on the chairman. If you are chairing a meeting, this is what you must do.

Prior to the meeting

Before the meeting starts, ensure that it has proper terms of reference and that the members are briefed on what to expect and what they should be prepared to contribute. Plan the agenda to provide for a structured meeting, covering all the issues in a logical order. Prepare and issue briefing papers that will structure the meeting and spell out the background, thus saving time going into detail or reviewing purely factual information during the meeting.

During the meeting

- Start by clearly defining the objective of the meeting, setting a timescale that you intend to keep.
- Go through each item of the agenda in turn, ensuring that a firm conclusion is reached and recorded.
- Initiate the discussion on each item by setting the scene very briefly and asking for contributions – ask for answers to specific questions (which you should have prepared in advance) or you may refer the matter first to a member of the meeting who can make the best initial contribution (ideally, you should have briefed that individual in advance).
- Invite contributions from other members of the meeting, taking care not to allow anyone to dominate the discussions.
- Bring people back to order if they drift from the point.
- If there is too much talk, remind members that they are there to make progress.
- Encourage the expression of different points of view and avoid crushing anyone too obviously if they have not made a sensible comment.
- Allow disagreement between members of the meeting but step in smartly if the atmosphere becomes too contentious.
- Chip in with questions or brief comments from time to time, but do not dominate the discussion.
- At appropriate moments during the meeting summarize the discussion, express views on where the committee has got to and outline your perception of the interim or final decision that has been made. Then check that the meeting agrees, amending the conclusion as necessary, and ensure that the decision is recorded exactly as made.
- Summarize what has been achieved at the end of the meeting, indicating who has to do what by when.
- If a further meeting is needed, agree the purpose of the meeting and what has to be done by those present before it takes place.

Remember that meetings can run in phases. For example, they start with an explanation, continue with a discussion of pros and cons, run into a sidetrack and have to be brought into line, generate more heat than light because of contending points of view, and eventually reach a point where you realize a decision has to be taken.

If you are chairing a meeting you may have to change your style accordingly. You may have to be decisive in bringing people to the point or business to a close, relaxed if you want to allow the discussion to keep going, or persuasive in order to draw people into the discussion.

Members

If you are a member of a meeting you should:

- Prepare thoroughly – have all the facts at your fingertips, with any supporting data you need.
- Make your points clearly, succinctly and positively – try to resist the temptation of talking too much.
- Remain silent if you have nothing to say.
- Keep your powder dry if you are not leading the discussion or if it is a subject you are not knowledgeable about. Listen, observe and save your arguments until you can make a really telling point. Don't plunge in too quickly or comprehensively – there may be other compelling arguments.
- If you are not too sure of your ground, avoid making statements such as 'I think we must do this.' Instead, pose a question to the chairman or other member of the meeting such as 'Do you think there is a case for doing this?'
- Be prepared to argue your case firmly, but don't persist in fighting for a lost cause. Don't retire in a sulk because you cannot get your own way; accept defeat gracefully.
- Remember that if you are defeated in committee, there may still be a chance for you to fight another day in a different setting.

37

How to negotiate

Negotiation is the process of coming to terms and, in so doing, getting the best deal possible for your firm, your union or yourself.

Negotiations involve a conflict of interest. Sellers prefer a high price to a low one and buyers prefer a low price to a high one. Unions want the highest settlement they can get, management wants the lowest. It can be a zero-sum game – what one side gains the other loses. No one likes to lose, so there is conflict, which has to be managed if an amicable agreement is to be achieved. And negotiators do, or should, try to end up on friendly terms, whatever differences of opinion have occurred on the way. After all, they may well meet again.

Another important feature of negotiations is that they take place in an atmosphere of uncertainty. Neither side necessarily knows what the other wants or will give.

There are two main types of negotiation – business and trade union.

Business negotiations

Business negotiations are mainly about the price and the terms for supplying goods or services.

In their simplest form they are no more than a haggle between buyer and seller, much the same as what happens when you trade in your car for a new one. At their more complex, they concern a package in which a number of extras are on offer along with the basic product. Sellers can usually offer a range of prices to suit the needs of the buyer: an 'ex-works' price, a delivered price, an installed price and a price that includes service. Various methods of staging payments or providing credit may also be offered.

Negotiations of this type usually start with the buyer producing a specification. The seller then produces a proposal and negotiation starts. The seller will have included a negotiating margin in the proposal and will be prepared to vary the price according to the package required.

Business negotiations are usually conducted in a friendly manner, and that's your major problem. You can too easily be seduced into accepting a less than satisfactory deal by the blandishments of the negotiator.

Trade union negotiations

Trade union negotiations can be much tougher. They may involve a simple pay settlement, but usually they involve a package. Extra benefits will be at issue, and can be traded for concessions if need be.

In this type of negotiation, both parties are probably quite clear as to the maximum they will give or the minimum they will accept. They will have predetermined their opening demands and offers, and their shopping list of extras will have been analysed to determine which points can be conceded in return for some benefit.

There are a number of bargaining conventions used in union negotiations, of which the following are the most generally accepted:

● Whatever happens during the bargaining, both parties hope to come to a settlement.

● Attacks, hard words, threats and (controlled) losses of temper are treated by both sides as legitimate tactics and should not be allowed to shake either party's belief in the other's integrity, or their desire to settle without taking drastic action.

● Off-the-record discussions (beneficial as a means of probing attitudes and intentions) should not be referred to specifically in formal bargaining sessions, unless both sides agree in advance.

● Each side should be prepared to move from its original position.

● It is normal, although not inevitable, for the negotiation to proceed by a series of offers and counter-offers that lead steadily towards a settlement.

● Concessions, once made, cannot be withdrawn.

● Firm offers must not be withdrawn, although it is legitimate to make and withdraw conditional offers.

● A third party should not be brought in until both parties are agreed that no further progress would be made without one.

● The final agreement should mean exactly what it says. There should be no trickery and the terms agreed should be implemented without amendment.

● If possible, the final settlement should be framed so that both sides can save face and credibility.

The process of negotiation

In both cases the process is much the same. Here each stage is illustrated by a summary of what took place in an actual trade union negotiation.

Stage 1: Preparation – Setting objectives (or drawing up specifications), assembling data, and deciding on negotiating strategy

The union's aim was to achieve a settlement at, or above, the current rate of inflation (8 per cent). Its strategy was to force management on to the defensive by asking them to make an offer without divulging what the union wanted. In addition, the union asked for a reduction of one hour in the working week, an extra three days' holiday and a Christmas bonus of one week's pay.

The management's objective was to settle at no more than the rate of inflation, and to concede nothing that would raise the total cost of the package above 8 per cent. There was some debate within the management team about strategy. One hawk wanted to pre-empt the union claim by starting with the final offer, allowing no room for bargaining. He was overruled on the grounds that this would cause a confrontation and hence long-term damage to relations with the union. The next question was how much room for manoeuvre should be allowed between the opening and closing offer. Some wanted to start as low as possible, say 3 per cent, so as to close well below the 15 per cent claim expected from the union. The prevailing view, however, was that too low an offer would prolong the negotiations unnecessarily. It was thought better to start at 5 per cent, so that, if it had to, the firm could take two steps of 1½ per cent before reaching its maximum of 8 per cent.

Stage 2: Opening – Negotiators reveal their initial bargaining positions to their opposite numbers

The union started by stating its case. It wanted a substantial increase to protect its members from inflation and to restore the differentials lost over the previous three years. The extras (reduced working week, etc) were thrown in almost as makeweights, giving management the clue that there might be scope for some trading later on.

Management stated that no 'substantial offer' could be expected. It emphasized the poor trading results of the firm and the fact that, overall, the pay of the union's members compared favourably with other workers. The point was also made (it was to be repeated many times in ensuing meetings) that the firm could not guarantee that pay increases would match inflation.

Having set out their opening positions and their main arguments, the two parties agreed to adjourn the meeting.

Stage 3: Bargaining

At this stage both parties have the same aims. As a negotiator you will be trying: a) to probe the weaknesses in the other side's case, and b) to convince the other side that they must abandon their position and move closer to your own. You will also be checking to see if your own position holds good in the light of information received from your opponents and their reactions to your case. Your original judgement may be confirmed or you may now have to adjust it. You may also decide to apply pressure or give concessions now in order to move towards a satisfactory conclusion.

In the bargaining stage three meetings were held. At each of them the arguments of both management and union teams were the same as in the opening phase.

Each party aimed to discover how strongly the other believed in their arguments and to what extent they were prepared to shift position. Every phrase was analysed to discover just what was behind it, both sides seeking hints as to how much support the other was getting – from the shop floor and top management respectively.

Management opened with a 5 per cent offer and got the usual reaction: it was 'derisory', 'insulting' and so on. The union refused to state exactly what it wanted, hoping to mystify and wrong-foot the management.

Between the second and third meetings the management team were agreed in the belief that the union was hoping to get 10 per cent but, if pushed, might settle for 8. It was decided that an offer to reduce the working week by 30 minutes might be made, but only as a last-minute trade-off if a reasonable settlement seemed unlikely.

At the third meeting, management increased its offer to 7 per cent, saying that this was as far as it could go. When pressed to state whether this was, or was not, their final offer, the management team refused to elucidate. The union rightly interpreted this to mean that there was more in the kitty and that top management would release it if pressed hard enough. The union demanded 10 per cent and the other concessions.

Stage 4: Closing

Each party judges whether the other side is determined to stick to its position or will settle for a compromise. The final moves are made. It is during this stage that final 'trade-offs' may lead to a settlement.

The final meeting lasted all day and into the night. Management stuck to its 7 per cent offer and made no other concessions. The union tried several tactics. Pleading, controlled loss of temper and threats of industrial action were all used. The management team finally judged that the only way to get a settlement was to attempt a trade-off. They offered 7 per cent plus one hour off the working week, in return for an agreement to abolish the customary five minutes' 'wash-up' time (a practice that had been consistently abused).

Management reiterated that this was the final offer and was as much as the firm could afford, and managed to convince the union by sheer force of argument that it meant what it said. The union accepted the offer after balloting its members.

Negotiating tactics

Preparation

1 Define your bargaining objectives as follows:
   - Ideal – the best you can hope to achieve.
   - Minimum – the least you would be prepared to settle for.
   - Target – what you are going to try for and believe, realistically, you have a good chance of achieving.
2 Consider how you might build up a package that would allow concessions to be exchanged. For example, could you accept a higher price for a concession on payment terms, or increase a pay offer if the union agrees to remove a restrictive practice?
3 Assess what the other party wants or is prepared to offer. For example, if you are a manufacturer negotiating terms with a store, it pays to know, say, that the buyer is constrained by company policy that insists on a three-times mark-up. Knowing the retail price that the store will want to charge, you will have a good idea of the maximum the buyer will pay. You can then judge whether you should press for a larger order to justify a lower selling price than you would normally accept.

   In a typical wage negotiation the union or representative body making the claim will come to the table with a predetermined target, minimum and opening claims. Similarly, you, as the employer, will have your own target, maximum and opening offer. The difference between their claim and your offer is the negotiating range. If your maximum exceeds their minimum this will indicate the settlement zone. This is demonstrated in Figure 37.1. In this example the chance of settlement without too much trouble is fairly high. It is when your maximum is less than their minimum, as in Figure 37.2, that the trouble starts.

FIGURE 37.1   Negotiating range with a settlement zone

FIGURE 37.2   Negotiating range without a settlement zone

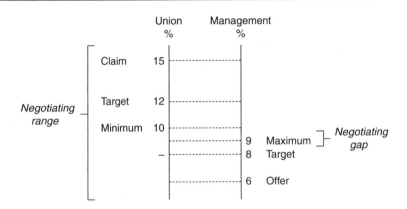

4 Decide on your strategy and tactics – your opening offer, the steps you are going to take, the concessions you are prepared to offer and the arguments you are going to use.

5 Collect the facts needed to support your case.

6 Assemble any documents you need, such as standard contract terms.

7 In a trade union negotiation:

  – Select the negotiating team. This should never have fewer than two members, and for major negotiations should have three or more: one to take the lead, one to take notes and feed the negotiator with any supporting information needed, and the others to observe their opposite numbers and play a specific part in negotiations in accordance with their brief.

  – Brief the members of the negotiating team on their roles and the negotiating strategy and tactics that are to be adopted. If appropriate, prepared statements or arguments should be issued at this stage to be used as required by the strategic plan.

- Rehearse the members of the team in their roles. They can be asked to repeat their points to other members and deal with responses from them; or someone can act as devil's advocate and force the leader or other members of the team to handle awkward points or negotiating ploys.

At this stage it may be possible to meet your opponents informally to sound out their position, while they sound out yours. You can use such a session as an 'early warning' system to get your opponents to modify their initial demands by convincing them of the strength of your own position or your determination to resist.

In a recent trade union negotiation these 'corridor tactics' met with success. The union concerned had asked management to introduce a new technology agreement with the usual clauses about consultation, job protection and health precautions.

During the first two meetings management stuck firmly to its view that all these requirements were catered for by existing agreements and published policies. But the union insisted that this was not so. The negotiation seemed to have reached an impasse. Whatever the union leader felt, he could not weaken too obviously during the actual meetings. Neither could the general manager who was heading the management team.

To break the impasse the general manager asked his industrial relations manager to hold an off-the-record meeting with the trade union leader. At this meeting it was made clear that the company would not agree to a separate new technology agreement in any circumstances. But the industrial relations manager suggested that the company would be prepared to add a stronger prior consultation clause to the existing agreement.

From previous experience, the union leader knew this man meant what he said. He saw no point in having a major confrontation on this issue and knew he would get little support from his members, who did not see new technology as a real issue. But he felt that if he had to give a concession he should get something back. In other words, he wanted a trade-off.

He therefore agreed to go along with the idea, so long as the company let the union monitor the introduction of any major new technology schemes over the next six months. This was accepted by the industrial relations manager. Both parties understood the convention that there was no commitment and that no reference would be made to their discussion in future formal meetings. They then cleared the informal understanding with their respective committees and, at the subsequent formal meeting, the terms were agreed without any difficulty. What looked like being a major problem had been solved by corridor negotiations.

Opening

Your tactics when opening the negotiation should be to:

- Open realistically and move moderately.
- Challenge your opponents' position as it stands, but on no account limit their ability to move.
- Explore attitudes, ask questions, observe behaviour and, above all, listen; assess your opponents' strengths and weaknesses, their tactics and the extent to which they may be bluffing.
- Make no concessions of any kind at this stage.
- Be non-committal about proposals and explanations (do not talk too much).

Bargaining

Your aim is to narrow the gap between the two initial positions and to persuade your opponents that your case is so strong that they must accept less than they had planned. You should:

- Always make conditional proposals: 'If you will do this I will consider doing that'.
- Never make one-sided concessions: always trade-off against a concession from the other party: 'If I concede x then I expect you to concede y.'
- Negotiate on the whole package: never allow your opponents to pick you off item by item; keep all the issues open so as to extract the maximum benefit from potential trade-offs.

Reading the signals

During the bargaining stage you must be sensitive to any signals made by the other party. Every time they make a conditional statement it shows that they are prepared to move. Explore the possibilities with questions. Try to get behind what people say and understand what they really mean. For example:

What they say	What they mean
That's as far as I can go.	I might be able to persuade my boss to go further.
We don't usually give more than 5 per cent discount.	We're prepared to give more if you give us something in return.
Let's think about that point.	I'm prepared to negotiate.
I need notice of that question.	It's difficult, but not impossible. Try again.
It will be very difficult for us to meet that requirement.	It's not impossible but we'll want a trade-off.
I shall certainly consider your offer.	I am going to accept it but I don't want to appear to be too easy a touch.
This is our standard contract.	We're prepared to negotiate on the terms.
We're prepared to offer you £x per 1,000 units.	The price is negotiable.
That's my final offer.	My boss might go further if pushed (or if it is made worth his while).
We couldn't meet your delivery requirements at that price.	I will negotiate on delivery or price.

Arguing

During the bargaining stage much of your time will be spent in arguing. Clear thinking (see Chapter 47) will help you to present your case and expose the fallacies in your opponent's arguments.

You should also consider the manner in which you argue. You are not there to beat your opponent into the ground. In fact, in the interests of future good relationships (which will benefit you as well as your opponent) it is wise to leave an escape route. As a leading trade unionist said: 'Always leave the other fellow the price of his bus ticket home.'

Avoid brow-beating your opponent. Disagree firmly, but don't shoot him down. Don't try to make your opponent look small. Score points, if you must, to discredit arguments or expose fallacious reasoning but never in order to discredit him or her as a person. If you indulge in personal attacks or abuse, your opponents will close ranks.

To argue effectively you must be prepared to listen both to the stated and to the implied points made by your opponent. Don't talk too much yourself; it will prevent you reading signals, and you may give too much away. Wherever you can, challenge your opponent to justify the case on an item-by-item basis. Put the onus on him or her by questioning for clarification. Answer a question with another question if you want time to consider.

Argue calmly and without emotion, but emphasize the points you really want to ram home either by raising your voice slightly and slowing down to highlight your argument, or by repetition.

Control your anger. Express yourself strongly, by all means, but you will lose everything if you lose your temper.

Always remember that you are not trying to win at all costs. If your opponent wants something that you cannot give, don't just say no. Offer an alternative package. If your opponent is asking for a higher specification than you normally provide for the price and wants a delivery date that you cannot meet without incurring extra overtime costs, say that you can meet the specifications and the delivery deadline as long as the other side is prepared to cover the costs.

Gambits

There are a number of standard bargaining gambits. Here are a few of the more common ones:

- *Uttering threats* – 'Agree to what I want or I'll call out the lads', or 'I'll take my custom elsewhere.' Don't over-react to such threats; simply treat them as part of the normal cut and thrust of negotiation and continue to address the point at issue.

- *No negotiation under duress* – 'We refuse to discuss your claim unless and until you cancel your overtime ban.' An excellent approach, if you can get away with it.

- *It will reflect badly on you* – 'Do you really want to get the reputation of being a heartless employer?' This is an emotional appeal and, as such, should be discounted.

- *The bluff direct* – 'I have two or three quotations lower than yours.' The answer to this gambit is to call your opponent's bluff – 'What are they offering for the price?' 'OK, why not accept them, why bother talking to me?'

- *The leading question* – 'Do you think it is a good idea to reward people according to merit?' 'Yes.' 'Then why do you insist on retaining this fixed incremental scheme that benefits everybody irrespective of how well they've done?' Never fall for a leading question.

- *The piecemeal or 'salami' technique* – In this your opponent will try to pick off the items one by one. 'That's the price agreed, now we can deliver in three months, OK?' 'Right, we've agreed the delivery terms;

now this is how we charge for maintenance.' Always negotiate the whole package. Don't allow yourself to be railroaded into a piecemeal approach.

● *The 'yes, but...' approach* – 'Yes, we agree to accept an increase of 8 per cent, but before we can agree to everything there is this other problem of compensation for redundancy we must tackle.' To avoid being caught in a 'yes, but' trap, always make offers on one part of a package conditional on accepting another part: 'We are prepared to consider a 4 per cent offer but only if you agree to drop your claim for enhanced redundancy pay.'

Closing

When and how you close depends on your assessment of the strength of your opponent's case and his or her determination to see it through. You may close by:

● Making a concession, preferably a minor one, and trading it off against an agreement to settle. The concession can be offered more positively than at the bargaining stage: 'If you will agree to settle at x, I will concede y.'

● Doing a deal: you might split the difference, or bring in something new – such as extending the settlement timescale, agreeing to back payments, phasing increases, making a joint declaration of intent to do something in the future (for example to introduce a productivity plan), or offering an incentive discount.

● Summarizing what has happened to date, emphasizing the concessions that have been made and the extent to which you have moved, and stating that you have reached your final position.

● Applying pressure through a threat of the consequences that will follow if your offer is not accepted.

● Giving your opponent a choice between two courses of action.

Do not say something is a final offer unless you mean it. If it is not really your final offer and your opponent calls your bluff, you will have to make further concessions and your credibility will be undermined. Your opponent will, of course, attempt to force you into revealing how close you are to your final position. Do not allow yourself to be hurried into this. If you want to avoid committing yourself and thus devaluing the word 'final', state as positively as you can that this is as far as you are prepared to go.

How to deal with office politics

Office politics – good or bad?

To be politic, according to the *Oxford English Dictionary*, you can be sagacious, prudent, judicious, expedient, scheming or crafty. So political behaviour in an organization could be desirable or undesirable.

Organizations consist of individuals who, while they are ostensibly there to achieve a common purpose, will, at the same time, be driven by their own needs to achieve their own goals. Effective management is the process of harmonizing individual endeavour and ambition to the common good. Some individuals will genuinely believe that using political means to achieve their goals will benefit the organization as well as themselves. Others will rationalize this belief. Yet others will unashamedly pursue their own ends. They may use all their powers of persuasion to legitimize these ends to their colleagues, but self-interest remains their primary drive. These are the corporate politicians whom the *Oxford English Dictionary* describes as 'shrewd schemers, crafty plotters or intriguers'. Politicians within organizations can be like this. They manoeuvre behind people's backs, blocking proposals they do not like. They advance their own reputation and career at the expense of other people. They can be envious and jealous and act accordingly. They are bad news.

But it can also be argued that a political approach to management is inevitable and even desirable in any organization where the clarity of goals is not absolute, where the decision-making process is not clear-cut and where the authority to make decisions is not evenly or appropriately distributed. And there can be few organizations where one or more of these conditions do not apply.

Andrew Kakabadse[1] recognizes this point when he says in *The Politics of Management*: 'Politics is a process, that of influencing individuals and groups of people to your point of view, where you cannot rely on authority.' In this sense, a political approach can be legitimate as long as the ends are justifiable from the viewpoint of the organization.

Political approaches

Kakabadse identifies seven approaches that office politicians adopt:

- Identify the stakeholders, those who have commitment to act in a particular way.
- Keep the stakeholders comfortable, concentrating on behaviour, values, attitudes, fears and drives that the individuals will accept, tolerate and manage (comfort zones).
- Fit the image – work on the comfort zones and align their image to that of the people with power.
- Use the network – identify the interest groups and people of influence.
- Enter the network – identify the gatekeepers, adhere to the norms.
- Make deals – agree to support other people where this is of mutual benefit.
- Withhold and withdraw – withhold information as appropriate and withdraw judiciously when the going gets rough.

Some of these precepts are more legitimate than others. Organizational life requires managers to identify the key decision-makers when they are involved in developing new approaches and getting things done. Before coming to a final conclusion and launching a fully fledged proposal at a committee or in a memorandum, it makes good sense to test opinion and find out how other people may react. This testing process enables managers to anticipate counter-arguments and modify their proposals either to meet legitimate objections or, when there is no alternative, to accommodate other people's requirements.

Making deals may not appear to be particularly desirable but it does happen, and managers can always rationalize this type of behaviour by reference to the end result. Withholding information is not legitimate behaviour, but people do indulge in it in recognition of the fact that knowledge is power. Judicious withdrawal may also seem to be questionable, but most managers prefer to live to fight another day rather than launch a doomed crusade.

Political sensitivity

Office politicians exert hidden influence to get their way, and 'politicking' in some form takes place in most organizations. If you want to get on, a degree of political sensitivity – knowing what is going on so that influence can be exerted – is desirable. This means:

- knowing how 'things are done around here';
- knowing how decisions are made, including the less obvious factors that are likely to affect decisions;
- knowing where the power base is in the organization – who makes the running; who are the people who count when decisions are taken;
- being aware of what is going on behind the scenes;
- knowing who is a rising star and whose reputation is fading;
- identifying any 'hidden agendas' – trying to understand what people are really getting at, and why, by obtaining answers to the question: 'Where are they coming from?'
- finding out what other people are thinking and seeking;
- networking – as Kakabadse suggests, identifying the interest groups.

Dangers

The danger of politics, however, is that it can be carried to excess, and can then seriously harm the effectiveness of an organization. The signs of excessive indulgence in political behaviour include:

- back-biting;
- buck-passing;
- secret meetings and hidden decisions;
- feuds between people and departments;
- paper or e-mail wars between armed camps – arguing by memoranda or e-mail, always a sign of distrust;
- a multiplicity of snide comments and criticisms;
- excessive and counterproductive lobbying;
- the formation of cabals – cliques that spend their time intriguing.

Dealing with office politicians

One way to deal with this sort of behaviour is to find out who is going in for it and openly confront them with the damage they are doing. They will, of course, deny that they are behaving politically (they wouldn't be politicians if they didn't), but the fact that they have been identified might lead them to modify their approach. It could, of course, only serve to drive them further underground, in which case their behaviour will have to be observed even more closely and corrective action taken as necessary.

A more positive approach to keeping politics operating at an acceptable level is for the organization to manage its operations as openly as possible. The aims should be to ensure that issues are debated fully, that differences of opinion are dealt with frankly and that disagreements are depersonalized, so far as this is possible. Political processes can then be seen as a way of maintaining the momentum of the organization as a complex decision-making and problem-solving entity.

Use of politics

There are occasions when a subtle appeal rather than a direct attack will pay dividends, and sometimes you have to exercise your powers of persuasion indirectly on those whose support you need. The following case study illustrates the legitimate use of politics.

James Hale was the personnel director of a large divisionalized group in the food industry. The rate of growth by expansion and acquisitions had been very rapid. There was a shortage of really good managers and a lack of coordination between the divisions in the group and between those divisions and head office. Hale believed that setting up a group management training centre would be a good way of helping to overcome these problems. He knew, however, that he would have to get agreement to this plan not only from the managing director, who would be broadly sympathetic, but also from his co-directors. The MD would not act without the support of a majority on his board. In any case Hale genuinely felt that there was no point in developing a facility of this sort for people who were not interested in it.

He therefore sat back and deliberately worked out a strategy for getting agreement to his proposal. He knew that a frontal attack might fail. Management development was perceived by his colleagues as a somewhat airy-fairy idea that had little relevance to their real concerns as directors. He therefore had to adopt a more subtle approach. He did not call it a political campaign, but that is what it was. He was setting out to influence people indirectly.

The basis of his plan was an individual approach to each of his colleagues, adjusted to their particular interests and concerns. In the case of the marketing director, he got the general sales manager to advocate the need for training in sales management for divisional sales staff. He ran several pilot courses in hotels and invited the marketing director to the winding-up session. He made sure that the marketing director was impressed not only by what the divisional sales staff had learnt from the course, but also by the new spirit of identification with group aims and policies engendered by the training. Casually, the personnel director let slip the thought that if the group had its own training centre this feeling of commitment could be developed even more strongly.

The same basic technique was used with the production director, who was nudged towards the view that a centre owned by the group could speed up the introduction of new ideas and provide a facility for communicating directly with key staff that was not available at present.

The finance director was a more difficult person to convince. He could easily assess the costs but found it difficult to accept largely subjective views of the potential benefits. In this case James Hale did not try too hard to persuade him against his will. He knew that the majority of the board, including the managing director, were now in favour of the plan. Hale felt safe in leaving his financial colleague in an isolated and ultimately untenable position. The qualitative arguments, as absorbed by the other members of the board, had the ring of truth about them that no purely quantitative arguments could overcome.

Hale was content that he had enough support. To clinch the argument he played his last political card by warning the marketing and production directors that there might be some financial opposition.

He then got them to agree with the thesis that they wouldn't allow 'Mr Money Bags' to adopt a narrow financial view and thus dictate the destiny of the firm.

James Hale had no difficulty in getting his proposal accepted at the next board meeting.

The non-legitimate use of politics

The following is an example of non-legitimate use of politics. Unfortunately, it is a fairly common one. In most organizations there are people who want to get on, and do not have too many scruples about how they do it. If it involves treading on other people's faces, then so be it.

Two directors of a company both aspired to be the next managing director. Mr Gray, the finance director, had the ear of the MD. Mr White, the technical director, was more remote.

Mr White had a number of ideas for introducing new technology and had proved, to his own satisfaction at least, that the pay-off was considerable. Unfortunately, he jumped the gun in order to anticipate comments from Gray, and presented a paper to the managing director that was not as well argued as it might have been. Gray carefully lobbied the MD and convinced him that the proposal was full of holes – he also hinted that this was yet another example of White's inability to understand the wider commercial issues.

The MD accepted this view more or less completely and agreed with Gray's suggestion that the whole proposal should be off-loaded on to a board sub-committee – a well-known device to delay if not to stifle new ideas. This was done, and the introduction of new technology was unnecessarily delayed by 18 months. But Gray had made his point as the practical man of affairs who would not allow the company to get involved in expensive and unrewarding projects.

Note

1 Kakabadse, A (1983) *The Politics of Management*, Gower, Aldershot

39 How to organize

An effective enterprise ensures that collective effort is organized to achieve specific ends. Organizing involves dividing the overall management task into a variety of processes and activities and then establishing means of ensuring that these processes are carried out effectively and that the activities are coordinated. It is about differentiating activities in times of uncertainty and change, integrating them – grouping them together to achieve the organization's overall purpose – and ensuring that effective information flows and channels of communication are maintained.

Organization design

Organization design is based on the analysis of activities, processes, decisions, information flows and roles. It produces a structure that consists of positions and units between which there are relationships involving cooperation, the exercise of authority and the exchange of information.

Within the structure there will be line managers who are responsible for achieving results in the organization's key areas of activity by managing teams and individuals, and specialists who provide support, guidance and advice to the line.

The structure must be appropriate to the organization's purpose and technology, and the environment in which it exists. It must be flexible enough to adapt itself easily to new circumstances – organization design is a continuous process of modification and change; it is never a one-off event. It must also be recognized that, although the formal organization structure may define who is responsible for what and the ostensible lines of communication and control, the way in which it actually operates will depend on informal networks and other relationships that have not been defined in the design process and arise from people's daily interaction.

The approach to organization design

Organization design aims to clarify roles and relationships so far as this is possible in fluid conditions. It is also concerned with giving people the scope and opportunity to use their skills and abilities to better effect – this is the process of empowerment.

Jobs should be designed to satisfy the requirements of the organization for productivity, operational efficiency and quality of product or service. But they must also meet the needs of individuals for interest, challenge and accomplishment. These aims are interrelated and an important aim of organization and job design is to integrate the needs of the individual with those of the organization.

When it comes to designing or modifying the structure a pragmatic approach is necessary. It is first necessary to understand the environment, the technology and the existing systems of social relationships. An organization can then be designed that is contingent upon the circumstances. There is always some choice, but designers should try to achieve the best fit they can. And in making their choice, they should be aware of the structural, human, process and system factors that will influence the design, and of the context within which the organization operates.

Organization design is ultimately a matter of ensuring that the structure, processes and methods of operation fit the strategic requirements of the business and its technology within its environment. Disruption occurs if internal and external coherence and consistency are not achieved. And, as Mintzberg[1] suggests: 'Organizations, like individuals, can avoid identity crises by deciding what they wish to be and then pursuing it with a healthy obsession.'

Organization design is always an empirical and evolutionary process for which absolute principles cannot be laid down. But there are a number of broad guidelines that should be taken into account even if they are not followed slavishly.

Organization guidelines

Allocation of work

Related activities should be grouped logically together into functions and departments. Unnecessary overlap and duplication of work, either horizontally or vertically within a hierarchy, should be avoided.

A matrix organization may be developed in which multidisciplinary project teams are created specially to accomplish a specified task but the members of those teams are responsible on a continuing basis to a functional leader who allocates them to projects, assesses their performance, provides rewards and deals with training and career development needs.

Close attention should be given to the processes within the business. These are the interconnected sequences of activities that convert inputs into outputs. Thus, 'order fulfilment' is a process that starts with an order as its input and results in an 'output': the delivery of the ordered goods. The organization design should ensure that the flow of such processes can proceed smoothly, efficiently and effectively.

Business process re-engineering can help to achieve this by subjecting the processes that link key organizational functions together – from initiation to completion – to critical examination and, as necessary, redesign. It is sometimes better to organize these processes properly before becoming over-involved in the design of rigid structures that can inhibit the flow of work.

The work that needs to be done and accountabilities for results should be defined and agreed with teams and individual jobholders.

Matters requiring a decision should be dealt with as near to the point of action as possible by individuals or self-managing teams. Managers should not try to do too much themselves, nor should they supervise too closely.

Levels in the structure

Too many levels of management and supervision inhibit communication and teamwork and create extra work (and unnecessary jobs). The aim should be to reduce the number of levels to a minimum. However, the elimination of middle managers and wider spans of control mean that more attention has to be paid to improving teamwork, delegation and methods of integrating activities.

Span of control

There are limits to the number of people anyone can manage or supervise well, but these vary considerably between different jobs. Most people can work with a far greater span of control than they imagine, as long as they are prepared to delegate more effectively, to avoid becoming involved in too much detail, and to develop good teamwork among the individuals reporting to them. In fact, wide spans of control are beneficial in that they can enhance delegation and better teamwork and free the higher-level manager to spend more time on policy-making and planning.

Limited spans of control encourage managers to interfere too much with the work going on beneath them and therefore constrain the scope that should be given to their subordinates to grow with their jobs.

One person, one boss

Generally speaking, individuals should be accountable only to one boss for the results they achieve, to avoid confusion on operational matters. But in a project-based or matrix organization, individuals might be responsible to their project leader for contributing to the outcome of the project while also being responsible to their departmental manager or the head of their discipline for the continuing requirements of their role and for achieving agreed standards of overall performance.

Individuals in functional roles such as finance or personnel may be directly responsible to a line manager but may also have a 'dotted line' relationship of responsibility to the head of their function on matters of corporate policy.

Decentralization

Authority to make decisions should be delegated as close to the action as possible.

Optimize the structure

Develop an ideal organization by all means, but also remember that it may have to be modified to fit in the particular skills and abilities of key individuals.

Relevance to organizational needs

The organization has to be developed to meet the needs of its situation. In today's conditions of turbulence and change, this inevitably means a tendency towards more decentralized and flexible structures, with greater responsibility given to individuals and an extension of the use of task forces and project teams to deal with opportunities or threats. This implies an informal, non-bureaucratic, organic approach to organization design – the form of the organization will follow its function, not the other way around.

The organization may be largely based on multidisciplinary project teams, as in a matrix organization, or greater emphasis will be placed on ensuring that flows of work involved in the key business processes are properly catered for rather than the creation of a traditional formal and hierarchical structure.

The process of organization design

The process of organization design is to:

- Define what the organization exists to do – its purpose and objectives.
- Analyse and identify the processes, activities or tasks required to achieve those objectives and, as appropriate, the flow of decision-making and work throughout the organization.

- Allocate related activities to teams and individual jobholders as appropriate.
- Group related activities carried out by teams and individual jobholders logically into organizational units, while ensuring that the flow of work across organizational boundaries is not inhibited.
- Provide for the management and coordination of the processes and activities at each level of responsibility.
- Ensure that attention is given to developing the processes of teamwork and communication.
- Establish reporting and communicating relationships.
- Recognize the importance of informal networks as means of communicating information and joint decision-making.
- Provide, as far as possible, for organizational processes to adapt to change.

Defining structures

Structures are usually defined by means of organization charts. Such charts have their uses in planning and reviewing organizations. They can indicate how work is allocated and how activities are grouped together. They show who is responsible to whom, and they illustrate lines of authority. Drawing up a chart can be a good way of clarifying what is currently happening: the mere process of putting the organization down on paper will highlight any problems. And when it comes to considering changes, charts are the best way of illustrating alternatives.

The danger with organization charts is that they can be mistaken for the organization itself. They are no more than a snapshot of what is supposed to be happening at a given moment. They are out of date as soon as they are drawn, and they leave out the informal organization and its networks. If you use little boxes to represent people, they may behave as if they were indeed little boxes, sticking too closely to the rule book.

Charts can make people very conscious of their superiority or inferiority in relation to others. They can make it harder to change things, they can freeze relationships, and they can show relationships as they are supposed to be, not as they are. Robert Townsend[2] said of organization charts: 'Never formalize, print and circulate them. Good organizations are living bodies that grow new muscles to meet challenges.'

Defining roles

Role definitions describe the part to be played by individuals in fulfilling their job requirements. They therefore indicate the behaviour required to carry out a particular task or the group of tasks contained in a job – they will set out the context within which individuals work as part of a team as well as the tasks they are expected to carry out.

The traditional form for defining roles is the job description, but, like organization charts, job descriptions can be too rigid and stifle initiative. It is better to use a role definition format along the following lines:

- job title;
- reporting relationships;
- main purpose of the role – a brief description of why the role exists;
- main areas of responsibility – defined in terms of the results expected, without any attempt to go into any detail of how the work is done;
- context – how the job fits in with others, flexibility requirements, decision-making authority, any particular requirements or pressures.

A role definition emphasizes the dynamic aspects of a job in terms of output, relationships and flexibility. It should focus on performance and delivery, not on tasks and duties.

Implementing structures

At the implementation stage it is necessary to ensure that everyone concerned:

- knows how they will be affected by the change;
- understands how their relationships with other people will change;
- accepts the reasons for the change and will not be reluctant to participate in its implementation.

It is easy to tell people what they are expected to do; it is much harder to get them to understand and accept how and why they should do it. The implementation plan should therefore cover not only the information to be given but also how it should be presented. The presentation will be easier if, in the analysis and design stage, full consultation has taken place with the individuals and groups who will be affected by the change. Too many organizational changes have failed because they have been imposed from above or from outside without proper consideration for the views and feelings of those most intimately concerned.

Implementation is often attempted by purely formal means – issuing edicts, distributing organization manuals or handing out job descriptions. These may be useful as far as they go, but while they provide information, they do not necessarily promote understanding and ownership. This can only be achieved on an informal but direct basis. Individuals must be given the opportunity to talk about what the proposed changes in their responsibilities will involve – they should already have been given the chance to contribute to the thinking behind the change, so discussions on the implications of the proposals should follow quite naturally. There is no guarantee that individuals who feel threatened by change will accept it, however much they have been consulted. But the attempt should be made. Departmental, team and interfunctional meetings can help to increase understanding. Change management is discussed in more detail in Chapter 26.

The implementation plan may have to cater for the likelihood that all the organizational changes cannot be implemented at once. Implementation may have to be phased to allow changes to be introduced progressively, to enable people to absorb what they will be expected to do and to allow for any necessary training. Changes may in any case be delayed until suitable people for new positions are available.

Notes

1   Mintzberg, H (1981) Organization design: fashion or fit, *Harvard Business Review*, January–February

2   Townsend, R (1970) *Up the Organization*, Michael Joseph, London

How to improve organizational capability

Organizational capability can be defined broadly as the capacity of an organization to function effectively in order to achieve desired results. Organizations are effective when they make the best use of their resources to achieve sustained high levels of performance, thus successfully achieving their purpose and objectives while also meeting their responsibilities to their stakeholders. These stakeholders consist of:

- the shareholders who own the organization, or the electorate who chose their representatives who run public bodies, or the trustees who oversee not-for-profit organizations;
- the employees who run the organization and carry out the activities required to achieve results and deliver services;
- the customers, clients or members of the public for whom the organization provides goods or services;
- the members of the community in which the organization operates.

Fundamental questions on organizational capability

Dave Ulrich and Dale Lake in their book on organizational capability[1] defined it as:

> A business's ability to establish internal structures and process that influence its members to create organization-specific competencies and thus enable the business to adapt to changing customer and strategic needs.

They posed the following six questions that they believed should be answered by anyone concerned with improving organizational capability:

- To what extent do we have leadership throughout the organization?
- To what extent do we have the capacity for change?
- To what extent do we have a shared mindset inside and outside the organization?
- To what extent does the business demonstrate world-class performance in the four main sources of uniqueness, namely: financial capability, technological capability, strategic capability and organizational capability?
- To what extent do we understand and meet customer needs?
- To what extent do we understand the economic and social conditions affecting the business?

Diagnostics to help the development of organizational capability

Increasing organizational capability is first a matter of using diagnostics to assess the strengths and weaknesses of the organization. Diagnostic models indicate the information that needs to be collected or the questions to be answered in studying an organization to judge its effectiveness under various headings, come to conclusions about any problems and their causes and inform remedial action. There are a number of diagnostic models available including those produced by Cummings and Worley,[2] Galbraith[3] and Weisbord.[4]

Cummings and Worley

The Cummings and Worley diagnostic model covers three levels: the organizational level, the group level and the individual level. Each level is analysed under three headings: inputs, design components and outputs, as shown in Table 40.1.

Galbraith

Galbraith's 'five star' model for diagnosing organizations is as follows:

- strategy to maintain direction;
- structure to determine the location of decision-making power;
- processes to manage the necessary flow of information and quality of decision-making;

TABLE 40.1 Cummings and Worley organizational diagnosis model

Level	Inputs	Design components	Outputs
Organizational	General environment Industry structure	Technology Strategy Structure Culture Human resources systems Management systems	Organizational effectiveness, eg: – performance – productivity – stakeholder satisfaction
Group	Organization design	Goal clarity Task structure Team functioning Group composition Group norms	Team effectiveness, eg: – performance – quality of working life
Individual	Organization design Group design Personal characteristics	Skill variety Task identity Task significance Autonomy Feedback about results	Individual effectiveness, eg: – performance – job satisfaction – absenteeism – personal development

- reward to provide motivation and incentives for performance and goal-directed behaviour;
- people (HR) policies to influence mindset and skill set.

Weisbord

Weisbord's six-box model for diagnosing organizations is as follows:

- purposes;
- structure;
- relationships;
- rewards;
- leadership;
- helpful relationships.

Checklist for assessing organizational capability

The models described above provide a useful basis for analysis. To bring everything together, use the following checklist to assess the extent to which there is:

- a clear and well-articulated vision of the purpose and future of the organization;
- a well-defined mission and goals and strategies to accomplish them;
- a value system that emphasizes performance, the need to value people as assets and treat them fairly in accordance with the principles of procedural and distributive justice, customer service, quality, teamwork and flexibility;
- strong, visionary leadership from the top;
- a powerful and well-qualified management team of effective leaders;
- a fully engaged, skilled and flexible workforce;
- continuous pressure to innovate and grow; to develop new business models or to change existing ones;
- the ability to respond fast to opportunities and threats;
- the capacity to manage, indeed to thrive on change;
- a strong financial base;
- effective systems for managing and controlling the business, especially IT;
- effective HR and reward systems.

Notes

1 Ulrich, D and Lake, D (1990) *Organizational Capability: Competing from the inside out*, Wiley, New York

2 Cummings, T G and Worley, C G (2009) *Organization Development and Change*, 9th Edition, South Western, Mason, OH

3 Galbraith, J R (1973) *Designing Complex Organizations*, Addison Wesley, Reading MA

4 Weisbord, M R (1976) Organizational diagnosis; six places to look for trouble with or without a theory, *Group and Organizational Studies*, 1, 430–37

41 How to plan and prioritize

Planning

Planning is the process of deciding on a course of action, ensuring that the resources required to implement the action will be available and scheduling the programme of work required to achieve a defined end result. It also involves prioritizing work – deciding the order in which to do things.

As a manager you will normally plan ahead over a relatively short period of time – up to one or, at most, two years. And your objectives, targets and budgets will probably have been fixed by the corporate plan or company budget.

You plan to complete tasks on time without using more resources than you were allowed. Your aim should be to avoid crises and the high costs that they cause, to have fewer 'drop everything and rush this' problems. Planning warns you about possible crises and gives you a chance to avoid them. Contingency or fall-back plans should be prepared if you have any reason to believe that your initial plan may fail for reasons beyond your control.

When you plan, you choose certain courses of action and rule out others; that is to say, you lose flexibility. This will be a disadvantage if the future turns out differently from what you expected – which is only too likely. Try to make plans that you can change at reasonable cost if you have to. It is a bad plan that admits no change.

Planning activities

As a manager, there are eight planning activities you need to carry out:

- *Forecasting:*
  - the sort of work that has to be done, how much and by when;
  - how the workload might change;
  - the likelihood of the department being called on to undertake specialized or rush jobs;

  – possible changes within or outside the department that might affect priorities, the activities carried out, or the workload.

- *Programming* – deciding the sequence and timescale of operations and events required to produce results on time.
- *Staffing* – deciding how many and what type of staff are needed and considering the feasibility of absorbing peak loads by means of overtime or temporary staff.
- *Setting standards and targets* – for output, sales, times, quality, costs or for any other aspect of the work where performance should be planned, measured and controlled.
- *Procedure planning* – deciding how the work should be done and planning the actual operations by defining the systems and procedures required.
- *Materials planning* – deciding what materials, bought-in parts or subcontracted work are required and ensuring that they are made available in the right quantity at the right time.
- *Facilities planning* – deciding on the plant, equipment, tools and space required.
- *Budgeting*.

Planning techniques

Most of the planning you do as a manager is simply a matter of thinking systematically and using your common sense. Every plan contains three key ingredients:

- *Objective* – the innovation or improvement to be achieved.
- *Action programme* – the specific steps required to achieve the right objective.
- *Financial impact* – the effect of the action on sales, turnover, costs and, ultimately, profit.

Figure 41.1 is an example of how a manufacturing plan could be set out.

Bar charts should be used to express plans more graphically wherever there is more than one activity and care has to be taken to sequence them correctly. The manufacturing plan illustrated in Figure 41.1 could be expressed as a Gantt chart (see Figure 41.2).

A more refined method of planning activities in a complex programme, where many interdependent events have to take place, is network planning. This requires the recording of the component parts and their representation in a diagram as a network of interrelated activities. Events are represented by circles, activities by arrows, and the time taken by activities by the length of the arrows. There can also be dotted arrows for dummy activities between events that have a time rather than an activity relationship. A critical path can be derived that highlights those operations or activities that are essential for the completion of the project within the allocated timescale. An illustration of part of a basic network is given in Figure 41.3.

There may be occasions when even more sophisticated planning techniques, using computer models, can be made available to help the manager, especially when large quantities of information have to be processed against a number of fixed assumptions or parameters, or where alternative assumptions have to be assessed. Plans can then be made to ensure that workers and machine capacity are available to deal with forecast work levels.

Action Programme

FIGURE 41.1   Example of a manufacturing plan

Action Programme

Steps	Responsibility	Completion by
1. Ensure recognition by supplier of problem with 'hard spots' in castings.	Purchasing Manager Production Manager	15 January
2. Negotiate price concession on all castings received during weeks when we return more than 10 bad castings.	Purchasing Manager	31 January
3. Set up storage area to accumulate ruined castings.	Facilities Manager	15 February
4. Establish procedures to record machine downtime and cutter breakage with individual castings.	Production Controller	1 March
5. Ensure XYZ Company agrees new arrangements.	Purchasing Manager	15 March

Profit impact

		£ 20... Profit increase (decrease)
Price concessions		7,000
Effect of improved quality	Scrap	8,500
	Overtime	3,500
	Expense tools	9,000
	Lost production	20,000
	Other	12,000
Modifications in storage area		(2,000)
Recording procedures		(1,000)
Other costs		(3,000)
	Total profit impact	£54,000

FIGURE 41.2 A Gantt chart

Step (detailed in action programme)	Responsibility	January	February	March
1. Get XYZ Company to recognize problem.	Purchasing Manager	▭		
2. Negotiate price concession.	Purchasing Manager	▭		
3. Set up storage area.	Facilities Manager	▭		
4. Establish downtime recording procedures.	Production Controller		▭	
5. Get XYZ Company to agree new arrangements.	Purchasing Manager			▭

FIGURE 41.3 Part of a basic network

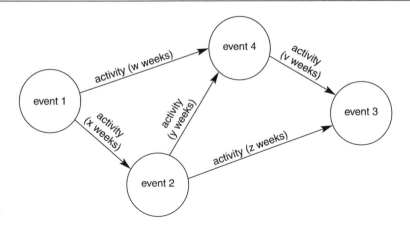

How to prioritize

Planning involves prioritizing work, which means deciding on the relative importance of a range of demands or tasks so that the order in which they are undertaken can be determined. The fragmented nature of managerial work and the sudden and often conflicting demands made on your time mean that you will constantly be faced with decisions on when to do things. There may often be situations when you have to cope with conflicting priorities. This can be stressful unless you adopt a systematic approach to prioritization.

Prioritization can be carried out in the following stages.

1 List all the things you have to do. These can be classified into three groups:
   - regular duties such as submitting a report, calling on customers, carrying out a performance review;
   - special requests from managers, colleagues, customers, clients, suppliers and so on, delivered orally, by e-mail, telephone, letter, or fax;
   - self-generated work such as preparing proposals on a new procedure.

2 Classify each item on the list according to:
   - the significance of the task to be done in terms of its impact on your work (and reputation) and on the results achieved by the organization, your team or anyone else involved;
   - the importance of the person requesting the work or expecting you to deliver something – less significant tasks may well be put higher on the priority list if they are set by the chief executive or a key client;
   - the urgency of the tasks – deadlines, what will happen if they are not completed on time;
   - any scope there may be for extending deadlines – altering start and finish times and dates;
   - how long each task will take to complete – noting any required or imposed starting and completion times that cannot be changed.

3 Assess how much time you have available to complete the tasks, apart from the routine work that you must get done. Also assess what resources, such as your own staff, are available to get the work done.

4 Draw up a provisional list of priorities by reference to the criteria of significance, importance and urgency listed at (2) above.

5 Assess the possibility of fitting this prioritized schedule of work into the time available. If this proves difficult, put self-imposed priorities on a back-burner and concentrate on the significant tasks. Negotiate delayed completion or delivery times where you believe this is possible, and if successful, move the task down the priority list.

6 Finalize the list of priorities and schedule the work you have to do (or you have to get others to do) accordingly.

Set out step by step like this, prioritization looks like a formidable task. But experienced managers go through all these stages almost unconsciously, although systematically, whenever they are confronted with a large work-load or conflicting priorities.

What many people do is simply write out a 'things to do' list at the beginning of the week or, in their mind, quickly run through all the considerations described in the above six-stage sequence and make notes on the order in which they should be tackled.

How to prepare a business plan

What is a business plan?

A business plan sets out what you or your business intends to achieve and how you intend to achieve it in order to attract any investment required. The plan includes financial projections of revenue and profit based on business forecasts covering the planned levels of sales or activity, the income they will generate and the investment required to get the expected results. In addition, it will provide information in sufficient but not excessive detail on how those results will be achieved.

Why have a plan?

A business plan may be required for any of the following reasons:

- to convince some person or organization, such as a bank, a finance company or a senior executive in the company, to invest in your business or idea;
- to convince someone to join with you in the business;
- to help in selling a business;
- to obtain a grant or regulatory approval.

Importantly, the discipline of producing a business plan and then using it as a point of reference can also provide a basis for driving and managing a business.

How should a business plan be structured?

The structure of a business plan will vary according to its purpose and the type of business it is dealing with. The following are typical headings, based on those suggested by Brian Finch in *How to Write a Business Plan* (Kogan Page):[1]

- summary;
- the business background;
- the proposal;
- financial projections;
- supporting information on the market, operations, finance, control systems, management and personnel;
- a risk assessment;
- conclusion.

Summary

This should be short (no more than one page long) and give anyone who may not be inclined to read a lengthy document the essential information they need to attract their attention. The key points to be made include a brief description of the business, the essence of the plan (what you intend to do), why you believe the plan will succeed, the investment of cash required and the return expected from that investment.

The business background

Describe the essence of the business – what is produced or what services are provided, its markets, customers and suppliers, and an outline of its trading history unless it is a start-up business.

The proposal

The proposal is the heart of the business plan. It sets out:

1 *What you intend to do* – this is an explicit statement describing what you expect to achieve in quantified terms and how the scale of your achievement will be measured.

2 *When you are going to do it* – the period of time covered by the plan. This should be realistic. A plan extending for more than five years is taking you too far ahead to be believable. Three years or so is often a more acceptable timetable.

3 *How you intend to do it* – this is a description of your plan of action, specifying the sequence of steps you will take.

4 *Why you believe you will be successful* – this is an important part of the proposal. The aim is to make a convincing case for your plan based on what you will be offering to customers, their likely response, an analysis of the competition and a description of the resources you will be able to

marshal when implementing the plan. This case is reinforced by the later sections of the plan covering finance, the market, operations, management and personnel, control systems and risk assessment.

5 *What you need to finance the plan* – this spells out how much cash you will need and when you will need it. If applicable, an indication is made of the amount of cash that you can already make available and, therefore, how much more you will need from an investor or investors. This should be a realistic sum – not too much and not too little.

6 *The financial returns your plan will generate* – this is a summary statement of the returns an investor can anticipate from an investment, which is expanded in the section on financial projections.

Financial projections

Financial forecasts are required over the period of the plan, say three years. They should state for each product or service group the anticipated sales and the gross profit or margin (the difference between sales revenue and the cost of goods sold) year by year. It is also helpful to include under the same headings a summary of trading results, if applicable, over the past two or three years. These projections should not go into elaborate detail. They can be expanded in an appendix.

It is necessary to explain the basis for the projections – why you think the sales and gross profit figures will be achieved. Refer as necessary to other sections in the plan where this is covered in more detail, for example a marketing plan. Figures that have been affected by such things as a change in the product mix, the injection of extra resources into marketing or streamlining production or distribution, or reductions anticipated in unit costs should also be explained.

The market

Describe:

- who your existing customers are and who your new customers will be;
- why they buy an existing product or service or will be keen to buy a new product or service, emphasizing any particular features that will persuade existing customers to buy more or will attract new ones;
- the current size of the market;
- trends in the size of the market – ideally it should be growing, but if it is static or declining you have to show convincingly that you can buck the trend and increase your market share or obtain a reasonable amount of market share on entry;
- the location(s) of the market – local, national or international;

- the competitors – who they are or might be, the existing and potential strength of the competition as measured by market share;
- why you believe you can achieve sustained competitive advantage and beat the competition with your product or service in terms of quality, cost, level of customer service, the uniqueness of your product or service, or the special characteristics of your operation in terms of the people you employ, the technology you use, your research and development expertise and the effectiveness of your distribution system;
- your pricing strategy;
- your marketing plans – sales, promotion, advertising and distribution.

Operations

Summarize the main processes used in your business so that investors can be confident that these will support the achievement of your business goals. Examples of processes include research and development, manufacturing, distribution, retailing, wholesaling, customer service, service operations, use of the internet, advertising and promotions. Indicate the extent to which your market assessments and sales projections have been based on rigorous market research and market testing.

Management and personnel

Give brief details of the qualifications, experience and achievement of yourself and the rest of the management team and why you have the collective expertise to achieve the plan. Also summarize the skills of your key workers and why they will contribute to the success of the enterprise.

Control systems

Outline the systems in place for managing and controlling the business in order to convince readers of the plan that you have the capability to run the operation effectively and efficiently. The systems could include accounting (budgeting and control), production control, service level control, quality control, sales analysis and control, and analysis of customer service levels.

Risk assessment

It is advisable to demonstrate in the plan that you are aware of any risks involved (no one believes that implementing business plans does not involve some risk) and how you intend to manage those risks. This shows that you have considered the plan from all the angles.

Conclusion

A brief conclusion is necessary that simply includes words to the effect that you commend the plan as being realistic, achievable and a basis for generating an acceptable return for anyone who invests in the business.

How should the plan be presented?

The plan needs to make a good impression and then hold the attention of the reader. To do this it must be clearly laid out with headings and sub-headings to provide signposts to take people through the text. Short sharp sentences should be used with action words saying what you will do and when. Avoid jargon.

The plan should be evidence based. Proposals should be supported by reliable and verifiable facts and figures wherever possible. As Brian Finch says in Kogan Page's *How to Write a Business Plan:*[1]

> Whatever you do don't waffle! It is common to read reports that go on at great length about the market, the opportunity, the history of the project and so on, but without any evidence. The plan may be badly or beautifully written but the attention of the business partner or divisional chief executive or financier will be lost at the beginning when they get bored and decide they don't believe the hype.

Note

1 Finch, B (2008) *How to Write a Business Plan*, Kogan Page, London

43 How to recover from setbacks

Even good managers have setbacks during their career, but the best managers recover from them quickly and go on to do even better. Here are some comments on coping with a reverse in your fortunes:

- 'Ever tried. Ever failed. No matter. Try again. Fail again. Fail better,' *Samuel Becket*.
- 'Regret nothing that's happened,' *Guy Browning* (2006).
- 'Dry one's eyes and laugh at a fall and baffled get up and begin again,' *Robert Browning*.
- 'The greater the difficulty, the more glory in surmounting it,' *Epicurus*.

Capturing these and other thoughts, the 10 things you can do to recover from a setback are:

- Learn from what has happened.
- If you have made a mistake, analyse how and why you did so and how you can avoid making it again.
- Accentuate the positive and build on what you know and can do and have already achieved.
- Assess your strengths and work out how you can use them more effectively in the future.
- Assess your weaknesses (but don't dwell on them) and what you need to do to overcome them.
- Although it is good to assess your strengths and weaknesses, avoid too much introspection – get into action.
- Seek the views of those you respect on what action you should take.
- Be clear about where you want to go and how you are going to get there.
- Enlist support from others in achieving your plans.
- Realize it's not the end of the world.

How to make effective presentations

44

A manager's job usually includes giving formal or informal presentations at meetings, and addressing groups of people at conferences or training sessions. To be able to speak well in public is therefore a necessary management skill that you should acquire and develop.

The four keys to effective speaking are:

- overcoming nervousness;
- thorough preparation;
- good delivery;
- appropriate use of visual aids (especially PowerPoint).

Overcoming nervousness

Some nervousness is a good thing. It makes you prepare, makes you think and makes the adrenalin flow, thus raising performance. But excessive nervousness ruins your effectiveness and must be controlled.

The common reasons for excessive nervousness are fear of failure, fear of looking foolish, fear of breakdown, a sense of inferiority and dread of the isolation of the speaker. To overcome it there are three things to remember and six things to do.

Three things to remember about nervousness

- Everyone is nervous. It is natural and, for the reasons mentioned earlier, a good thing.
- Speaking standards are generally low. You can do better than the other person.
- You have something to contribute. Otherwise why should you have been asked to speak?

Six things to do about nervousness

- Practise. Take every opportunity you can get to speak in public. The more you do it, the more confident you will become. Solicit constructive criticism and act on it.
- Know your subject. Get the facts, examples and illustrations that you need to put across.
- Know your audience. Who is going to be there? What are they expecting to hear? What will they want to get out of listening to you?
- Know your objective. Make sure that you know what you want to achieve. Visualize, if you can, each member of your audience going away having learned something new that he or she is going to put into practical use.
- Prepare.
- Rehearse.

Preparation

Allow yourself ample time for preparation in two ways. First, leave yourself plenty of low-pressure time; start thinking early – in your bath, on the way to work, while mowing your lawn, any place where you can freely develop new ideas on the subject. Second, you should leave yourself lots of time actually to prepare the talk. There are eight stages of preparation.

1. Agreeing to talk

Do not agree to talk unless you know you have something to contribute to this audience on this subject.

2. Getting informed

Collect facts and arguments for your talk by: brainstorming and writing down all the points as they occur, reading up the subject, talking to colleagues and friends, and keeping cuttings and files on subjects you may have to speak on.

3. Deciding what to say

Start by defining your objective. Is it to persuade, inform, interest or inspire? Then decide the main message you want to put across. Adopt the 'rule of three'. Few people can absorb more than three new ideas at a time. Simplify your presentation to ensure that the three main points you want to convey come over loud and clear. Finally, select the facts and arguments that best support your message.

Never try to do too much. The most fatal mistake speakers can make is to tell everything they know. Select and simplify using the rule of three.

4. Structuring your presentation

Good structure is vital. It provides for continuity, makes your thoughts easy to follow, gives the talk perspective and balance, and, above all, enables you to ram your message home.

The classic method of structuring a talk is to: 'Tell them what you are going to say – say it – tell them what you have said'. This is the rule of three in action again, as applied to attention span. Your audience will probably only listen to one-third of what you say. If you say it three times in three different ways they will at least hear you once.

You were no doubt told at school that an essay should have a beginning, a middle and an end. Exactly the same principle applies to a talk.

Tackle the middle of your talk first and:

- Write each main message on a separate postcard.

- List the points you want to make against each main message.

- Illustrate the points with facts, evidence and examples, and introduce local colour.

- Arrange the cards in different sequences to help you to decide on the best way to achieve impact and a logical flow of ideas.

Then turn to the opening of your talk. Your objectives should be to create attention, arouse interest and inspire confidence. Give your audience a trailer to what you are going to say. Underline the objective of your presentation – what they will get out of it.

Finally, think about how you are going to close your talk. First and last impressions are very important. End on a high note.

Think carefully about length, reinforcement and continuity. Never talk for more than 40 minutes at a time. Twenty or 30 minutes is better. Very few speakers can keep people's attention for long. An audience is usually very interested to begin with (unless you make a mess of your opening), but interest declines steadily until people realize that you are approaching the end. Then they perk up. Hence the importance of your conclusion.

To keep their attention throughout, give interim summaries that reinforce what you are saying and, above all, hammer home your key points at intervals throughout your talk.

Continuity is equally important. You should build your argument progressively until you come to a positive and overwhelming conclusion. Provide signposts, interim summaries and bridging sections that lead your audience naturally from one point to the next.

5. Prepare your notes

Your notes will be based on what you have already prepared. If you are giving a talk without the use of PowerPoint you can record your notes (the main messages and the supporting bullet points) on postcards so that they can easily be referred to in your presentation. It is often a good idea to write out your opening and closing remarks in full and then learn them by heart so that you can begin and end confidently. Clearly, they both have to be succinct.

If you are using PowerPoint (most people do), the text on the slides should correspond to the main points you want to make, with the proviso that you do not overload the slides (see penultimate section in this chapter). You can then print the PowerPoint slides full size and use them as your notes, with some brief and easily read annotations if you need them. The slides can also serve as handouts. Audiences are accustomed to these and no longer expect lots of prose, which they don't read anyhow.

At conferences it is usual to issue the handouts in advance. This can be slightly disconcerting to the speaker, as members of the audience may bury their heads in the handouts and appear to be paying little attention to what is being said. Some speakers insist on the handouts being issued after the presentation, but this is not always allowed by the conference organizer. In these circumstances, it is up to you to make what you say as interesting as possible so the audience does pay attention.

6. Prepare visual aids

As your audience will only absorb one-third of what you say, if that, reinforce your message with visual aids. Appeal to more than one sense at a time. PowerPoint slides provide good backup, but don't overdo them and keep them simple. Too many visuals can be distracting, and too many words, or an over-elaborate presentation, will distract, bore and confuse your audience. (See penultimate section of this chapter on the uses and abuses of PowerPoint.)

7. Rehearse

Rehearsal is vital. It instils confidence, helps you to get your timing right, enables you to polish your opening and closing remarks and to coordinate your talk and visual aids.

Rehearse the talk to yourself several times and note how long each section takes. Get used to expanding your notes without waffling. Never write down your talk in full and read it during rehearsal. This will guarantee a stilted and lifeless presentation.

Practise giving your talk out loud – standing up, if that is the way you are going to present it. Some people like to tape record themselves but that can be off-putting. It is better to get someone to hear you and provide constructive criticism. It may be hard to take but it could do you a world of good.

Finally, try to rehearse in the actual room in which you are going to speak, using your visual aids and with someone listening at the back to make sure you are audible.

8. Check and prepare arrangements on site

Check the visibility of your visual aids. Make sure that you know how to use them. Test the projector. Brief your projector operator and get them to run through the slides to ensure there are no snags.

Be prepared for something to go wrong with your equipment. You may have to do without it at short notice. That is why you should not rely too much on visual aids.

Before you start your talk, check that your notes and visual aids are in the right order and to hand. There is nothing worse than a speaker who mixes up their speech and fumbles helplessly for the next slide.

Delivery

With thorough preparation you will not fail. You will not break down. But the way you deliver the talk will affect the impact you make. Good delivery depends on technique and manner.

Technique

Your *voice* should reach the people at the back. If you don't know that you can be heard, ask. It is distracting if someone shouts 'speak up'. Vary the pace, pitch and emphasis of your delivery. Pause before making a key point, to highlight it, and again afterwards to allow it to sink in. Try to be conversational. Avoid a stilted delivery. This is one reason why you should never read your talk. If you are your natural self the audience is more likely to be on your side.

Light relief is a good thing if it comes naturally. People are easily bored if they feel they are being lectured, but you should never tell jokes unless you are good at telling jokes. Don't drag them in because you feel you must. Many effective and enjoyable speakers never use them.

Your *words* and *sentences* should be simple and short.

Your *eyes* are an important link with your audience. Look at them, measure their reaction and adjust to it. Don't fret if people look at their watches; it's when they start shaking them to see if they've stopped that you should start to worry!

Use *hands* for gesture and emphasis only. Avoid fidgeting. Don't put your hands in your pockets.

Stand naturally and upright. Do not stand casually. Be and look like someone in command. If you pace up and down like a caged tiger you will distract your audience. They will be waiting for you to trip over some equipment or fall off the edge of the platform.

Manner

Relax and show that you are relaxed. Convey an air of quiet confidence. Relaxation and confidence will come with thorough preparation and practice. At the beginning of your presentation look around at the audience and smile at them.

Don't preach or pontificate to your audience. They will resent it and turn against you.

Show sincerity and conviction. Obvious sincerity, belief in your message, positive conviction and enthusiasm in putting your message across count more than any technique.

Using PowerPoint

Most speakers rely on PowerPoint to back up their presentations. The slides are easy to prepare and because they enforce the use of bullet points they encourage the development of succinct and easily followed expositions and arguments. They also enable handouts to be produced easily. But PowerPoint slides can be over-used, and present a number of dangers that can reduce rather than enhance the impact of a presentation. The following are 10 guidelines on their preparation and use:

- Don't use too many slides. It's very tempting as they are so easy to prepare, but if they proliferate they can divert the attention of the audience from the key points you want to make (remember the rule of three). In a 40-minute presentation you should aim to keep the number of slides down to 15 or so – never more than 20. And the number should be reduced pro rata for shorter talks.
- Don't clutter up the slides with too many words. The rule of six should be adopted – no more than six bullet points and no more than six words per bullet point. Keeping slides down to this number concentrates the mind wonderfully.

- Make the font size as large as possible (another good reason for keeping the number of words to a minimum). Try to ensure that the heading is not less than 32 points and the text not less than 24 points. Ensure that the text can be seen against whatever background you select (yellow text on a deepish blue background stands out quite well).

- Use diagrams wherever you can, on the basis that every picture can tell a story better than a host of words. Diagrams break up the presentation. There is nothing more boring than a succession of slides that are entirely bullet-pointed.

- Use the PowerPoint facility for cascading bullet points (custom animation/appear) with discretion. It offers the advantage of making sure that each point can be dealt with in turn and is thus given greater significance. If the whole list of points is displayed at once the audience will be tempted to read it as a whole rather than listening to each point separately. But cascading every list of bullet points can bore and distract the audience. Save this approach for slides in which you have to elaborate on each point separately. Also use the other PowerPoint facilities with discretion. The 'fly' facility provides a variation in the way in which bullet points are presented to an audience, but does not add much if you use it every time. It is also helpful if you want to build up a diagram or flow chart to emphasize the sequence of points, but overdoing it can be messy and create confusion. It is tempting to use the 'dissolve' facility to provide elegant variation; but again, it can simply distract an audience who have come to hear what you have to say rather than to be present at a demonstration of PowerPoint tricks.

- Do not try to be either too slick or too clever. Consultants often make this mistake when making presentations to clients. They attempt to overwhelm their audience with an over-sophisticated presentation and the people subjected to it are not impressed. They may prefer presenters who can get their points across without being propped up by PowerPoint – it shows that they can express themselves without recource to a visual aid. There is often a reaction against over-slick or clever-clever presentations.

- PowerPoint slides provide useful notes, but don't just read them out point by point. Your audience may well ask themselves the question: 'What's the use of listening to this person who is simply telling me something that I can equally well read?'

- It is sometimes a good idea to show a slide with a series of bullet points and give the audience the chance to read it. Then elaborate as necessary or, better still, get some participation by encouraging them to make comments or ask questions.

- Never use the pre-packaged PowerPoint presentations. It always shows and it reveals the speaker as someone who cannot think of anything original to say. Never use other people's slides. You need to present your own ideas, not theirs.

- Rehearse using the slides (the handouts if you do not have a projector) to ensure that you can elaborate as necessary, and to indicate where you might get the audience to read them, with follow-up questions from yourself. You must be quite clear about the sequence of slides, and it is a good idea to prepare bridging remarks in advance to link slides together. A succession of unconnected slides will not impress.

Conclusion

- You can learn to become an effective speaker with practice. Seize every opportunity to develop your skills.
- Nervousness can be controlled by preparation and knowledge of technique.
- Good preparation is more than half the battle.
- Technique is there to help you to exploit your personality and style to the full, not to obliterate them.

How to solve problems

45

Problems and opportunities

It is often said that 'there are no problems, only opportunities'. This is not universally true, of course, but it does emphasize the point that a problem should lead to positive thinking about what is to be done now, rather than to recriminations. If a mistake has been made, the reasons for it should be analysed, to ensure that it does not happen again. But it is then water under the bridge.

Faced with a continuous flow of problems you may occasionally feel utterly confused. We all feel like that sometimes.

Improving your skills

How can you improve your ability to solve problems? There are a few basic approaches you should use.

Improve your analytical ability

A complicated situation can often be resolved by separating the whole into its component parts. Such an analysis should relate to facts, although, as Peter Drucker[1] points out, when trying to understand the root causes of a problem you may have to start with an opinion. Even if you ask people to search for the facts first, they will probably look for those facts that fit the conclusion they have already reached.

Opinions are a perfectly good starting point as long as they are brought out into the open at once and then tested against reality.

Analyse each hypothesis and pick out the parts that need to be studied and tested.

Mary Parker Follett's[2] (1924) 'law of the situation' – the logic of facts and events – should rule in the end. And although you may start out with a hypothesis, when testing it use Rudyard Kipling's six honest serving men:

I keep six honest serving men
(They taught me all I knew)
Their names are What and Why and When
and How and Where and Who.

Use your imagination

A strictly logical answer to the problem may not be the best one. Use lateral thinking, analogies and brainstorming to get off your tramlines and dream up an entirely new approach.

Keep it simple

One of the first principles of logic is known as Occam's razor. It states that 'entities are not to be multiplied without necessity.' That is, always believe the simplest of several explanations.

Implementation

A problem has not been solved until the decision has been implemented. Think carefully not only about how a thing is to be done (by whom, with what resources and by when) but also about its impact on the people concerned and the extent to which they will cooperate. You will get less cooperation if you impose a solution. The best method is to arrange things so that everyone arrives jointly at a solution freely agreed to be the one best suited to the situation (the law of the situation again).

Ten steps for effective problem-solving

1 *Define the situation* – establish what has gone wrong or is about to go wrong.

2 *Specify objectives* – define what is to be achieved now or in the future to deal with an actual or potential problem or change in circumstances.

3 *Develop hypotheses* – develop hypotheses about what has caused the problem.

4 *Get the facts* – find out what has actually happened and contrast this with an assessment of what ought to have happened. Try to understand the attitudes and motivation of those concerned. Remember that people will see what has happened in terms of their own position and feelings (their framework of reference). Obtain information about internal or external constraints that affect the situation.

5 *Analyse the facts* – determine what is relevant and what is irrelevant. Diagnose the likely cause or causes of the problem. Do not be tempted to focus on symptoms rather than root causes. Test any assumptions. Dig into what lies behind the problem.

6 *Identify possible courses of action* – spell out what each involves.

7 *Evaluate alternative courses of action* – assess the extent to which they are likely to achieve the objectives, the cost of implementation, any practical difficulties that might emerge and the possible reactions of stakeholders. Critical evaluation techniques as described in Chapter 7 can be used for this purpose.

8 *Weigh and decide* – determine which alternative is likely to result in the most practical and acceptable solution to the problem. This is often a balanced judgement.

9 *Plan implementation* – timetable project management resources required.

10 *Implementation* – monitor progress and evaluate success.

Notes

1 Drucker, P (1967) *The Effective Executive*, Heinemann, London
2 Follett, M P (1924) *Creative Experience*, Longmans Green, New York

46 How to be strategic

It is often said that managers must be strategic if they want to get on. But what is the process of 'being strategic'? To answer this question it is necessary to understand what is meant by strategy and strategic management and, in the light of this understanding, to describe what managers do when they are being strategic.

What is strategy?

Strategy can be defined as the continuous process of defining a sense of purpose and direction. It aims to match the organization's capabilities and resources to the opportunities available in the external environment in the most advantageous way and to ensure that different aspects of the strategy cohere and are mutually supportive.

Strategy has often been defined as a logical, step-by-step affair, the outcome of which is a formal written statement that provides a definitive guide to the organization's long-term intentions. Many people still believe that this is the case, but it is a misrepresentation of reality. In practice the formulation of strategy is never the rational and linear process described by some writers or attempted by some managers. Strategies often tend to be fragmented, evolutionary and largely intuitive. They emerge in response to evolving situations in the shape of actions and reactions. This does not mean that a strategic approach to management as described below is inappropriate or unachievable. It may not be such a formal process as some people think but it is still desirable to assess continuously where you want to go and how you intend to get there and to consider how this can best fit in with the achievement of the organization's goals.

Strategic management

The purpose of strategic management as defined by Rosabeth Moss Kanter[1] is to 'elicit the present actions for the future' and become 'action vehicles

– integrating and institutionalizing mechanisms for change'. Their main concern is to identify the broader issues they are facing and decide on the general directions they must take to deal with these issues and achieve future business objectives. They do not take a narrow or restricted view.

Strategic management deals with both ends and means. As an end it describes a vision of what something will look like in a few years' time. As a means, it shows how it is expected that the vision will be realized. Strategic management is visionary management, concerned with creating and conceptualizing ideas of where the organization should be going. But it is also empirical management that decides how in practice it is going to get there. This means getting things right now.

Businesses and managers must perform well in the present to succeed in the future. Strategic management is about the future but it is also about integrating activities now so that they are mutually supportive in the pursuit of immediate and longer-term goals.

Strategic managers

Managers who act strategically will think about what the organization wants to be and become and what they can do to ensure this happens. They will have a broad view of where they are going and are capable of seeing 'the big picture', looking beyond the confines of their immediate problems to what lies ahead and how what they do supports the efforts of other people. But they will also be aware that they are responsible, first, for planning how to allocate resources (people and money) in ways that contribute to the implementation of strategy, and second, for managing these resources so that they significantly add value to the results achieved by the firm.

Ten things to do if you want to manage strategically

- Understand the business and its competitive environment.
- Be aware of the goals of the business and its plans to attain them.
- Align what you are doing with the organization's business strategy.
- Know where you are going and how you are going to get there.
- Remember that formal strategic plans do not guarantee success; it is the implementation of the plans that delivers results.
- Know how to plan the use of resources to make the best use of business opportunities.

- Understand how you can contribute to the achievement of the objectives of the key functions in the business and support the strategic activities of your colleagues.
- Be able to foresee longer-term developments, envisage options and their probable consequences, and select sound courses of action.
- Rise above the day-to-day detail.
- Challenge the status quo.

Note

1 Kanter, R M (1989) *When Giants Learn to Dance*, Simon & Schuster, London

How to think clearly

47

Clear thinking is logical thinking. It is a process of reasoning by which one judgement is derived from another and correct conclusions are drawn from the evidence. Clear thinking is analytical: sifting information, selecting what is relevant, establishing and proving relationships.

If you say people are logical, you mean that they draw reasonable inferences – their conclusions can be proved by reference to the facts used to support them. They avoid ill-founded and tendentious arguments, generalizations and irrelevancies. Their chain of reasoning is clear, unemotional and based on relevant facts.

Clear thinking – a logical approach to problem-solving, decision-making and case presentation – is an essential attribute of an effective manager. This does not mean that it is the only way to think. Edward de Bono has made out an incontrovertible case for lateral (ie creative) thinking as a necessary process for innovative managers to use alongside the more traditional vertical or logical thinking pattern. But a logical approach is still an essential requirement.

A further attribute of a good manager is the ability to argue persuasively and to detect the flaws in other people's arguments. To think clearly and to argue well, you need to understand: first, how to develop a proposition or a case from basic principles; second, how to test your proposition; and third, how to avoid using fallacious arguments and how to expose the fallacies used by others.

Developing a proposition

The first rule is to 'get the facts'. It is the starting point for clear thinking. The facts must be relevant to the issue under consideration. If comparisons are being made, like must be compared with like. Trends must be related to an appropriate base date, and if trends are being compared, the same base should be used. Treat opinions with caution until they are supported by evidence. Avoid a superficial analysis of surface data. Dig deep. Take nothing for granted. Sift the evidence and discard what is irrelevant.

Your inferences should be derived *directly* from the facts. Where possible, the connection between the facts and the conclusion should be shown to be justified on the basis of verifiable and relevant experience or information on similar relationships occurring elsewhere.

If, as is likely, more than one inference can be deduced from the facts, you should test each inference to establish which one most clearly derives from the evidence as supported by experience. But it is no good saying 'it stands to reason' or 'it's common sense'. You have to practise evidence-based management, ie produce the evidence that proves that the inference is reasonable and you have to pin down the vague concept of common sense to the data and experience upon which it is based. It was Descartes who wrote: 'Common sense is the best distributed commodity in the world, for every man is convinced that he is well supplied with it.'

Testing propositions

Susan Stebbing[1] in *Thinking to Some Purpose* wrote: 'We are content to accept without testing any belief that fits in with our prejudices and whose truth is necessary for the satisfaction of our desires.' Clear thinking must try to avoid this trap.

When we form a proposition or belief we generalize from what is observed – our own analysis or experience – and thence infer to what is not observed. We also refer to testimony – other people's observations and experience.

If your proposition or belief is derived from a generalization based upon particular instances, you should test it by answering the following questions:

- Was the scope of the investigation sufficiently comprehensive?
- Are the instances representative or are they selected to support a point of view?
- Are there contradictory instances that have not been looked for?
- Does the proposition or belief in question conflict with other beliefs for which we have equally good grounds?
- If there are any conflicting beliefs or contradictory items of evidence, have they been put to the test against the original proposition?
- Could the evidence or testimony lead to other, equally valid conclusions?
- Are there any other factors that have not been taken into account that may have influenced the evidence and, therefore, the conclusion?

If your belief is based on testimony, you should test the reliability of the testimony, its relevance to the point, and whether or not your belief follows logically from the evidence: that is, it can reasonably be inferred from the facts.

Fallacious and misleading arguments

A fallacy is an unsound form of argument leading to a mistake in reasoning or a misleading impression. The main fallacies to avoid or to spot in other people's arguments are:

- sweeping statements;
- potted thinking;
- special pleading;
- oversimplification;
- reaching false conclusions;
- begging the question;
- false analogy;
- using words ambiguously;
- chop logic.

These are discussed briefly below.

Sweeping statements

In our desire for certainty and to carry the point, we often indulge in sweeping statements. We sometimes then repeat them more and more loudly and angrily in order to convince our opponent. If we do it often enough and forcibly enough we can even deceive ourselves. It has been said that 'It's never fair, it's never wise, it's never safe to generalize.' But that is a generalization in itself. Scientific method is based on generalizations. They can be valid if they are inferred properly from adequate, relevant and reliable evidence.

Generalizations are invalid when they have been produced by oversimplifying the facts or by selecting instances favourable to a contention while ignoring those that conflict with it. The classic form of a fallacious generalization is the contention that if some A is B then all A must be B. What frequently happens is that people say A is B when all they know is that some A is B or, at most, A tends to be B. The argument is misleading unless the word 'some' or 'tends' is admitted.

Many of the fallacies considered below are special cases of unsafe generalization, the most common symptom of unsound reasoning.

Potted thinking

Potted thinking happens when we argue using slogans and catch phrases, when we extend an assertion in an unwarrantable fashion.

It is natural to form confident beliefs about complicated matters when we are proposing or taking action. And it is equally natural to compress these beliefs into a single phrase or thought. But it is dangerous to accept compressed statements that save us the trouble of thinking. They are only acceptable if fresh thinking has preceded them.

Special pleading

If people say to you: 'everyone knows that', 'it's obvious that' or 'it's indisputably true that', you can be certain that they have taken for granted what they are about to assert.

We indulge in special pleading when we stress our own case and fail to see that there may be other points of view, other ways of looking at the question. Special pleading happens when we cannot detach ourselves from our own circumstances. We often blunder because we forget that what is true of one of us is also true of the other in the same situation.

A safeguard against this mistake is to change 'you' into 'I'. Thus, I feel that you can't see what is straight in front of your nose; you feel that I can't see what is on the other side of my blinkers. A rule that appears to be sound when I apply it to you may seem to be unsatisfactory when you ask me to apply it to myself.

Of course, thinking for too long about other points of view is a recipe for indecision. There are not necessarily two sides to every question and even if there are, you eventually – and often quickly – have to come down firmly on one side. But before you do this, check in case the other points of view or the alternative approaches are valid, and take them into account.

Oversimplification

Oversimplification is a special form of potted thinking or special pleading. It often arises in the form of what Susan Stebbing terms 'the fallacy of either black or white', the mistake of demanding that a sharp line should be drawn, when in fact no sharp line can be drawn. For example, we cannot ask for a clear distinction to be drawn between the sane and the insane, or between the intelligent and the unintelligent. Our readiness to make this mistake may be taken advantage of by a dishonest opponent, who insists that we define precisely things that do not permit such definition.

Reaching false conclusions

One of the most prevalent fallacies is that of forming the view that because some are or may be, all are. An assertion about several cases is twisted into an assertion about all cases. The conclusion does not follow the premise.

The most common form of this fallacy is what logicians call the 'undistributed middle', which refers to the traditional syllogism consisting of a premise, a middle term and a conclusion.

A valid syllogism takes the following form:

Premise: All cows are quadrupeds.
Middle term: All quadrupeds are vertebrates.
Conclusion: Therefore, all cows are vertebrates.

This may be represented as:

Premise: All A is B.
Middle term: All B is C.
Conclusion: Therefore, all A is C.

This is logical. The middle term is fully distributed. Everything that applies to A also applies to B, everything that applies to B also applies to C, therefore everything that applies to A must apply to C.

An invalid syllogism would take the following form:

All cows are quadrupeds.
All mules are quadrupeds.
Therefore, all cows are mules.

This may be represented as:

All A is B.
All C is B.
Therefore, all A is C.

This is false because, although everything that applies to A and C also applies to B, there is nothing in their relationship to B that connects A and C together.

The difference between the true and false syllogism may be illustrated in Figure 47.1. In the false syllogism, A and C could be quite distinct although still contained within B. To link them together goes beyond the original evidence. The fact that two things A and B are related to another thing, C, does not necessarily mean that they are related together. In forming arguments, we too often jump to the conclusion that some means all.

FIGURE 47.1   The difference between true and false syllogisms

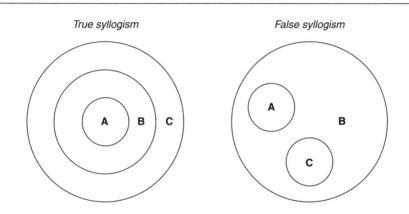

Allowing the conclusion to go beyond the evidence can also take the form of assuming that because we are aware of the effect (the consequent), we also know the cause (the antecedent). But this assumption may be incorrect. An effect can have many different causes. This fallacy of the consequent, as it is termed, can be illustrated by the following example:

> If she won the lottery she would go to the West Indies.
> She has gone to the West Indies.
> Therefore she has won the lottery.
>
> ie If P then Q.
> Q.
> Therefore P.

But there are a number of other reasons why she could have gone to the West Indies besides winning the lottery. A clear inference can only be drawn if the cause is directly related to the effect, thus:

> If she wins the lottery she will go to the West Indies.
> She has won the lottery.
> Therefore she will go to the West Indies.
>
> ie if P then Q.
> P.
> Therefore Q.

A further danger in drawing conclusions from evidence is to forget that circumstances may alter cases. What has happened in the past will not necessarily happen again unless the circumstances are the same. You may be able to infer something from history but you cannot rely on that inference. Times change.

Begging the question

We beg the question when we take for granted what has yet to be proved. This can take the form of assuming the point in dispute without adequate reason; what the logicians call *petitio principii*.

If you spot anyone taking for granted a premise that is not contained in the conclusion you must challenge the assumption and ask for information about the premises upon which the conclusion is based. You can then assess whether or not the conclusion follows logically from those premises.

Challenging assumptions is a necessary part of thinking clearly. You should challenge your own assumptions as well as those made by others.

False analogy

Analogy forms the basis of much of our thinking. We notice that two cases resemble each other in certain respects and then infer an extension of the resemblance. Analogies also aid understanding of an unfamiliar topic.

Analogies can be used falsely as vivid arguments without any real evidence. Just because A is B, where both are familiar matters of fact, does not mean that X is Y, where X and Y are unfamiliar or abstract. When we argue by analogy we claim that if:

x has properties of p1, p2, p3 and f,
and y has properties of p1, p2 and p3,
therefore y also has the property of f.

This could be true unless y has a property incompatible with f, in which case the argument is unsound.

Analogies may be used to suggest a conclusion but they cannot establish it. They can be carried too far. Sometimes their relevance is more apparent than real.

Use argument by analogy to help support a case but do not rely upon it. Don't allow anyone else to get away with far-fetched analogies. They should be tested and their relevance should be proved.

Using words ambiguously

The Lewis Carroll approach – 'When I use a word it means just what I choose it to mean, neither more nor less' – is a favourite trick of those who aim to deceive. People use words that beg the question; that is, they define a word in a special way that supports their argument. They shift the meaning of words in different contexts. They may choose words that have the same meaning as each other but that show approval or disapproval.

There is a well-known saying that the word 'firm' can be declined as follows: 'I am firm, You are obstinate, He is pigheaded.'

Chop logic

'Contrariwise,' continued Tweedledee, 'if it was so, it might be, and if it were so, it would be; but as it isn't, it ain't. That's logic.'

Chop logic is not quite as bad as that, but it can be equally misleading. It includes such debating tricks as:

- selecting instances favourable to a contention while ignoring those that conflict with it;
- twisting an argument advanced by opponents to mean something quite different from what was intended – putting words in someone's mouth;
- diverting opponents by throwing on them the burden of proving something they have not maintained;
- deliberately ignoring the point in dispute;

- introducing irrelevant matter into the argument;
- reiterating what has been denied and ignoring what has been asserted.

Note

1 Stebbing, S (1959) *Thinking to Some Purpose*, Penguin Books, Harmondsworth

How things go wrong and how to put them right

48

Things can go wrong through events beyond your control or through incompetence. It is difficult and very rare for anyone to admit that they are incompetent, but this is why things most frequently go adrift. It is therefore useful to know something about the causes of incompetence so that you can put them right.

You should also know about troubleshooting so that you can tackle problems, whether or not they are of your own making. Theodore Roosevelt once said: 'Do what you can, with what you have, where you are.' The trouble is, people don't always take this advice. Things go wrong because people do less than they are capable of, misuse their resources or choose an inappropriate time or place in which to do it. Situations are misjudged and the wrong action is taken.

Studies of incompetence

There have been two interesting analyses of incompetence that, if studied, will give you some clues about how to avoid or at least minimize mistakes. The first of these is *The Peter Principle* by Dr Lawrence J Peter;[1] the second is *On the Psychology of Military Incompetence* by Norman F Dixon.[2]

The Peter Principle

In *The Peter Principle*, Dr Lawrence Peter suggested that in a hierarchy, individuals tend to rise to the level of their own incompetence. This somewhat pessimistic view was based on his experience that the system encourages this to happen because people are told that if they are doing their job efficiently and with ease, the job lacks challenge and they should move up. However, as Peter says, 'the problem is that when you find something you can't do very well, that is where you stay, bungling your job, frustrating your co-workers, and eroding the effectiveness of the organization.'

The Peter Principle has only been accepted as common parlance because it reflects a fundamental problem when assessing potential. We know, or we think we know, that someone is good at his or her present job. But does this predict success in the next one up? Perhaps yes, perhaps no; however, we cannot be sure because the skills needed by, for example, a first-rate research scientist are quite different from those required by the leader of a research team. Technical competence does not necessarily indicate managerial competence.

Beating the Peter Principle – for yourself

Can the Peter Principle be beaten? The answer is yes, but with difficulty. People don't usually refuse promotion. If they do, they become suspect. It is thought that they should be made of sterner stuff. It is, however, perfectly reasonable to check on what is involved if you are promoted. You should obtain precise answers to questions on what you will be expected to achieve, the resources you will be given to achieve it and the problems you will meet. If you think these demands are unreasonable, discuss the job to see if they can be modified.

Don't take a job unless you are satisfied that you can do it, or at least that you can learn how to do it within an acceptable period of time. You can quite properly ask what training and help you will be given in the early stages. If your predecessor failed, you can ask what went wrong, so that you can avoid making the same mistakes.

Beating the Peter Principle – for others

If you are in a position of offering promotion or a new job, you have to be aware of the Peter Principle and how to circumvent it. You need to match the capacities of the candidate to the demands of the job, and your starting point for this process should be an analysis in depth of the skills required. These should be classified under the headings of MATCH:

- *Managerial* – making things happen, leading, inspiring and motivating people, team building and maintaining morale, coordinating and directing effort, using resources productively, and controlling events to achieve the required results.
- *Analytical* – dissecting problems and coming up with the right conclusions about what is happening and what should happen.
- *Technical/professional* – an understanding not only of all the tricks of the trade but also of how to use other people's knowledge effectively.

- *Communications* – putting the message across.
- *Human resource management/personnel* – the ability to persuade, enthuse and motivate; trustworthiness, integrity, dedication.

When you have drawn up the specifications, measure the candidate against each of these criteria. Obtain whatever evidence you can about his or her performance in the present job that gives any indication of potential competence in these areas. Ask for information on successes and failures and why they occurred.

This matching process should identify any potential weaknesses. You can then discuss these and decide on any help the individual needs in the shape of coaching, training or further experience.

Monitor the progress of the individual carefully in the initial months. Your aim should be to spot dangerous tendencies in good time so that swift remedial action can be taken.

Military incompetence

Norman Dixon suggests that there are two basic types of military incompetents. The first group includes Generals Elphinstone (first Afghan war), Raglan (the Crimean War), Butler (Boer War) and Percival (Singapore). These were all mild, courteous and peaceful men, paralysed by the burden of decision-making under fire. The second group includes people like Haig, Joffre and a number of other First World War generals. They are characterized by overweening ambition coupled with a terrifying insensitivity to the suffering of others. Far from being paralysed by decisions, they were active, but active in vain, devious, scheming and dishonest ways. Alistair Mant[3] in *Leaders We Deserve* quotes the example of the catastrophic results achieved in the Crimean War when an incompetent in the first group (Raglan) has authority over someone in the second group (the Earl of Cardigan, reputed by one contemporary to possess the 'brains of a horse').

The elements of military incompetence are listed by Norman Dixon as:

- serious wastage of human resources;
- fundamental conservatism and clinging to outworn tradition or to past successes;
- tendency to reject or ignore information that is unpalatable or that conflicts with preconceptions (as with company 'yes men');
- tendency to underestimate the enemy;
- indecisiveness and a tendency to abdicate from the role of decision-maker;
- obstinate persistence in a given task despite strong contrary evidence;
- failure to exploit a situation gained and a tendency to 'pull punches';
- failure to make adequate reconnaissance;

- a predilection for frontal assaults, often against the enemy's strongest point (reference the gross overcrowding of once profitable markets);
- belief in brute force rather than the clever ruse;
- failure to make use of surprise or deception;
- undue readiness to find scapegoats;
- suppression or distortion of news from the Front, usually deemed necessary for morale or security;
- belief in mystical forces – fate, bad luck, etc.

Examples of all these can be found in the actions or inactions of business leaders and managers:

1 *Wasting resources* – most businesses are overstaffed, to the tune of 10 per cent or more.

2 *Conservatism* – 'That's the way it has always worked. We have been market leaders for the last 20 years, why change?'

3 *Rejecting unpalatable information* – 'What did you say about our losing market share? I don't believe it; these desk surveys are always inaccurate.'

4 *Underestimating the enemy* – 'What's this? Bloggs & Co have introduced a new product in our range. And you think it will compete? Forget it. They're useless. They couldn't run a winkle stall.'

5 *Indecisiveness* – 'We need to think a bit more about this.' 'I need more information.' 'I sometimes think that if you put problems like this in the "too difficult" section of your pending tray, they will go away.' 'It seems to me that we have several alternative routes ahead of us. Let's call a meeting next week or sometime to look at the pros and cons.' 'This is something for the Board.'

6 *Obstinate persistence* – 'Don't confuse me with the facts.' 'That's the way it's going to be.'

7 *Failure to exploit a situation* – 'OK, you think we're going to exceed budget on our launch and you want to accelerate the programme. But let's not get too excited, we mustn't overstretch ourselves.'

8 *Failure to reconnoitre* – 'I don't believe in market research.'

9 *A predilection for frontal assaults* – 'Bloggs are doing particularly well in widgets. Yes, I appreciate we know nothing about widgets, but we can soon find out. Let's get in there fast and topple them from their perch.'

10 *A belief in brute force* – 'Tell the union they can either take 5 per cent or do the other thing... What's this about a productivity package? I don't believe in messing about. It's a straight offer or nothing... They'll come out? I don't believe it.'

11 *A failure to make use of surprise* – 'I don't like playing about. Let's get this show on the road... You think we'll get off to a better start if we

keep the competition guessing? Forget it, we're miles better than they are!'

12 *Scapegoating* – 'It's not us, it's the rate of exchange.' 'This xxxx government has screwed us up!' 'Why am I surrounded by incompetent fools?'

13 *Suppression of news* – 'Don't tell them about how well we're doing. They'll only ask for more money.'

14 *A belief in mystical forces* – 'I just feel in my bones we must do this thing.'

Why things go wrong – a summary

The main reasons for things going wrong are:

- inability to learn from mistakes;
- sheer incompetence through over-promotion;
- poor selection and inadequate training;
- overconfidence;
- under-confidence;
- carelessness;
- laziness;
- lack of foresight.

What can you do about it?

You may be forced to carry out a troubleshooting exercise as described in Chapter 49, but there are other things you can remember and do as set out below.

Inability to learn from mistakes

Remember Murphy's Law, which states that if anything can go wrong it will. Mistakes will happen. The unforgivable thing is to make the same mistake twice. You learn from your mistakes by analysing what went wrong – no excuses, no alibis – and making notes of what to do and what not to do next time.

Incompetence

This is something you should minimize in your subordinates by a constant drive to improve selection and performance standards and by training and coaching aimed at correcting specified weaknesses.

If you have doubts about your own ability, analyse your own strengths and weaknesses and grab every opportunity you can to get extra training and advice from people you believe in. If that still does not work, get out in good time.

Poor selection, inadequate training

If you pick the wrong person for the job they will under-perform and make mistakes. You must ensure that you specify exactly what you want in terms of experience, qualifications, knowledge, skills and personality, and that you do not settle for second best. Your interview should be planned systematically to find out what the candidate has to offer under each of the headings of your specification. Ensure by probing questions that you establish whether or not the experience is of the right sort and at the right level. Ask for details of achievements. Check that the candidate has had a progressive career with no record of failures or mysterious gaps. Check by telephone with the present or previous employer that the candidate has told you the truth about his job, period of employment and, where appropriate, reason for leaving.

If you have failed to provide proper induction training, or to take the right steps to identify and meet individuals' training needs, you should not be surprised if they are not up to the job. Guidance on approaches to developing your staff is given in Chapter 14.

Overconfidence

This is the most difficult problem to eradicate. It is always said in the Royal Air Force that the most accident-prone pilots are the over-confident ones. You need confidence in yourself and your staff. How can it be controlled from going over the edge?

It takes time to understand or demonstrate that misjudgements occur because you are so certain that you know all the answers that no attempt is made to foresee or take care of the unexpected. Over-confident people tend to have tunnel vision – they can see quite clearly to the end but they take no notice of what is happening on either side or beyond. And if they see the light at the end of the tunnel they may not appreciate that it is the light of an oncoming train.

Under-confidence

This can be overcome as long as the individual is fundamentally competent. People who lack confidence often need help from someone who can underline achievements and provide encouragement to do more of the same. Mentors can help, as can a deliberate policy of extending people steadily so that they are not suddenly faced with a daunting leap in the level of work they have to do. Start by giving the under-confident tasks that are well within their capabilities and progressively increase demands, but only in achievable steps.

Carelessness

This is a universal problem. It can happen through overconfidence, but we all make mistakes under pressure or because we think the task is easier than it is. Sadly, reputations can be damaged, even destroyed by relatively minor mistakes. If you submit a report to your board with a glaring arithmetical error in it, the credibility of your whole report may be damaged, even if the mistake, although obvious, was not significant. Never submit a report or write a key letter without checking every figure and every fact at least once. If possible, ask someone else to do it as well.

Laziness

No one would ever admit to being lazy. But lazy people do exist, either because they are naturally indolent or because they have not been given sufficient leadership and a well-defined role in the organization. If one of your staff is lazy, put the boot in. It cannot be tolerated.

Lack of foresight

This is a common reason for errors. As a manager, one of your prime responsibilities is to think ahead. You must try to anticipate all the eventualities and make contingency plans accordingly. You won't get it right every time and you may find yourself occasionally in a crisis-management situation. But you will at least be better prepared if thought has been given to some of the eventualities, even if you could not anticipate them all.

Notes

1 Peter, L J (1972) *The Peter Principle*, Allen & Unwin, London
2 Dixon, N F (1979) *On the Psychology of Military Incompetence*, Futura, London
3 Mant, A (1985) *Leaders We Deserve*, Blackwell, London

49

How to troubleshoot

No matter what you do, things will sometimes go wrong. As a manager, you will often be called upon to put them right, or to employ other people to do it for you.

Troubleshooting requires: diagnostic ability, to size up the difficulties; know-how, to select the required solution and decide how to implement it; and managerial skill, to put the solution into effect. It can be divided into three main parts:

- planning the campaign;
- diagnosis;
- cure.

Planning the campaign

Even if you decide to do it yourself without using management consultants, you can still take a leaf out of the consultant's book. A good management consultant will go through the following stages:

- Analysis and diagnosis of the present situation: what has happened and why.
- Development of alternative solutions to the problem.
- Decision as to the preferred solution, stating the costs and benefits of implementing it.
- Defining a method of proceeding: how and over what timescale the solution should be implemented, who does it and with what resources. If a staged implementation is preferred, the stages will be defined and a programme worked out.

The most important task at the planning stage is to define the problem, and clarify objectives and terms of reference. A problem defined is a problem half solved. And it is the difficult half. The rest should follow quite naturally if an analytical approach is adopted.

Once you know what the problem is you can define what you want done and prepare terms of reference for those who are conducting the investigation, including yourself. These should set out the problem, how and by whom it is to be tackled, what is to be achieved and by when. All those concerned in the exercise should know what these terms of reference are.

The next step is to programme the troubleshooting assignment. Four points need to be decided: the information you need, where you get it from, how you obtain it and who receives it. Draw up lists of facts required and the people who can supply them. Remember you will have to deal with opinion as well as fact; all data are subject to interpretation. List those who are likely to understand what has happened and why; those who might have good ideas about what to do next.

Then draw up your programme. Give notice that you require information. Warn people in plenty of time that you want to discuss particular points with them and that you expect them to have thought about the subject *and* have supporting evidence to hand.

Diagnosis

Diagnosis means finding out what is happening – the symptoms – and then digging to establish why it is happening – the cause. There may be a mass of evidence. The skilled diagnostician dissects the facts, sorts out what is relevant to the problem and refines it all down until he or she reveals the crucial pieces of information that show the cause of the problem and point to its solution.

Analytical ability – being able to sort the wheat from the chaff – is a key element in diagnosis. It is a matter of getting the facts and then submitting each one to a critical examination, in order to determine which is significant.

During the process of diagnosis you must remain open-minded. You should not allow yourself to have preconceptions or to be over-influenced by anyone's opinion. Listen and observe, but suspend judgement until you can arrange all the facts against all the opinions.

At the same time, do whatever you can to enlist the interest and support of those involved. If you can minimize their natural fears and suspicions, those close to the problem will reveal ideas and facts that might otherwise be concealed from you.

Troubleshooting checklist

Base your diagnosis on an analysis of the factors likely to have contributed to the problem: people, systems, structure and circumstances.

People

- Have mistakes been made? If so, why? Is it because staff are inadequate in themselves or is it because they have been badly managed or trained?
- If management is at fault, is the problem one of system, structure or the managers themselves?
- If the people doing the job are inadequate why were they selected in the first place?

Systems

- To what extent are poor systems or procedures to blame for the problem?
- Is the fault in the systems themselves? Are they badly designed or inappropriate?
- Or is it the fault of the people who operate or manage the systems?

Structure

- How far has the organization or management structure contributed to the problem?
- Do people know what is expected of them?
- Are activities grouped together logically, so that adequate control can be exercised over them?
- Are managers and supervisors clear about their responsibilities for maintaining control and do they exercise these responsibilities effectively?

Circumstances

- To what extent, if any, is the problem a result of circumstances beyond the control of those concerned? For example, have external economic pressures or changing government policies had a detrimental effect?
- If there have been external pressures, has there been a failure to anticipate or to react quickly enough to them?
- Have adequate resources (people, money and materials) been made available, and if not, why not?

Cure

The diagnosis should point the way to the cure. But this may still mean that you have to evaluate different ways of dealing with the problem. There is seldom 'one best way', only a choice between alternatives. You have to narrow them down until you reach the one that, *on balance*, is better than the others.

Your diagnosis should have established the extent to which the problem is one of people, systems, structure or circumstances. Fallible human beings may well be at the bottom of it. If so, remember not to indulge in indiscriminate criticism. Your job is to be constructive: to build people up, not to destroy them.

Avoid being too theoretical. Take account of circumstances – including the ability of the people available now to deal with the problem, or, if you have doubts, the availability of people from elsewhere who can be deployed effectively. Your recommendation should be practical in the sense that it can be made to work with resources that are readily available and within acceptable timescales.

You must make clear not only what needs to be done but *how* it is to be done. Assess costs as well as benefits and demonstrate that the benefits outweigh the costs. Resources have to be allocated, a timescale set and, above all, specific responsibility given to people to get the work done. Your recommendations have to be realistic in the sense that they can be phased in without undue disruption and without spending more time and money than is justified by the results.

Take care when you apportion blame to individuals. Some may clearly be inadequate and have to be replaced. Others may be the victims of poor management, poor training or circumstances beyond their control. Their help may be essential in overcoming the trouble. It is unwise to destroy their confidence or their willingness to help.

Using management consultants to troubleshoot

A management consultant has been described, or dismissed, as someone with a briefcase 50 miles from home. Robert Townsend[1] describes consultants as people 'who borrow your watch to tell you what time it is and then walk off with it'.

Calling in consultants in desperation can indeed be an expensive and time-wasting exercise. But they have their uses. They bring experience and expertise in diagnosis. They can act as an extra pair of hands when suitable people are not available from within the organization. And, as a third party, they can sometimes see the wood through the trees and solve problems or unlock ideas within the company that, sadly, are often inhibited by structural or managerial constraints.

There are, however, a number of rules, as set out in the table below, which you should be aware of when contemplating bringing in consultants.

DO	DON'T
Get tenders from two or three firms and compare, not only their fees, but their understanding of your problem and the practical suggestions they have on how to tackle it.	Be bamboozled by a smooth principal who is employed mainly as a salesperson.
Check on the experience of the firm and, most important, of the consultant who is going to carry out the assignment.	Go for a big firm simply because it has a good reputation. It may not have the particular expertise you want.
Brief the firm very carefully on the terms of reference.	Accept any old consultant who comes along. Many redundant executives have set up as consultants without having a clue about how to do it. There is a lot of skill in being an effective consultant. Check that the firm is a member of the Management Consultants Association or that the principal is a member of the Institute of Management Consultancy (for UK-based firms). These provide a guarantee of professional status.
Get a clear statement of the proposed programme, total estimated costs (fees plus expenses) and who is actually going to carry out the assignment.	
Meet and assess the consultant who is going to carry out the work.	
Insist on regular progress meetings.	Allow the consultant to change the programme without prior consultation.
Ensure that the outcome of the assignment is a practical proposal that you can implement yourself, or with the minimum of further help.	Leave the consultant to his or her own devices for too long. Keep in touch. Appoint a member of your staff to liaise or even to work with the consultant.

Note

1   Townsend, R (1970) *Up the Organization*, Michael Joseph, London

How to write reports

50

The ability to express oneself clearly on paper and to write effective reports is one of a manager's most important skills. As often as not, it is through the medium of reports that you will convey your ideas and recommendations to your superiors and colleagues and inform them of the progress you are making.

What makes a good report?

The purpose of a report is to analyse and explain a situation, to propose and gain agreement to a plan. It should be logical, practical, persuasive and succinct.

To be an effective report writer you start by having something worthwhile to say. Clear thinking (Chapter 47), creative thinking (Chapter 9) and problem-solving (Chapter 45) techniques will all help. Your analysis of opinions and facts and your evaluation of options should provide a base for positive conclusions and recommendations.

There are three fundamental rules for report writing:

- Give your report a logical structure.
- Use plain words to convey your meaning.
- Remember the importance of good, clear presentation of material.

Structure

A report should have a beginning, a middle and an end. If the report is lengthy or complex it will also need a summary of conclusions and recommendations. There may also be appendices containing detailed data and statistics.

Beginning

Your introduction should explain why the report has been written, its aims, its terms of reference, and why it should be read. It should then state the sources of information upon which the report was based. Finally, if the report is divided into various sections, the arrangement and labelling of these sections should be explained.

Middle

The middle of the report should contain the facts you have assembled and your analysis of those facts. The analysis should lead logically to a diagnosis of the causes of the problem. The conclusions and recommendations included in the final section should flow from the analysis and diagnosis. One of the most common weaknesses in reports is for the facts not to lead on naturally to the conclusions; the other is for the conclusions not to be supported by the facts.

Summarize the facts and your observations. If you have identified alternative courses of action, set out the pros and cons of each, but make it quite clear which one you favour. Don't leave your readers in mid-air.

A typical troubleshooting report would start by analysing the present situation; it would then diagnose any problems or weaknesses in that situation, explaining why these have occurred before making proposals on ways of dealing with the problem.

End

The final section of the report should set out your recommendations, stating how each of them will help to achieve the stated aims of the report or overcome any weaknesses revealed by the analytical studies.

The benefits and costs of implementing the recommendations should then be explained. The next stage is to propose a firm plan for implementing the proposals – the programme of work, complete with deadlines and names of people who would carry it out. Finally, tell the recipient(s) of the report what action, such as approval of plans or authorization of expenditure, you would like them to take.

Summary

In a long or complex report it is very helpful to provide an executive summary of conclusions and recommendations. It concentrates the reader's mind and can be used as an agenda in presenting and discussing the report. It is useful to cross-reference the items to the relevant paragraphs or sections of the report.

Plain words

> If language is not correct, then what is said is not what is meant; if what is said is not what is meant, then what ought to be done remains undone. (Confucius)

The heading of this section is taken from Sir Ernest Gowers' *The Complete Plain Words*.[1] This book is required reading for anyone interested in report writing. Gowers' recommendations on how best to convey meaning without ambiguity, and without giving unnecessary trouble to the reader, are:

● Use no more words than are necessary to express your meaning, for if you use more you are likely to obscure it and to tire your reader. In particular do not use superfluous adjectives and adverbs, and do not use roundabout phrases where single words would serve.

● Use familiar words rather than the far-fetched if they express your meaning equally well, for the familiar are more likely to be understood.

● Use words with a precise meaning rather than those that are vague, for they will obviously serve better to make your meaning clear; and in particular, prefer concrete words to abstract for they are more likely to have a precise meaning.

You will not go far wrong if you follow these precepts.

Presentation

The way in which you present your report affects its impact and value. The reader should be able to follow your argument easily and not get bogged down in too much detail.

Paragraphs should be short and each one should be restricted to a single topic. If you want to list or highlight a series of points, tabulate them or use bullet points. For example:

Pay reviews
Control should be maintained over increments by issuing guidelines to managers on:

● the maximum percentage increase to their payroll allowable for increments to individual salaries;

● the maximum percentage increase that should be paid to a member of staff.

Paragraphs may be numbered for ease of reference. Some people prefer the system that numbers main sections 1, 2, etc, subsections 1.1, 1.2, etc, and sub-sub-sections 1.1.1, 1.1.2, etc. However, this can be clumsy and distracting. A simpler system, which eases cross-referencing, is to number each paragraph, not the headings, 1, 2, 3, etc; sub-paragraphs or tabulations are identified as 1(a), 1(b), 1(c), etc and sub-sub-paragraphs if required as 1(a)(i), 1(a)(ii), 1(a)(iii), etc (or use bullet points).

Use headings to guide people on what they are about to read and to help them to find their way about the report. Main headings should be in capitals or bold and subheadings in lower case or italics.

A long report could have an index listing the main and subheadings and their paragraph numbers like this:

	Paragraphs
PAY ADMINISTRATION	83–92
Pay structure	84–88
Job evaluation	89–90
Pay reviews	91–92

Your report will make most impact if it is brief and to the point. Read and re-read your draft to cut out any superfluous material or flabby writing. Use bullet points to simplify the presentation and to put your messages across clearly and succinctly.

Do not clutter up the main pages of the report with masses of indigestible figures or other data. Summarize key statistics in compact, easy-to-follow tables with clear headings. Relegate supporting material to an appendix.

Note

1 Gowers, Sir E (1987) *The Complete Plain Words*, Penguin, London

Positive or negative indicators of performance

Manage performance

Do things well and achieve the objectives and standards agreed for the role

Positive indicators

- Carries out work as required.
- Completes work on time.
- Meets quality/service standards.
- Works accurately.
- Sees things through.
- Asks for ground rules.
- Is committed to achieving high-quality results.
- Shows commitment to make it happen.
- Seeks to raise quality standards.
- Puts measures in place.
- Actions match words.
- Takes ownership of things to be done.
- Evaluates and revises deadlines as necessary.
- Takes responsibility for outcomes.
- Always has a follow-up course of action.
- Makes contingency plans.
- Does everything possible to ensure that things get done to the best of his or her ability.
- Confronts issues.

Manage performance
Do things well and achieve the objectives and standards agreed for the role

Negative indicators
- Frequently forgets things.
- Has to be chased to meet deadlines.
- Is not concerned with quality.
- Does not learn from mistakes.
- Does not follow instructions.
- Is often late in delivering expected results.
- Work not up to standard.
- Makes too many mistakes.
- Does minimum he or she can get away with.
- Relies on others to complete actions.
- Has no pride in the job.
- Blames others for personal failure.
- Conceals situations when things go wrong.
- Focuses on less important activities.
- Builds achievements to be greater than they are.
- Agrees unrealistic deadlines.
- Prioritizes badly.

Manage oneself
Making decisions, solving problems, taking initiative, managing time, improving own performance, working to support the organization's values and goals

Positive indicators
- Gets on with work without supervision.
- Is ready to learn.
- Acts in line with the organization's values.
- Solves problems effectively.
- Seeks opportunities for learning.
- Schedules and uses time effectively.
- Quickly identifies the right thing to do.
- Continuously develops expertise.
- Actively promotes the organization's values.
- Acts decisively, taking a broad view.
- States problems clearly.
- Evaluates conflicting priorities.
- Reaches clear conclusions based on understanding of underlying issues.
- Deals with crisis situations effectively.
- Demonstrates understanding of critical issues.
- Makes quality strategic decisions.

Negative indicators
- Needs constant supervision.
- Is not interested in doing better.
- Is unaware of organization's values.
- Is unwilling to act on own initiative.
- Takes no steps to improve performance.
- Makes snap decisions without thinking.
- Does not keep skills and knowledge up to date.
- Is indecisive, takes a superficial and narrow view.
- Offloads decisions to others.
- Focuses on symptoms, not causes.
- Cannot cope with pressurized situations.
- Fails to make timely decisions.
- Does not consider long-term impact of decisions.

Manage others

Getting results through people; exercising leadership; managing performance; providing feedback; implementing performance management; developing staff

Positive indicators	
	• Cooperates well with team leader and colleagues.
	• Responds positively to suggestions and feedback.
	• Rises to the occasion when leadership required.
	• Accepted in leadership role by team members.
	• Gives clear direction.
	• Offers firm support and guidance.
	• Knows what's going on and takes swift corrective action.
	• Takes an active interest in staff development.
	• Carries out thorough and helpful performance reviews.
	• Encourages team members to take joint responsibility for their achievements.
	• Lets people know that they are valued.
	• Uses performance management processes to the full.
	• Encourages open, honest and constructive behaviour that helps the team to find its way.
Negative indicators	
	• Not a team player; disruptive.
	• Is unwilling to work towards team goals.
	• Ignores feedback.
	• Is reluctant to take on responsibility for team performance.
	• Cannot win respect of team members.
	• Doesn't explain why things need to be done.
	• Fails to clarify team goals and standards.
	• Seldom if ever gives feedback.
	• Imposes own views on team.
	• Operates a 'blame culture'.
	• Takes no interest in developing people.
	• Is unable to create shared vision for team.
	• Adopts a 'command and control' approach.

Manage relationships

Exerting influence; building and maintaining effective relationships with colleagues and stakeholders; participating in or running meetings

Positive indicators

- Gets on well with colleagues and customers.
- Takes part in team activities; fully accepted by team colleagues.
- Views others positively.
- Builds good relationships with internal and external customers.
- Gets on well with people.
- Shows tact, sensitivity and support.
- Offers support through regular contact; makes time for people.
- Offers ideas, suggestions and advice relevant to the needs of the individual.
- Expresses point of view clearly in order to reach agreement.
- Expresses views and proposals persuasively.
- Is sensitive to other people's needs and wants, and adjusts proposals and recommendations accordingly.
- Listens, reflects and checks own understanding.
- Presents proposals that are logical, practical and persuasive.
- Contacts are spread throughout the organization and with key external people.
- Looks for shared ways to get round problems and disagreements.
- Marshals powerful and compelling arguments that clearly address the issue and are developed logically from the facts.
- Networks widely to get a strategic overview.
- Works to achieve consensus, rather than force own direction.
- Is seen and used as an important contact by key people inside and outside the organization.

Manage relationships
Exerting influence; building and maintaining effective relationships with colleagues and stakeholders; participating in or running meetings

Negative indicators
- Courtesy depends on mood.
- Is often difficult to deal with.
- Does not contribute much to team activities.
- Is unresponsive to others' contributions, feelings and concerns.
- Is tactless, says things without considering effect.
- Takes no real interest in the concerns of others.
- Pursues own agenda, irrespective of others.
- Does not listen to or encourage contributions from others.
- Produces an unconvincing case or weak arguments when making a proposal or suggestion.
- Fails to build up or maintain good relationships.
- Doesn't treat people as equals.
- Arguments supporting proposals are not thought through and do not hang together.
- Finds it difficult to get others to accept complex or controversial proposals.
- Makes little attempt to network with other people, inside or outside the organization.
- Proposals are ill-prepared and lack conviction.
- Proposals fail to address the issues that concern recipients.
- Goes own way, irrespective of the needs of other people.

Manage communications
Communicate orally or in writing to colleagues, customers/ clients and external individuals or organizations

Positive indicators
- Speaks clearly and audibly and gains the attention of those he or she is talking to.
- Written information is presented clearly.
- Uses language that other people can understand.
- Delivers concise communications that are readily understood, simple to interpret and avoid jargon.
- Speaks persuasively and with conviction.
- Delivers concise communications that are readily understood, simple to interpret and avoid jargon.
- Actively listens.
- Acknowledges other people's feelings and emotions.
- Tailors message to recipient.
- Expresses ideas lucidly and presents arguments in a logical manner.
- Written communications are easy to follow, well constructed and have an internal logic.
- Gains the complete attention of those to whom he or she is speaking.
- Letters, memoranda and reports are concise, lucid and to the point.
- Selects most appropriate means of communication.

Negative indicators
- Uses language poorly.
- Does not readily communicate or share with others.
- Communications are vague and irrelevant.
- Letters and memoranda are badly constructed and written.
- Sends lengthy, verbose, ambiguous messages.
- Tends to waffle.
- Uses language poorly and expresses ideas in a 'woolly' manner.
- Reports, memoranda and presentations lack structure and are unclear.
- Conclusions are not well justified.

Manage customer service

Provide high level of service to internal and external customers in accordance with exacting standards

Positive indicators
- Meets expressed needs of internal customers.
- Handles customers' queries effectively and knows where to channel queries within the organization.
- Understands customer problems.
- Identifies potential opportunities to help customers.
- Asks customers how services could be improved.
- Builds collaborative relationships with customers.
- Establishes high level of trust amongst customers, as confirmed by customer feedback.
- Develops extensive customer networks.
- Sets standards of customer service and ensures that they are met.
- Actively involved in promoting high levels of customer service across the organization.
- Continuously monitors customer service levels and takes swift corrective action when necessary.

Negative indicators
- Has no appreciation of customer needs or pressures.
- Doesn't listen to customers.
- Is unaware of customer needs.
- Passes on enquiries when he or she could have taken action him/herself.
- Fails to respond to customer requests or queries.
- Does not deliver standard of service customers have the right to expect.
- Customer enquiries and complaints are not attended to swiftly.
- Gets negative feedback from customers.
- Too little concerned with setting and monitoring customer service standards within function.
- Takes a narrow view of customer service: not concerned with wider issues.

TITLES BY THE SAME AUTHOR

Armstrong's Essential Human Resource Management Practice, 2010
Armstrong's Handbook of Human Resource Management Practice, 11th edn, 2009
Armstrong's Handbook of Management and Leadership, 2nd edn, 2009
Armstrong's Handbook of Performance Management, 4th edn, 2009
Armstrong's Handbook of Reward Management Practice, 3rd edn, 2010
Armstrong's Strategic Human Resource Management, 5th edn, 2011
Evidence-Based Reward Management (with Duncan Brown and Peter Reilly), 2010
A Handbook of Management Techniques, revised 3rd edn, 2006
How to Manage People, 2008
Human Capital Management (with Angela Baron), 2008
The Reward Management Toolkit (with Ann Cummins), 2011

ALSO PUBLISHED BY KOGAN PAGE

The 30 Day MBA, 2nd edn 2011, Colin Barrow
Decision Making and Problem Solving Strategies, 2010, John Adair
Develop Your Leadership Skills, 2010, John Adair
Develop Your Presentation Skills, 2011, Theo Theobald
Dealing With Difficult People, Revised edn, 2010, Roy Lilley
Disaster-Proof Your Career, 2010, Patrick Forsyth
Effective Business Writing, 2009, Patrick Forsyth
Effective Customer Care, 2010, Pat Wellington
Effective Financial Management, 2010, Brian Finch
Effective NLP Skills, 2011, Richard Youell and Christina Youell
How to Deal with Stress, 2nd edn, 2010, Stephen Palmer and Cary Cooper
How to Manage Meetings, 2nd edn, 2011, Alan Barker
How to Motivate People, 2nd edn, 2010, Patrick Forsyth
How to Negotiate Effectively, 3rd edn, 2010, David Oliver
How to Sell Yourself, 2010, Ray Grose
How to Write a Marketing Plan, 3rd edn 2010, John Westwood
How to Write Reports and Proposals, 2nd edn, 2010, Patrick Forsyth
Improve Your Coaching and Training Skills, 2008, Patrick Forsyth
Improve Your Communication Skills, 2nd edn, 2010, Alan Barker
The Innovative Leader, 2007, Paul Sloane
The Inspirational Leader: How to motivate, encourage and achieve success, 2009, John Adair
The Mindful International Manager, 2010, Jeremy Comfort and Peter Franklin
The New Boss, 2008, Peter Fischer
Not Bosses But Leaders: How to lead the way to success, 3rd edn, 2009, John Adair
Successful Interviewing and Recruitment, 2010, Rob Yeung
Successful Project Management, 3rd edn, 2010, Trevor Young
Successful Time Management, 2nd edn 2010, Patrick Forsyth

The above titles are available from all good bookshops or direct from the publishers. To obtain more information, please contact the publisher at the following address:

Kogan Page
120 Pentonville Road
London N1 9JN

Tel: 020 7278 0433
Fax: 020 7837 6348

www.koganpage.com

INDEX